Painted Diaries

Painted Diaries

A Mother and Daughter's Experience through Alzheimer's

Kim Howes Zabbia

Fairview Press
Minneapolis

Library of Congress Cataloging-in-Publication Data

Zabbia, Kim Howes.
    Painted diaries : a mother and daughter's experience through Alzheimer's / Kim Howes Zabbia.
    p.   cm.
    ISBN 1-57749-007-X
    1. Howes, Margaret Lou—Health. 2. Alzheimer's disease—Patients—Family relationships. 3. Zabbia, Kim Howes. I. Title.
    RC523.2.Z33   1996
    362.1'96831'0092—dc20
    [B]   96-17789
                                                                 CIP

Cover design by Richard Rossiter.

First Printing: October 1996
Printed in the United States of America

00 99 98 97 96   7 6 5 4 3 2 1

Publisher's Note: Fairview Press publishes books and other materials related to the subjects of family and social issues. Its publications, including *Painted Diaries*, do not necessarily reflect the philosophy of Fairview Hospital and Healthcare Services or their treatment programs.

The paper used in this publication meets the minimum requirements of American National Standard for Information Sciences—Permanence of Paper for Printed Library Materials, ANSI Z329.48-1984.

To Mom,
of course

Illustrations

Bert Howes and Lou Hendry Howes, August 1945, one month after their wedding

Pop and Mom down the river, 1977

Zab with newborn Kate, February 1982

Mom and Kate, February 1982

Four generations of strong women, April 1982. Bigmama, 83; Mom, 57; Kim, 30; Kate, 9 weeks.

Family portrait, Christmas 1985, one month after Lou's diagnosis. Ricky, Kim, Fan, Pop, and Mom.

Kate giving Mom memory tests, October 1987

Lou's writing of "I love yoow," fall 1989

Kate helping Mom down her back steps, 1990. The yellow tape on the stairs made them clearer.

Kim and Mom at Kim's L.S.U. reception for her M.F.A. exhibit, March 1992

Kim in her studio, 1991

Mom and Kim in Kim's studio, May 1992

Stadium I. © 1989, 34" x 46", collection of the artist.

Stadium IV. © 1989, 33" x 44", collection of the artist.

Searching for Words. © 1989, 29" x 58", collection of the artist.

Tangled Memories I. © 1990, 27" x 35", collection of Dr. and Mrs. Rick Richoux, New Orleans, Louisiana.

Even the Sky Moves I. © 1990, 26" x 32", collection of Merle and Joe Suhayda, Baton Rouge, Louisiana.

Hallucination I. © 1990, 26" x 34", collection of Merle and Joe Suhayda, Baton Rouge, Louisiana.

Lost in the Park I. © 1990, 27" x 35", collection of Beth and

Bob Daly, Fairfax, Virginia.

Private War I. © 1990, 25" x 35", collection of Dr. Louise Baenninger, Mandeville, Louisiana.

Private War III. © 1990, 17" x 24", collection of Ruth Speirer, New Orleans, Louisiana.

Lost in the Park III. © 1990, 32" x 44", collection of Ruth Hamilton, Moosejaw, Saskatchewan, Canada.

Visions at the Foot of the Bed IV. © 1991, 42" x 50", collection of the artist.

The War Within III. © 1991, 44" x 51", collection of the artist.

Constricted Messages. © 1991, 50" x 97", collection of the artist.

To the Bright Light of Death I. © 1991, 43" x 51", collection of Beth and Bob Daly, Fairfax, Virginia.

To the Bright Light of Death II. © 1991, 42" x 49", collection

of Merle and Joe Suhayda, Baton Rouge, Louisiana.

To the Bright Light of Death III. © 1991, 43" x 51", collection of the artist.

Nerves Kiss Before They Die II. © 1991, 40" x 47", collection of Dr. Alan Stevens, Birmingham, Alabama.

In Search of Rebirth II. © 1992, 45" x 50", collection of Stacy Wilson, Sulphur, Louisiana.

Reaching the Womb I. © 1992, 44" x 50", collection of the artist.

Acceptance I. © 1993, 20" x 28", collection of Ellen Elmes, Jewell Ridge, Virginia.

Reaching the Womb III. © 1994, 38" x 44", collection of the artist.

To Deny the Inevitable. © 1994, 28" x 48", collection of the artist.

The Ultimate Release, August 27, 1994. © 1994, 48" x 96", collection of the artist.

❦ Acknowledgments ❦

If it weren't for Alan Stevens, Ruth Speirer, Mike Howes, Bunnie Sutton, Vernon Weldy, and Merle Suhayda, my paintings would still be in the studio.

If it weren't for the late Bill Kelly, Fan Disher, Rita Neal, Beth Daly, Betty Morgan, and Katusha Zeller, this book would have remained a thesis paper.

If it weren't for Ann Serff, Robbie Braun, Joe Dziemianowicz, Barbara Tardo, Gail Hood, and John Kemp, no one would have known about this adventure in the first place.

If it weren't for Margaret Ellis, Mary Cunnane, Gwen and Robert Barsley, my agent—David Hendin, my chopper—John Land, and my editor—Robyn Hansen, this book would still be a manuscript in a red and black box.

If it weren't for Pop, and especially for Zab and Kate, I would never have survived any of this.

October 1993

I could see Mom's upturned face interrupted by the shine of a cold chrome bed railing. I watched quietly, waiting for her pale blue eyes to stop staring at the speckled ceiling, to turn slowly on that white pillow, to recognize me as her daughter, her second child, her Kim. That seldom happens anymore. She smiles every once in a while. She sings sometimes. Yesterday, she even tried to whistle.

The smell in this nursing home isn't too bad. The faint stench of wet diapers dissolves into the pungent springtime-fresh deodorizers that splash my senses each time I walk through the front door. In February, when Pop and I visited this "living center" for the first time, I remember remarking that it didn't have a typical nursing home smell. It was pleasant and unexpected. Now, the smell burns sad memories into my sinuses, memories of what will be Mom's final months of coping with Alzheimer's disease.

She doesn't get out of bed anymore. I can feel my forefingers and thumbs touch when I place them around Mom's thigh, her stretched skin hanging like moss through my other fingers. For this 5'9" former newspaper reporter who now weighs only ninety pounds, I don't think our voyage back to the womb will take much longer.

Mom will be 69 in a couple of weeks. It's been eight years since she was diagnosed, eight years of disappearing memory and wild hallucinations, eight years since our big adventure turned into an emotional journey backward in time. The two of us saw these years unfold, first in Mom's journals, then in my paintings as her symptoms floated through my soaked fingers onto the paper.

I kissed Mom on the forehead, careful not to say, "I have to go." I knew she would forget my visit in a few minutes. She may already have forgotten. I breathed deeply after closing the swinging front door of the lobby, hoping to cleanse that penetrating smell from my head, only to catch the scent of jasmine on a bush by the sidewalk. White jasmine lined the asphalt driveway to Mom and Pop's home, long before I grew up there, long before I married Zab and moved down the street, long before I was pregnant with Kate. The jasmine aren't there anymore.

Spring 1982

Our kitchen table was built into the wall four years before my sister and brother and I were even born. In 1961, Pop spruced it up with new turquoise Formica. When the Formica accidentally cracked on the edge of the table, Pop cut an eight-inch star out of white Formica and embedded it into the original to cover the crack. Gold flecks of glitter twinkled from the star, and company always asked why it was there. Everyone thought Pop had planned to put the star in the table in the first place.

Other than that, the turquoise Formica was in pretty good shape considering it survived twenty-one more years of scratchy forks, Corningware casseroles, and the shells of boiled crawfish. Its glossy surface echoed the sun's rays as they shot through the picture window that rose from the white star. It was a heavy wooden window whose hidden weights made a rumbling sound whenever I raised the glass. My designated place at the half-oval table was right next to that window. When we ate supper each night, I could look over my left arm at the back yard and kick my brother, Ricky, under the table at the same time. He had the spot directly across from me, and our eyes met between every bite. My sister, Fan, sat on the curved end, separated from us by Mom and Pop. This chair gave her the privilege of getting up for any forgotten item from salt to milk. Fan thought she should sit there anyway because she was the oldest, and this was the only head of the table.

Sitting next to Ricky, Pop could correct him easily with his right hand. Fan, he could discipline with his left hand, but I was the farthest away. Luckily for Pop, he had been perceptive enough to build a drawer that ran under the table both ways between Ricky and me. It was convenient for the phone book and napkins, but it also served as Pop's third hand. When I tried to stash my half-chewed round steak under the rim of my plate, for example, Pop just quietly reached in front of Ricky and pushed the drawer into my stomach. It wasn't painful; it just got my attention.

I thought of that drawer now, twenty years later, as my pregnant stomach pushed it into the lap of my husband, Zab. He was sitting in Ricky's spot across the table; Pop and Mom filled their usual places. Fan's chair was empty. Since we only lived two blocks down the street from my parents, Mom invited us to join them for supper every once in a while. Tonight was not a special occasion; they were just frying up some of the shrimp Zab and Pop caught trawling last summer in Lake Pontchartrain.

When the conversation hit its first lull, Zab automatically stood up to put his plate in the sink and clean up the kitchen. It was an old habit instilled in him and his two older brothers long before I ever entered his picture.

Pop said, "Sit down. Kim'll get those."

Zab flashed a grin my way and quickly sat back in his chair. I stood up, pregnant belly first, and began to pick up the dishes.

"Come on, little momma," Mom said as she began scraping the leftovers into a bowl for their dog. "It won't take long."

I watched Mom as she passed me on her way to the dishwasher. She had changed very little since I slept in this house eight years ago, the night before my wedding and the end of an era: no more kids at home.

Looking at her tonight, I could see that she was the same sentimental toughie she had been back then. Mom seldom wore any jewelry other than her wedding ring and kept her brown hair cropped short and away from her face. Pop had always hated bangs. A born-and-bred tomboy, Mom didn't care about sissy stuff like the color pink or ruffles on the edge of flowered curtains. I remember she bucked the idea of adding a touch of lace to the cuffs of the formal-length dress she had to wear for my wedding. In spite of her lack of vanity, Mom discreetly primped a bit just for Pop. She actually set her hair in pin curls each time she washed it, even though it was naturally curly. Every once in a while, her femininity would creep through in the form of lipstick or an occasional necklace.

When we were growing up, she was exactly what

we wanted for a mother. She did everything from showing us how to throw a football to faking a girlie squeal when we wanted to scare her with a live cricket or a roly-poly doodlebug from outside. Besides that, Mom was smart. She could organize an entire town of Girl Scout troops, substitute almost daily at the high school for any subject, and still have enough time to write for the weekly newspaper. Mom was a go-getter, a born volunteer, a take-charge girl. She made firm decisions about almost anything, that is, as long as Pop said it was OK first.

Bert Howes and Lou Hendry were married for two years before they had enough money to build the house on North Seventh Street where they still live. When they bought the corner lot for $1,200, it was one hundred by two hundred feet of strawberry rows and short pine trees, even though it was located only four blocks from the downtown bustle of a 1947 Louisiana town called Ponchatoula. They paid a man $15 per thousand board feet to cut timber at Grandpa's farm and haul it to the mill. Then they hired Pop's uncle to be the contractor for $1.25 an hour. It took them only nine months to build the house, but it took Mom and Pop six years to make a baby.

In 1950, when Mom finally became pregnant with their first child, Pop planted an acorn by the window next to the kitchen sink. That live oak is still there. On May 31, 1951, after sixty hours of labor, Fay Ann was born. She was named Fay after Pop's middle name, but was called Fan because that's what Fay Ann sounded like if you said it fast. The summer solstice of the following year brought me, Margaret Kim, named after Mom, Margaret Lucille, and *Kim* by Rudyard Kipling. In the book, Kim is an East Indian boy, not a girl, which suited my own tomboy instincts just fine.

On December 18, 1953, Mom and Pop received just what they wanted for Christmas; the baby boy for whom they had hoped long before Fan and I ever came along. We weren't disappointments per se; we were just the wrong sex. His birth certificate reads Richard Bert, but they called him Ricky. They kept Richard on the official document in case he wanted to be a doctor when he grew up. He might not like being called Dr. Ricky Howes, for example. Dr. Richard Howes sounded more appropriate, they imagined, even though Ricky grew up to work for a bank instead of the medical profession and never goes by the name of Richard, not even in the phone book.

Pop and Mom believed that we three children could do anything we set our minds to, especially because they had taught us how to juggle. We were always challenged to see how much life we could handle, the family being the epitome of the word *active*, constantly making use of idle time.

We three kids were just as active during and after school as our parents were. Fan could sing, I could draw, and Ricky could play the trumpet. We learned what it meant to be involved. We ran track, played basketball and softball, and practically lived in the water when we were at the camp down the river. We hadn't yet heard of the word *stress*, much less *stomach acid* or *tension headache*. We all three had a sneaking feeling that life could be cut short at any minute, so we had better make a difference while we had the chance.

Pop was a sales manager during the day and a jack-of-all-trades by night. He was always coming up with new ideas. He seldom spoke out loud, but inside that bald head of his, there was a noisy brainstorming session taking place. When he sparked an idea, I could practically see the wheels churning as he silently completed an entire project in his mind before he cut the first piece of wood.

He created in the "boathouse," his word for his workshop that used to house the fifteen-foot wooden boat that he built to take us to the camp down the river. Pop had built the boathouse, too, tucking it under the protective shade of a giant oak tree, its delicate leaves now accustomed to the whirring sound of his power tools. When I was little, I would sit nearby, trying to guess which tool he wanted next and hand it to him before he had to ask for it. If he did have to ask, I knew I had better know the difference between a crescent wrench and a socket wrench, and I did.

To the average passerby, Pop looked like a gruff, old codger who disliked the nuisance a little kid might bring, but Pop wasn't like that at all; he was really a softie inside. Mom used to call him her "rough, tough cream puff." Kids could see through that hard crust too, as the neighborhood brood was drawn to the boathouse like mosquitoes to a porch light. As much as Pop liked to act the loner, he really preferred to have a kid around, watching him work, "oohing" and "aahing" at each new invention. He would invite us to join him by saying, "Maybe you'll learn something."

I still remember him helping me make my first boat out of wood. It was about eight inches in length and had a metal washer for a steering wheel. When I was finished, Pop looked at it as if it had been all my idea and said, as he always said, "Girl! You know some stuff!" and I beamed.

Even when Pop wasn't building something, his brain remained in high gear. He was known about town as the expert scrounger because he could visualize a finished product out of any piece of scrap. His pride in his work rested just as much on which parts of it he could make with scrounged materials as it did on his craftsmanship. He made us a merry-go-round out of pipes and one-by-twelve pine, and a high-jump bar out of two sticks, two dowels, and a cane fishing pole.

"When are you ever going to start charging?" I asked him one day.

"Nah," he said, "if you charge people, that gives them the right to find fault with it. If you give it to 'em free, they just can't believe it, and they tell you how wonderful it is." He paused, then smiled at me. "Besides, I like to see the look on their face when I give it to 'em. That's enough."

Journal Entry
February 18, 1976

I haven't been keeping up with this journal as much as I'd like. I only get to write when Bert and I are at the camp because it's so hectic at home. As I remember it, I was recapping some of the highlights in our very full life. Let's see. Kim and Ricky were still in high school, and Fan had just started college, so I must have left off with 1969. Yes, November of 1969 brought a big change into our lives: Fan married Bren Disher. They lived in the playroom at our house while they attended Southeastern Louisiana University in nearby Hammond. Our first grandchild, Christopher Brennan, appeared by the end of the summer and started a new way of life for us all. Of course, I think he is absolutely adorable and love him to pieces—a feeling shared by this whole family. After graduation, the three of them moved to Morgan City where Bren got a job with Texaco Oil Co. and Fan started teaching 7th & 8th grade Math. In the summer of '75, another adorable grandchild arrived: Chad Edward Disher. I went to Morgan City and took care of him and Fan for two weeks. He is adorable (I said that): a fine, fat, big-blue-eyed smiling baby. At this writing, he is almost 6 months old—scooting around on his stomach, probably crawling by now. Chris adores him—has ever since he found out he was in his mommy's stomach. He has never shown any jealousy toward Chad at all, and Chad lights up like a Christmas tree when Chris walks in.

Lou Howes

When Fan told me in fourth grade that she kind of liked Brennan Disher, Jr., I was floored. Mom was their teacher at St. Joseph's that year, and she told me that Bren had cussed one day. I wasn't sure if Fan had made the right decision; but since he was her first love, I would never stop her. I'd never stop my idol.

We shared a small bedroom next to our brother's, and Pop had built us trundle beds. During the day, my bed was stored under Fan's, and every night, I'd roll it out to go to sleep. I guess that's why I learned to make up my bed: we couldn't move about the room as long as it was out. Each night, we would talk ourselves to sleep, Fan looking down at me from her high bed, our dolls tucked neatly under the edges of the sheets. I was usually scared of the dark because I believed that the devil lived in our attic and that the Easter Bunny was eight feet tall. Fan, however, would convince me that the noises I heard were just creaks from the pine floorboards adjusting to the shifting house. I would invariably fall asleep before the end of her practical analysis, but she knew I would.

As a matter of fact, it was Fan who pragmatically explained away the Easter Bunny by telling me that he was really two people—our parents. Regardless of how much I defended my beliefs, she just reinforced her theory by throwing in, "By the way, the Rat is Mom, too." I was devastated. Most kids had the Tooth Fairy; we had the Rat. Either way, I couldn't bear the thought that I had left my baby teeth to a human. When I ran to tell Mom, I could hear Fan yell behind me, "While you're at it, ask her about Santa Claus!"

Fan found out about sex in the fourth grade when she asked Mom what the big "F" word meant. Unlike most mothers, Mom was delighted to tell her. Mom never did have reservations about discussing the facts of life with any of us. I did, however, and it took Mom five more years to corner me with the notorious facts.

I was so modest that I used to get dressed every morning under my nightshirt and seldom saw myself naked without feeling awkward. The rest of my family, though, seemed to be quite comfortable with their own bodies. I used to think how neat it was that Mom and Pop could walk in front of each other without any clothes on and be completely at ease. I remember thinking that I hoped by the time I got married, I would have found out how they got to that point. As soon as I turned thirteen, Mom decided I couldn't put her off any longer, so she came into the bathroom while I was taking a bath. She refused to leave until I promised her I would listen as soon as I got out. I promised, got out of the tub, covered up with my robe,

and went into her room where she was waiting for me. I listened. I have to say, the facts of life put the Easter Bunny story to shame.

Fan was relieved when she found out that Mom had finally told me about sex because I hadn't let her tell me either. I guess she felt we were on the same wavelength then, but I knew we always had been. I did what Fan did. We had our braces put on and our wisdom teeth taken out at the same time. We joined the same Girl Scout troop at the same time and stayed with it for ten years. I probably even wanted to become a teacher because Fan wanted to become a teacher. My first memory in life is of Fan and me lying in twin hospital beds in 1955, waiting to get our tonsils removed. The memory ends with the ether mask coming down over my nose and mouth, but only after it had come down over Fan's.

I would like to say I was happy that Fan and Bren were getting married, but I cried when she told me. It wasn't Bren; he had turned out all right in spite of my earlier reservations. In fact, I was looking forward to having him for a brother-in-law. No, I cried because I felt that I was being ripped from my Gemini twin, the better half of our duet—my sister! I tried to laugh through my tears and reminded her of our theme song: "Lord help the mister that comes between me and my sister."

She just sang back to me the next line, "Lord help the sister that comes between me and my man." We both laughed, but I honestly believed our close relationship would end at that point. It survived, however, and even strengthened in 1981 when we both became pregnant at the same time. I would be giving birth to my first child, but this would be Fan's third.

Journal Entry
May 31, 1982

Cary Ann Disher was born on December 3, a natural birth, 8 lbs., and no trouble at all. I got over there the afternoon of the birth and Cary was all combed and made up waiting for Brennan to bring the boys after school. Brennan had been with Fan through the whole labor and birth, and everybody was so happy with that girl. The boys would hurry home from school and argue over who was going to hold her

first. Chris was so good with her; he would change her diaper even when she was dirty.

The big February news is the arrival, February 6, of Kate Frances Zabbia, 8 lbs., 6 1/4 oz. Kim had the Lamaze method, like Fan, and Zab was in the delivery room the whole time. He even took pictures. She was born with a head full of coal black hair.

June 1, 1979

Let me backtrack a bit to tell you about Ricky's marriage to Gwen Bardwell in the spring of 1973. It was a small family wedding with a pretty ceremony, very impressive, and a nice reception at the Bedico Community Center afterwards. They lived in the playroom where Fan & Bren had started out their married lives nearly four years earlier.

Jan Michelle was born on November 9, 1973—a beautiful, little tiny 5 lb., 10 oz. doll. They all lived with us until January or February of 1974 when Gwen went back to work at the bank and they moved to a trailer in Hammond. Jan has beautiful golden curls and is a clown. She had to wear a bar to straighten her feet when she was little, but they are fine now. Her only problem is a runny nose, probably from an allergy.

Ricky graduated in May 1976 with a B.A. in Business Administration and took a full-time job at the bank. We were all very proud of him.

A great surprise for all of us was the early arrival of Ryan Blake Howes on April 22, 1979, instead of June 9. He weighed 3 lbs., 11 oz. and stayed at the hospital for five weeks. Now he is doing fine. They brought him home to their new house on Marley Drive in Hammond.

Lou Howes

When my younger brother, Ricky, was born in 1953, the ring and middle fingers on his left hand were joined. Because I was only eighteen months old at the time, I don't remember him as a baby, but I do remember his web fingers. They were not surgically separated until he was three, and Mom told him that he would never be able to wear a wedding ring on his left hand. That didn't seem to bother him much.

As we three were growing up, Mom was there to spray Bactine, blow our noses, and fix our lunches. Ricky and I would stand on the vinyl kitchen chairs to watch Mom make egg salad sandwiches. We scooped mayonnaise from the quart jar with a long spoon and ate it before it could make its way to the salad bowl. Fan told us that it was pronounced *my-nez*; we took her word as the gospel truth. We believed everything Fan told us because she was the oldest and smartest, and she felt it her duty to boss us around.

On special occasions, we dressed up in our trick-or-treat costumes, or in any big clothes we could find, and staged lengthy productions on top of the cedar chest in our parents' bedroom. We improvised constantly and changed characters as often as we rewrote the action. When we grew tired of masquerades, we pulled out the baseballs, badminton, or croquet sets and tried to keep up with Ricky. A born sportsman, Ricky could out-hit, out-shoot, and out-ski all of us. He was little and skinny and could beat me in any race. He even learned to waterski barefoot, while I could only slalom. The only thing Fan and I could win was the high jump because Ricky stayed short for so long. His coach wouldn't let him play basketball, so he quit the team in ninth grade. When Ricky shot up to six feet, one inch between his sophomore and junior years, the coach asked him to come back to the team, but Ricky said no.

When Fan got on our nerves, Ricky and I would go off together to Memorial Park. I asked him how he could shoot a rifle so well, and he said he didn't know, but added, "If I put in seventeen bullets and only kill sixteen ducks, I feel like I'm wasting ammunition." I was in awe, to say the least.

I was also amazed at Ricky's ability to talk his way in and out of almost any situation. He told me that anybody would believe anything if you just approached it right. He was a master salesman, whether he was selling Boy Scout raffle tickets or Kiwanis pancakes. When he greeted the neighborhood ladies at the door with a kiss on the cheek and a big grin, he would have a sure sale. If they just so happened to turn him down, he would say, "Well, if you won't buy a raffle ticket, how about some Girl Scout cookies for my sisters?"

The one thing that nearly drove us all to distraction was that Ricky couldn't sit still. He always felt the need to move; he would jerk his head, clear his throat, or sniff. He might shrug his shoulders for no reason one minute and blink his lashes in rapid succession the next, or he might do both at the same time. He would walk past a chair on one side and insist on passing the same side of the chair on his return. When I asked him why in the Sam Hill he had to do that, he told me, "Because it feels like there's an invisible rubber band that pulls me back if I go on the other side."

When I started teaching at Ponchatoula High in 1974, Ricky stopped in to see me. I was in the main office and my principal invited us into his office for a chat. I felt Ricky watching me as we talked, and afterwards, he asked me, "How do you stay so still like that?" When I told him I didn't know, he just shook his head. "I could never sit still like that."

Journal Entry
February 18, 1976

Kim dated Bobby Zabbia for most of her last three years in college and graduated with honors in May of 1974. She has had a good English-journalism education, an excellent social education, and a leader education, both from her extracurricular activities and her classwork. Kim got a job at

Ponchatoula High School teaching junior English, started planning her wedding for November, and she and Zab started building their house—just two blocks from us.

Added Note: I failed to mention Kim's growing ability as an artist. She had dabbled at art all her life, picking up a little here and there and a couple of sketching courses at SLU. During the summers she earned money drawing charcoal and pastel portraits. Excellent work!

On November 23, 1974, after many weeks of planning, showers, teas, activities of all sorts, Zab & Kim were married in a big wedding at St. Joseph. Father Charles Johnston married them. (Father Johnston also performed our wedding 29 years earlier when he was a young assistant in Amite.) Fan sang in the wedding and was matron of honor, Chris was the ring bearer, and Ricky was an usher. It was a fine family affair with Mr. Zabbia as the best man and both his brothers as groomsmen. And of course, Bert gave the bride away. Me? I was just the mother of the bride.

Lou Howes

Spring 1983

It was late, at least ten o'clock before I arrived home. I had just given a talk on freelancing commercial art at Southeastern, and the question-and-answer period went on longer than I had expected. As I got out of the car, I could smell the March air coming through the pecan leaves in the back yard and wondered how long it would last before the muggy summer washed it away. As I put my satchel on the dining room table, I caught a glimmer of a lamp coming from the front of the house. In the living room, I found Zab asleep on the sofa, Kate's little body asleep on his chest, and Cedar, our Siamese, snoozing on the carpet below. Even though Kate was only one year old, her snoring was louder than her daddy's.

"Zab," I whispered as I shook his arm, "Zab, I'm home." I gently lifted Kate from his chest, and her little fingers wrapped automatically around my neck. It was easy to see why Zab had not laid her in her crib, for she was warm nestled against my shoulder.

"How'd it go?" Zab asked as his socked feet slid onto the floor by Cedar's tail.

"Fine. Lots of interesting questions," I said, and turned toward Kate's room, knowing Zab would follow as soon as he had scratched Cedar's stomach.

"Let me change that diaper first before you put her down," Zab said. "We drank a ton of apple juice."

"OK, she's awake anyway." I lifted Kate up in the air to face me. "Hi, sweetheart. Did you and Daddy have fun?" I laid her on the padded changing table that doubled as a chest of drawers, and Zab made motorboat noises with his lips as he worked on the side snaps of her pajamas.

"Real daddies change dirty diapers, huh, Kate." Zab smiled down at his dark-haired, black-eyed beauty who reached for his cheeks with both hands. Zab took one whiff, then jumped back. "Ooh, a good one!"

A nice old lady once told me that if I wanted to stay married for a long time, I had to find someone who liked pets, kids, and old people. That advice seemed to have worked for me. Zab likes cats and cows, dearly loves our daughter Kate, and could sit for hours listening to every long-winded story delivered by any of the legendary residents of our hometown of Ponchatoula. Zab just loves everything there is to love about the small town: Paul's Cafe, the Feed Store, the Kiwanis Log Cabin—and all within walking distance from his dad's engineering office where he works.

As I was growing up just two blocks north of where I now live, I used to think that when I got big, I wanted to live in a small town just like Ponchatoula, but not Ponchatoula. I didn't think I should stay in the same town because that would mean that I hadn't grown intellectually, that I hadn't become worldly enough. I guess I assumed that just by moving to another small town, I would instantly become a worldly intellectual whose life was rich and full. I would nostalgically reflect upon those warm, childhood days in that little nonworldly, nonintellectual community in Louisiana. Even though I thought this same naive way throughout my four years in college, I had not prepared myself for one thing: falling in love with a man who was himself in love with Ponchatoula.

After Zab rocked Kate to sleep, he placed her gently on her stomach in the crib, and we crept out of the room. I don't ever remember wondering before we were married whether or not Zab would have made a good father. I just liked what I saw: dark hair, brown eyes, cheek bones and jawline that looked as if they had been chiseled from granite, and 5'10" of intelligence. It didn't hurt that we could talk to each other for hours or that his sharp features were easy for me to capture on canvas.

Journal Entry
December 30, 1980

I think one of the highlights of the first months of 1980 was Kim and her posters. The Kiwanis are in charge of the Strawberry Festival Poster, and this year they decided to have a contest to choose who would design the poster. Kim's poster won. Since then she has drawn the Hammond Hot Air Balloon Festival Poster and the Italian Festival Poster. Also she was commissioned by Mrs. Russell Long to draw a poster for Senator Long's supporters. It's been exciting to be on the fringe of all of her activity. I think she also wants to get into advertising. At this writing she has finished her art certification and has gotten the art teaching job at Ponchatoula High. She was going back to English teaching until the art teacher there had to quit. So, once again, Kim came out with

what she really wanted. She will do an excellent job, I know.
Lou Howes

I received my first easel for Christmas when I was twelve, but I cannot remember not being able to draw. Mom told me I even doodled in my diapers. I assume she meant I doodled while I was in diapers, but I guess it doesn't matter now. As ingrained in me as it was, however, I didn't take an art course until I entered college in 1970, and even then it was not my major. By that time, I guess, art was already one of my internal organs, and its newness had long ago worn off. At the time, I was more interested in my goal of becoming a high school teacher. I really didn't care what subject I taught. I just knew I wanted to teach.

Since Southeastern didn't have an Art Education degree then, I majored in English and Journalism Education. I already had a small yearbook scholarship and I loved to write, so I figured I could schedule art courses during my slow semesters. Unfortunately, I only had two slow semesters. Now, I can see that my years of involvement with the yearbook, as well as one year as art editor of the university's newspaper, turned my future toward graphic design and commercial art, a turn I never intended to make. In the nine years since my graduation, I have become what I can only describe as a small-town artist. Being a small-town artist means that I am called upon to create any number of artistic works, regardless of shape, size, concept, or medium, simply because there are not many freelance artists in town. Doubling as the high school art teacher, I am asked to move freely from portraits to logos, from interior design consulting to architectural renderings, from caricatures to silk-screen posters. It is typical of our breed to tackle several of these commissions simultaneously and for minimum wages. Most jobs are freebies, mainly because some clients believe we shouldn't charge money for a God-given gift. Even my family thinks I actually want to be in this commercial field. This is real art to them, the kind that has a purpose.

Nevertheless, at the present time, I am in the midst of a creative slump, and I have no idea how to get out of it. Maybe pregnancy did it; maybe turning thirty did it; maybe eighteen editions of posters in three years did it. I don't know. I just know that I feel like a robot with a paintbrush in both hands, pumping out impersonal commission after commission, signing my name five hundred times with each new poster. I feel reproduced, rather than unique. I watch cowardly as one of my paintings multiplies and spreads its same image throughout the South. I am tired of walking into a Wendy's in Florida three states away and seeing one of my posters on the wall above the extra napkins, the same poster that decorates kitchens in Mississippi and blends with every sofa in Louisiana.

Originally, I saw posters through a teacher's eyes, thinking they would be useful from an educational standpoint. Viewers would learn that an inspector in 1910 would randomly choose a pint of strawberries from the center of a wooden crate and pour them into his hand to check for damaged fruit, or that a Greek dancer would hold a white handkerchief in his right hand. I liked that idea, that I was teaching through my artwork. Then I became disillusioned when I discovered that some people were buying them sight-unseen just because they went up in value so rapidly. I wanted the buyer to identify with the image, not see dollar signs. Nevertheless, I shouldn't complain about the money end of it all. The fee for a commissioned poster is respectable and in balance with the number of hours I put in. I am sure I'll accept more jobs simply to help pay the bills from the addition to the house. It's difficult to justify to Zab the need for a studio if it doesn't help pay for itself monetarily. Yet, what I really want my studio to do is pay for itself emotionally. I want my paintings to speak, to move the viewer to another world. I want my paintings to make the viewer think more deeply than what's on the surface, to probe his own sensibilities, to question her own emotions. My work now doesn't even come close to this.

Journal Entry
July 9, 1981

For some time in the last few weeks of May, I had some strange feelings in my head, like I might pass out or something. Sometimes it was just a large pressure that felt terrible. I went to see Dr. Walker and he decided to run a bunch of tests to see why this was happening.

I took the glucose tolerance test—no diabetes. They also tested my blood for about five things—all negative. I had a brain scan; which is nuclear medicine, and an EEG, electroencephalograph. Then I had to see a neurologist from New Orleans who comes to Seventh Ward Hospital every Thursday.

Well, the diagnosis was that a calcium buildup in the back of my neck was constricting the flow of blood to my head, therefore causing the pressure and dizziness. He prescribed Hydergine which is a circulation medicine specifically for the head.

At this writing, I have been back to see him once, the pressure is gone, and he's pleased with the results. I'm to see him again in August. Most of the family had already decided I was crazy, but I guess that will come later.

Lou Howes

Summer 1983

I knew Bigmama was expecting me to stop by this afternoon, for she left her front screen door unlatched. In spite of the fact that she had been living in Ponchatoula for sixteen years now, my 5'7" grandmother still locked her door to ward off the same hoboes that had frequented the railroad tracks by her home in Arcola. There, she single-handedly brought up four children, my mother being the third. Situated about thirty miles north of here, Arcola was so small that Mom used to tell us that the city limits sign said "Welcome to Arcola" on one side and "Hurry Back" on the other, but I never saw it.

When Bigmama retired from her job as head, and only, librarian in Roseland, a couple of miles south of Arcola, two of her sons-in-law built her this house on the back corner of Mom and Pop's lot. She was seventy-three years old then, and this was the first new house she had ever had.

From inside the front door, I could see into three of the tiny rooms. Usually at this time of the day, Bigmama is sitting in her favorite overstuffed chair watching "Days of Our Lives" on her TV set eighteen inches in front of her. Since arthritis has brittled both of her knees, she prefers to sit close enough for her gnarly fingers to reach the dial. All the furniture in Bigmama's house is situated close together, just far enough apart to form a pathway. This tight format eliminates the need for her cane inside. She just creeps from sofa to television to chair to table to kitchen counter.

Today, Bigmama was taking an early nap, so I entered with caution, my sketchbook planted firmly under my left arm. Bigmama was my favorite model because she could sit for an hour without moving a bone in her body, except her jaws. As long as I was willing to let her talk, she would pose for me all day long. She loved the company, especially since I was one of her thirteen grandchildren.

This afternoon, I had to draw in complete silence, however, interrupted only by the soft sound of her snoring. She lay deathly still on her left side, her rosary draped gently over her hand, her face turned toward the foot of the bed and me. I could see her legs, covered tightly in support hose, flowing from the bottom of her dress, ending in toes that had long ago twisted around each other to form two triangles. Bigmama still warns me about wearing pointed shoes, showing her own deformed feet as a direct result of her youthful vanity.

As I drew the slow contours of Bigmama's hunched shoulders with my pencil, I thought about her colorful stories of the home in which she grew up as Lucille Whittington. It was a white wooden house with a massive front porch that faced those same railroad tracks in Arcola, just two doors south of where she would later live as an adult. She and her six surviving brothers and sisters were reared by an iron-fisted Papa and his strong mother. In 1920, Lucille was whisked away by an Arcola man named Warren Douglas Hendry, Jr., who, thirteen years and four children later, brought her back to that gravel road by the tracks and filed for divorce.

Bigmama rolled over with a start and even without her glasses could tell that someone was in the room.

"It's just me, Bigmama," I reassured her. "Did you forget I was coming over this afternoon?"

"No, angel. I was just resting," she slid her feet to the floor and reached for her glasses on the bedside table. I put down my sketchbook and knelt at her feet to help her put on her orthopedic shoes. I looked up at her white-white hair, trimmed short for convenience, yet long enough to soften the deep crevices by her brown eyes. She could see me clearly now, and her face brightened as I relieved her of the job she hated: getting on those "darn shoes."

"Where's my little Kate?" Bigmama asked as I helped her to stand. She took one step to grasp the wooden railing Pop had built on the wall by her bed.

"She's playing inside with Mom. We'll go over there if you like," I said as I picked up my sketchbook. "I've been drawing you while you were asleep. Look."

"Good Lord, I look like I'm dead," she said and smiled at me.

"I know. Isn't that spooky?"

"You've been here a long time then?" Bigmama took my hand. I grabbed her cane behind me as we headed for the door.

"Not long enough," I said, "but I can finish this later." We walked across the yard to Mom's back door. "Hey, I almost forgot. Next month at this time, the backyard will be filled, remember? Are you looking forward to your grandkids coming?"

"You know I am."

Bigmama's four children and their thirteen off-spring have always had a wonderful habit of getting together for any family occasion, from weddings to graduations, from blind dates to broken fingernails. When we were small, our list of vacation spots was limited to two trips outside the city limits of Ponchatoula. We could go to Arlington, Virginia, to visit Mom's sister Betty or Melbourne, Florida, to visit Mom's sister Tricia. Since their older brother, Dodo, lived just thirty miles away in Covington, his family wasn't on the list because we could visit them all year long.

This summer, Bigmama's entire crew is coming to Ponchatoula for our first official reunion. It didn't matter if this reunion were official or not. We would still do the same thing we always do: talk about each other. All the first cousins are approximately the same age; most of us spent weeks of our summer vacations in Arcola, so we share similar childhood memories of Blip the dog, the twins named Terry and Gerry next door, and the books we inhaled at Bigmama's library. Most of us dated during the Sixties, married in the Seventies,

and produced great-grandchildren for our Bigmama from then on.

Fall 1983

Yesterday's rain did little to cool the sticky Louisiana climate, yet I knew Bigmama would still take her sweater to church this morning. In spite of the fact that she is eighty-seven, Bigmama is mentally alert and, if I don't count thin veins, arthritis, and a spastic stomach, physically able. She wants to live for as long as her thirteen grandchildren and twelve great-grandchildren want her to live, forever.

Today, she opened the screen door as soon as she heard my car door slam. She had her pocketbook slung over one arm, her sweater over the other, and both hands clinched onto the arms of her aluminum walker. I gave her a kiss as I helped her cross the threshold.

"How's my angel?" she asked, smiling up at me. Her frame had long ago slumped in stature, the hump in her shoulders becoming more pronounced every year. The pink dress that Betty had made her for her birthday hung several inches below her knees, but only in the front.

"Just fine. I see Mom's already left for church," I said as I glanced at the empty parking spot under my parents' carport across the yard.

"Yes, she has to commentate today. She doesn't have to commentate all the time, about once a month. She does such a beautiful job, too, but she can't commentate when she's down the river, just when she's home," Bigmama explained as I placed her folded walker on the back seat. She was already in the middle of a sentence by the time I opened the door on the driver's side.

". . . just has a beautiful voice. You know, she was the first woman to commentate here. People are always telling me how much they love to hear Lou sing. Even when she was young, we'd go to Mass every Sunday, and Bert would always be waiting for her when we got home and—" Bigmama paused to take a breath before continuing her train of thought. The family teases her about saying "and" before she breathes, just to keep someone from interrupting her chance to finish; however, Bigmama seldom finishes voluntarily.

"You know, your daddy's not Catholic," she went on, "but that's OK. Bert agreed to raise you all Catholic, so that made it all right, and he would always make sure Lou and the kids got to church even if ya'll were down the river. He's a good man and—" Bigmama stopped for another breath, but I broke in before she could continue.

"We're here. I'll come around to get you." The church is only four blocks from Bigmama's house, so there wasn't much time for a lengthy conversation.

"OK, darlin'."

As I opened St. Joseph's massive double doors, I looked up quickly to see if the front pews were still available. Luckily for me, one was. Luckily for Bigmama, it was the one directly in front of Mary's statue, her favorite spot. She and the Virgin Mary had always been friends. I often overheard Bigmama whisper prayers to her—that is, whenever she wasn't having an in-depth chat with St. Jude.

Bigmama handed me her walker as she slid slowly into the front pew, her poor knees crackling as she sat down. Arthritis had long ago deprived her of the luxury of kneeling. As I leaned the folded walker against the edge of the pew, I saw Bigmama take out her rosary and begin whispering her prayers.

When Mom appeared at the lectern directly in front of us, she winked at me and opened her hymnal. Mom was an excellent reader as well as singer, so parishioners were relieved to see that it was her turn to commentate. Some of the men that have been commentating lately have holy intentions, but so-so reading skills, and their singing is even worse. Sometimes I imagine Mary's statuesque ceramic shoulder slowly lifting to her ear to block the din of a poor commentator. Today, however, she looked relaxed on her tiny pedestal in the air, knowing that she would be enjoying an hour of Mom's clear voice.

Even though Bigmama could no longer read without her magnifying glass, she had no problem keeping up with the Mass. She knew all the prayers by heart, even the priest's part, and recited them in her soft low voice. Bigmama still had that noticeable habit of saying the prayers one syllable behind the rest of the con-

gregation, but I guess it made her feel more devout.

As we sat down for the readings, I put Bigmama's sweater over her shoulders. Her low blood pressure runs in the family, her thin blood making her cold when everyone else is sweating. We watched as Mom stood up to read. Both readings floated into the ears of the waiting parishioners like the tinkling of fine crystal. Many did not follow along in their own missalettes, choosing instead to watch the expression on Mom's face as she read aloud.

Mom then announced the number of the next hymn, and the organist cranked up the pipes to begin. As the ushers marched up the center aisle to pass the collection baskets, Mom sang out the first line of "Faith of Our Fathers," and I thought to myself that Judy Garland would be proud. Most of the church was singing along, but there were a few who remained quiet just to listen to Mom sing.

She began the next verse as strongly as she had the first, yet when she reached the second line, she began singing different words to the music. She didn't realize she was out of sync with the rest of the congregation until she reached the third line. I could tell she felt awkward when she smiled down at me and shrugged her shoulders. She waited for the organist to reach the third verse before singing again.

After Mass was over, Bigmama and I met Mom by her car, for she was taking Bigmama home. When she saw us, she just shook her head.

"Definitely not my day, huh?"

"No big deal, Mom," I reassured her. "Happens to the best of us."

"Well, it's been happening to me too often lately. Do you realize what I did?"

"You just sang the wrong words."

"It was more than that. When I was supposed to sing the second line of the second verse, I sang the first line of the third verse. Why? I don't know. I guess I'm just getting old," she said as she opened her door. I helped Bigmama into the front seat of Mom's car.

"Old? I wouldn't call fifty-nine old," I laughed. "Bigmama, now you're going to have to say a novena for Mom too."

"Yeah," Mom added, "who's the patron saint for old people?"

Bigmama looked at both of us and smiled. "All of them."

"Great!" Mom said facetiously and waved good-bye as they drove out of the parking lot.

Journal Entry
March 1, 1984

I have been having some circulation problems—causing a memory problem—anyway, the neurologist had me take a CT scan; it was normal. Dr. Walker, our family doctor, put me on some more circulation medicines—I don't know yet if they are helping. I think a lot of it would be better if I didn't have so many people depending on me and so little time to do what I'd rather be doing. Doesn't that sound selfish?

Lou Howes

Spring 1984

Kate and I found Mom at Bigmama's house helping her take down her Christmas decorations, two weeks into January. The house was steaming hot, but Bigmama had a crocheted shawl over her knees and her sweater buttoned up to the neck. Mom, on the other hand, looked hot and bothered, as Bigmama would describe it. To me, she just didn't seem to be in the best of moods, in spite of the fact that Kate hugged her tightly around the neck when we came in.

"You're just taking down Christmas, Bigmama?" I said as I kissed her hello. Mom looked at me as if that were the sore subject of the day.

"Yes," Bigmama said, "you know the three wise men didn't come until last week."

"Then they should have come to take it down for you," Mom said in a huff as she picked up a windowsill full of Christmas cards.

"What's eating you, Mom?" I asked.

"Nothing, except Bigmama's got diarrhea again and Bert's mama called me to come over there for some little old thing and now I'm taking it out on these Christmas decorations," she said as she put bits of garland into a musty cardboard box.

Bigmama added, "I told her she didn't have to do that today, but she insisted." Then she turned to Kate, "Come here, my little Katie. Yes, you can hold it." Kate walked to Bigmama's side slowly, carrying a tiny porcelain statue from the nativity scene.

"Careful, Kate, it'll break," I said. "Hand it to Bigmama."

"No, sweetie, you can hold it. It's the baby Jesus. Can you say baby Jesus?" Bigmama looked at Kate who didn't take her eyes off the statue.

"Baby cheese," Kate said.

"Good," Bigmama smiled at her. "That's my big two year old."

"Not for three more weeks, Bigmama," I said. "Mom, did I tell you I'm taking an art history course at Southeastern this semester?"

"I don't see how you can handle all that and teach too," she said.

"That's nothing compared to what you do." I was surprised at her negative attitude. "It starts at 3:15. I'll have to book it to get there on time."

"Then don't take it," she snapped.

"No, I really want to take it," I said, then changed the subject. "Bigmama, did I tell you how much I liked the ornament you gave me for Christmas?"

"Yes, you did, sweetie," she said, then continued talking to Kate.

Suddenly, Mom stopped her packing frenzy and looked at me in a totally different mood. "I always try to make your ornament different from the rest and that's the one Bigmama wants to see first. I don't know if she even remembers the rest of them. This year, I think I mailed them all without even showing them to her."

"Mom," I said, "it's one thing to buy them for her, but don't you think she'd at least like to see them?"

"I know. I just forgot, I guess." Her eyes cast in the air looking straight through me. Mom's left eye has been blind since birth, but it was unnoticeable to anyone who didn't know. Her glasses made both eyes look normal. I walked around the table to hand her a manger light. Mom placed the last of the ornaments in the box and taped down the lid.

"Don't forget Baby Cheese," I said, but Bigmama stopped me.

"Leave him out, so Kate can play with him when she comes again."

"OK, as long as you don't care if he gets broken." Kate actually looked at me as if she were offended. "OK, OK," I said and placed him back on the table.

"Mom, did you finish that article for the *Enterprise?*"

She stopped with the box in midair and glared at me. "No, I decided not to write it."

"Why?"

"I just did, that's all," she snapped. When she saw the puzzled look on my face, she placed the box back on the table and said, "My hands just wouldn't cooperate. I couldn't get my typewriter to work, so I gave up. Which reminds me, would you commentate for me next month?"

"Sure, why?"

Mom picked up the box again and brought it into Bigmama's utility room closet. From there, she sounded like her voice was in a fog. "I just think it's time for the younger ones to take over."

Journal Entry
March 30, 1984

My association with the Enterprise *began back in my college days at Southeastern in 1944. As associate editor of the college newspaper, I came down to Ponchatoula each Tuesday with the editor and the sponsor, and we "made up" the paper. In those days, all the copy was set on the linotype machine. "Making up the paper" then meant putting the columns of "hot type" in the forms, setting the heads by hand from loose type, and, above all, learning to read the made up pages upside down and backwards. You actually got to the point of being able to read it as well as the printed paper.*

When I graduated in June 1944, I went to work at the Enterprise. *I found that my education had just begun. During the two years I worked there, my job included being a news reporter, society editor, feature writer, sports editor, bookkeeper, and janitor.*

After a fifteen-year lapse, I went back to work at the Enterprise *in the Sixties on a part-time basis. I sold advertising for the new editor, and I wrote a series of articles entitled "In Our Community," which were profiles of various people in Ponchatoula and the surrounding area. I guess I wrote over a hundred of those articles, even won an award for "Best Feature Story" from the Louisiana Press Association.*

Many weeks, when the editor was elsewhere, I was acting editor, and in charge of getting out the weekly paper and writing her weekly column under my by-line. During that time the transition began from "hot type" to off-set paste up and my education continued.

When the paper was sold to a new owner, I continued to do some feature stories and coverage of activities at the high school. When the paper was sold a second time, I hung up my typewriter and Polaroid, and my 25-year, sometimes part-time journalist career came to an end.

April 21, 1984

Ricky has changed jobs. He is now selling insurance. He had left the bank to sell communication systems for quite a while, but is doing much better in insurance. Starting out on a new career right around his 30th birthday—I hope he is very successful in it. This month's big news is Ricky and Gwen moving to Ponchatoula. They bought a house on the other side of the block from Kim's. Their back yards almost meet, but Kim is one lot south of Ricky's. Kim is on 7th Street and Ricky is on 8th Street, facing in the opposite direction.

Lou Howes

Fall 1984

It's still funny being able to see Ricky and Gwen come and go every day. Ever since April, when my brother and his wife bought the blue house on the corner behind us, their lives have been an open book to us. Whether we like it or not, we can see them, and they can see us. Maybe one day, they'll build a fence or plant a row of azaleas. At least now Ricky is close enough to help if Mom or Pop needs him.

I've been preoccupied anyway, planning a major project to commemorate the last year in our sixty-year-old high school: a written history compiled from fifty to sixty interviews of former students and teachers. The resulting articles will be printed in Ponchatoula High's 1985 yearbook, *The Last Hurrah*, as one of the students on the staff suggested we name it.

This whole project seemed right up Mom's alley—interviewing interesting people, digging through mounds of research, piecing together this journalistic history puzzle. Yet, sometimes she was interested in it; sometimes, not. I never knew what to expect.

I shut her back door quietly behind me, not sure of the direction Mom's mood would take today. All summer, no matter what we did or said, we could not lift her spirits. She was negative about every comment, whether it pertained to her or not, so much so that even her friends remarked that she was not the same old Lou. The old Lou was optimistic, but not naive. She was the gal who laughed at cynicism and dared its bitterness to rub off on her.

From where I stood, I could see through the open dining room to the kitchen table where Mom was sitting in Pop's chair, poring over some papers in front of her. She had not heard me come in, and I hesitated before walking any closer. A memory from May displaced this scene, the memory of her in that same chair moving papers around, trying to organize the church directory she had volunteered to produce. I remembered tears in her eyes that day, along with her words, "I can't do this," over and over. The day after, Mom returned the materials to the priests at St. Joseph, conceding defeat.

Now seemed almost an echo of that incident four months ago, except that today, Mom wasn't crying. She was angrily concentrating on her bank statement, trying to make sense of what appeared to her to be chaos. I startled her as I sat down across from her at the table.

"Hey, I didn't hear you come in." Mom gave me a weak smile.

"Just thought I'd stop in to say hi."

"Good," she said awkwardly and began folding her half-balanced statement into its envelope and pushing it to the side, toward the glittery white star in the turquoise Formica.

"I took back the movie camera for Pop yesterday," I told her when she stopped shuffling papers. "I still think you should have kept it."

"No, I can't work that thing."

"I guess I should have gotten a camcorder instead. Those eight-millimeter movie cameras are really antiques now."

"That's not the point," she said shaking her head.

"But it was something you said you always wanted." Pop had given me the money to buy it for their thirty-ninth anniversary in June.

"I wanted it to film you three when you were growing up. It's too late for that now."

"You could film your grandkids now," I argued.

"I said no! I don't want it, OK?" Mom looked flustered.

It was at that moment that I decided this bitterness had gone on long enough.

"Mom, you have really been a bitch lately!" I half expected her to grab me by the arm, whisk me to the porcelain sink and scrape a bar of Ivory soap across my tongue even though I was thirty-two years old. Instead, she broke into tears and proceeded to drag out a mound of papers and pamphlets onto the table in front of me.

"I know," she sobbed. "I don't know what's going on, but I think I've narrowed it down to this—depression. It's a real disease, you know. It's not just feeling sorry for yourself. Here, look at these symptoms."

She pushed a ripped-out article on depression from *Good Housekeeping* toward me. "This describes me to a tee. Look: jumpiness, getting no pleasure out of anything in life, unexplainable crying spells—that's me."

"You cry for no reason?" I asked through my own tears.

"Sometimes I wake up crying and don't know why," she sobbed. "The only thing I can't figure is that line: 'difficulty in remembering.' I'm worse than that. I can't remember *anything* anymore. Did you know that I sat in the bank parking lot for forty-five minutes at dusk the other day, just looking for the light switch in that damn car? Now, that's pretty bad!"

My insides sunk as I thought of her sitting there alone not knowing what to do, then spending hours alone, researching her own problem.

"What does Dr. Walker say about all this?"

"He thinks it might still be circulation, the brain not working because the blood isn't getting to it fast enough."

"I wish you would have told me. I could have helped you find out something, anything. I don't know."

Mom shook her head. "I feel like I'm losing my mind."

"OK, this is it," I said, clearing my voice, getting it under control. "This is what we'll do. We'll go back to Dr. Walker and have him recommend a psychiatrist, someone who can treat depression. There's medication for this. I know there is. People have this all the time and live to joke about it. Besides, it's the latest fad in diseases, Mom; you'll really be with it."

"You think so?" she smiled, knowing I was just trying to cheer her up.

Mom made an appointment the next day with a psychiatrist who happened to agree with her diagnosis and prescribed an antidepressant.

Mom's sister, Tricia, and her husband, Hank, invited Mom and Pop to join them for Thanksgiving at their new cabin in the North Carolina mountains. They said that Betty, Dodo, and his wife Olive, would be there, too, and tried to convince them that the mountains would provide a peaceful getaway. Mom and Pop took them up on their offer and returned from the trip feeling good, raving about the fire-colored leaves and the clean mountain springs. Unfortunately, the trip for Mom's sisters and brother was not quite as pleasant.

In the first week after Thanksgiving, I received a phone call from Aunt Tricia who wanted to know what was wrong with Mom. I explained that she was being treated for clinical depression and that I thought she was handling it the best way she knew how. Tricia said that Mom's behavior was stranger than depression, that she had to keep reminding Mom how to find the bathroom or how to make apple pie.

"She does have a lot on her mind lately," I told Tricia in an effort to ease her concern. "This week, Grandma had to go back in the hospital—chest pains again. So Mom's under pressure taking care of Bigmama and Grandpa, as well as keeping up with Grandma's health."

A week later, Betty's call began with a cheerful "Merry Christmas" but eventually turned to the same subject.

"Tricia told me that Bert's mother was in the hos-pital. How is she?"

"Grandma died Tuesday," I began. "I just haven't had a minute to call you, what with the wake Wednesday night and the funeral the next day."

"I'm sorry to hear that. How's Bert taking it?"

"He's OK. It seems like both Grandma and Grandpa have come close to death so many times that it was a shock when it really happened."

"I know," Betty said. "At least now, Mrs. Howes won't be calling Lou every day expecting her to come running. And how is your mom really doing?"

"So-so. Why?" I was trying not to second-guess her.

"Well, she was acting unusual at Thanksgiving."

"I know. Tricia's already called," I said. "She's still taking medicine for depression. Was she just moody?"

"No. In fact, she was in a good mood. She just couldn't *do* anything. She couldn't remember how to make up her bed; her room was a mess." There was a long pause before Betty continued, "We had to watch her; she kept missing steps on the stairs. We were afraid she was going to fall."

When I didn't say anything, Betty said, "We even

went for a ride in the car. Lou would say things like, 'Well, this is the way we came' over and over, and it really wasn't the same road. I don't know what was wrong. She just kept making these strange comments."

"They're both at the camp down the river this weekend, and you know how much they love it down there," I reassured her. "Maybe Mom just needed a vacation. I know she's been running ragged lately with the old people and not knowing if Pop is going to retire or what. This week, in spite of the funeral, she's been frantically searching the house for some stocking gifts she ordered months ago. Apparently, they came in, but she can't remember where she hid them."

"Expensive gifts?"

"No, just little tablets to put in our stockings. She was so proud of them because she had our names printed on them. I've helped her look, but I couldn't find them either. It's little things like that that really set her off."

"Well, give her my love, honey, and keep me posted," Betty said.

Summer 1985

Kamp Kim sits about a mile from the mouth of the Tangipahoa River where it pours into Lake Pontchartrain. Swamp water runs under the back of the camp, swirling around the creosote posts that raise it to safety. Thin strings of grass grow between the white shells in the ground, clam shells Pop had shoveled in from the lake to fill in a levee. The levee created a small front yard that separated the camp from the river, and a "Pop-made" break-wall still keeps the wake of passing skiffs from washing away the edge of the swamp. Treadless tires have been nailed to the sides of the wharf to bounce off docked boats when they dance in the waves.

When we were kids, we would wait for a boat to pass on the unwrinkled river before cannonballing in to catch the waves of its wake. Our inner tubes would ride the swells, pushing us back to the wharf and the waiting ladder. Even though the river was so muddy it would yellow a white bathing suit, we'd still dive in expecting to be able to see underneath. We would dive out far enough to stay away from the possibility of a stump or a trotline tangled on a cypress knee.

When Mom and Pop spent their honeymoon at the camp in 1945, they didn't even have electricity or indoor plumbing. During the six years before we were born, they probably didn't have much to do except sleep a lot. I guess they fished, walked the plank to the outhouse, and shot at bottles with the rifle Pop gave Mom for their anniversary. Pop likes to tell the story of the case of bullets he bought for $1.70, ten boxes at 17¢ a box. He would jam kitchen matches in the crack of a log on the river bank, and he and Mom would sit on the front steps of the camp with her rifle in hand.

"Your mama could strike them with her shots; make them light," he would say proudly, "and she only has one eye, you know. I could cut them in half, but I couldn't strike 'em."

Mom taught me to shoot a .22 rifle down the river. We would stand up old bottles on a two-by-four at the back of the camp where the swamp grass met the pump shed, and we would shatter them one at a time. Pop taught me to skin a catfish and set a worm on a hook down the river. Fan would sooner die than touch an earthworm, so I was always careful to allow plenty of time for the oozing thing to squirm, and long enough to be assured that she had witnessed the entire gruesome spectacle.

One night, we even spent the night on Lake Pontchartrain with mosquito netting wrapped around the bars of the canvas tarp. When the sun came up, the wind blew tiny whitecaps on the lake, and Ricky liked to jump off the boat and climb back in by walking up the dead propeller in the stern. Once, when he was tiny, he dove in wearing his lifering and couldn't flip over. I was too young to realize he was in trouble; I just thought it funny that his skinny legs were wiggling in the air above the water. The next thing I knew, a fully clothed Pop was diving over the motor into the lake after him. I asked Mom why Pop didn't take off his clothes first, but she didn't hear me; she just kept hugging Ricky and drying him with a towel.

I wasn't worried. Nothing could happen to any of us as long as Pop was around. He always has been the luckiest man I know. One night, his flat boat threw him into the river when it hit a log. In Pop-like fashion, he was not wearing a life jacket, but, with Pop's typical luck, he remained conscious and held onto his seat cushion. The boat just moved on about ten feet, and then the motor killed. Pop climbed in, started the partially broken motor and puttered home.

When Pop and Mom had saved enough money, they were able to purchase a used fiberglass Cruiser, Inc., twenty-one feet long. They called it the Mama Lou. On its last Thanksgiving trip down the river, Pop heard an explosion and saw fire coming from both the bow and stern. Making Mom jump overboard for safety, he waited to be sure she came up for air before he jumped in. By the time she did, the burning boat had floated to the shore, and Pop simply stepped out. The boat continued to burn on the site, while a dry Pop and a very wet Mom looked on.

Pop was even lucky when he caught Legionnaires' disease this spring and almost died. About a week before Pop was to retire from his sales manager job, Mom called me to come to the house immediately because Pop was talking out of his head. He was stumbling around the house, murmuring under his breath.

Mom was frantic, which is totally out of character for her; she is normally clear-headed in a crisis. I drove both of them to the emergency room at the hospital three miles away, and for the first time, Mom depended on me to take charge. This was so new to me, making the decisions in situations where my parents were concerned. Both of them were in their early sixties; it seemed too soon for me to be stepping in.

Pop stayed in intensive care, seemingly forever. When his head cleared, he wrote me a note that I still have. It reads: "They didn't tell me I couldn't talk." For the first time in his sixty-three years, I think he was feeling his own vulnerability. He seemed to realize that he was not invisible to oncoming boats or bronzed against the forces of the swamp. Pop discovered he was human.

By the time summer rolled around, Pop was back to his normal self, free of any signs of Legionnaires' disease. Mom, on the other hand, had gotten worse. Her behavior seemed far more bizarre than what I understood defined depression. Mom was never in a crisis like Pop had been. It was just something that built up slowly and began to occur more and more.

Pop knew there was something wrong with Mom long before I ever did. He just didn't say much about it. That's not unusual though; Pop doesn't say much about anything. His way of expressing love for Mom consists of a quiet pat on the shoulder when he passes or a half smile when she walks up to hug him all over. When we were little, we learned early how to read his mind. In the mornings before he went to his salesman job, a thrust-out elbow meant he wanted his short sleeves rolled up twice. At night, if Fan and I forgot to put out all the silverware for supper, Pop would silently begin eating with his butter knife until we noticed that he didn't have a fork. This summer, however, it became tough to decipher Pop's thoughts. I tried to read between the few lines that he did vocalize.

"Seems she's forgotten how to drive," he said as he passed through the kitchen where Fan and I were discussing Mom's memory lapses.

Or, "Pop, are there any more paper towels?" I'd ask.

"Nope, but there's a ton of toilet paper at the camp. Mom just keeps buying it."

When Mom complained about not being able to keep track of their insurance payments, bank statements, and bills, as well as the finances of Bigmama and Grandpa, I told Pop that I'd take over the bookwork. He just said, "I've already done that." Now, Pop handling the family finances told me that he knew much more than he was letting on. Not that he couldn't easily handle finances; he had graduated from college with a major in math. It was just that Mom had always done everything when it came to running the household. She took care of us three kids as well as three of my grandparents.

Ours was a typical Fifties household, complete with embroidered "Master" and "Slave" towels hanging in the bathroom: father working the 8 AM-to-5 PM desk job, mother working the 7 AM-to-10 PM housewife job. They reared their three children much the same way. Pop used to say jokingly that he had two daughters just so they could clean up the kitchen and change the channel. Fan and I were the very first remote controls. My brother's job was a man's job: taking out the garbage. Anyway, Pop taking over the bill paying meant something was definitely changing on North Seventh Street.

In September, Fan brought me her son's August issue of *Discover* magazine. It contained a thorough, easy-to-understand article that described a disease none of us had ever heard of. After reading it, I called Fan at her home in Morgan City. We both agreed that it described Mom's condition perfectly. In fact, it seemed like the article had been written about Mom, not that other woman. Fan suggested that I keep it from Mom, but I thought she would be relieved to have more insight into her problem. We were both right: she was at once excited and scared to death. I knew better than to give it to Pop to read. I would never know if he in fact had read it only because Pop would never say so. I decided to just tell him about it.

I stepped down Pop's two concrete stairs making sure I closed the back door quickly behind me. In Louisiana, an outside door open for more than thirty seconds flashes a welcome sign to any mosquito or roach that happens by at the time. Pop was already on the carport sitting in one of Mom's inherited rocking chairs.

I sat down in a second rocker next to Pop and thought how unusual it was that he was actually motionless in the middle of the day. Mom called Pop's chronic condition "ants in the pants," her words for his endless urge to be doing something, anything. Pop just took all the energy that most people put into talking and put his into quiet tinkering.

"You know, Pop," I began my prepared speech trying to sound casual. "Fan and I think Mom might have something called Alzheimer's disease."

His eyes didn't move from the St. Augustine grass in the backyard. I rocked my chair back and forth a few times. "It's a disease where she just starts to reverse. She gradually becomes a child, more and more helpless. We read a great article about it in one of Chad's magazines."

"Hmm," he nodded.

"Well, anyway," I continued, "we can make an appointment with the doctor, but apparently it's a hard disease to diagnose. . . . They almost have to use process of elimination; if you don't have anything else, it might be Alzheimer's."

I paused, expecting Pop to say something, but his face looked like I wasn't telling him anything new. He just waited for me to continue.

"You know, if this is it, if Mom does have Alzheimer's, it's eventually going to mean she won't be able to do anything. She'll get to the point where someone will have to do everything for her."

Pop studied the oak tree root that had cracked its way through the carport concrete, then said in his slow, Southern drawl, "I'm retired, got nothin' left to do but take care of her."

Fall 1985

I leisurely walked to six o'clock Mass to fulfill my commentating duties. Mom's name still appears on the schedule, but she doesn't commentate anymore. I substitute for her, but she thinks I have the job more often than the rest. Mom has also given up substituting at the high school. Now that we're in an entirely new building, I guess she would have had to give it up any-

way. Even I'm still having trouble finding my way around that massive complex.

As I stepped up to the lectern, I spied Mom and Bigmama sitting in the front pew, of course on the same side as the statue of Mary. Bigmama was whispering her prayers as usual, running the beads on her glass rosary. Mom just smiled up at me, happy to see her daughter following in her footsteps. She'll be sixty-one in October, I thought at the time, only sixty-one.

During the Mass, I could hear Mom singing in front of me, stopping every once in a while to hand Bigmama a Kleenex or help her with her sweater. I could have been wrong, but I thought I saw Mom make the sign of the cross backwards. Then, later, coming back to her seat from Communion, she passed up the front pew and walked down about five rows before she knew she was wrong. She turned around, trying to remember her pew, looking down each one for Bigmama's seated figure. I tried to imagine how I could leave the lectern in the middle of the song I was leading and step down to help Mom find her seat. Finally, a lady stood up from the third pew and walked Mom back to the front row and Bigmama. I could see Mom's face flush with embarrassment, and I felt a lump slowly form in my throat. I began mouthing the words to the song and was relieved when it was time to sit down.

Chad's magazine article had moved us into the wait-and-see stage of this Alzheimer's disease idea. The symptoms were slow coming on, and we afforded ourselves the luxury of some denial time, as well as the opportunity to investigate on our own before seeking a doctor's advice.

"Well, Fan, what do you think?" My calls to Morgan City were routine since we could talk longer on my nickel. Fan's oldest son Chris still swears that the first word his mother taught him was "frugal."

"I don't know," she said. "What has she done now?"

"Same old thing. Pop and I were putting together some frames, and he asked her to get some nails. She started walking out of the kitchen, then turned around and said, 'What am I looking for?' But get this," I added, "Pop was actually patient with her. He even

had to tell her three times."

"Really?" Fan paused. "Did you read a couple of weeks ago about the man in Florida that shot his wife who had Alzheimer's? He called it a mercy killing."

"Sounds like he put himself out of misery, too. Mom went to see Dr. Walker again last week," I said. "While she was in the waiting room, she made a list of all of her symptoms, including not being able to follow a recipe or drive at night. She even has to stand in the middle of the kitchen and concentrate to remember where a certain pot is."

"What did he say about all the forgetting?"

"Mom said he sounded concerned, but the tests he gave her turned out to be normal, nothing wrong. Maybe Mom really does have Alzheimer's, Fan, but if she does, wouldn't Dr. Walker have told her to see some kind of specialist or something? I don't know. Ricky thinks it might be thyroid."

"Thyroid. Where did he get that?" Fan asked.

"Something on TV. Speaking of TV, there's a movie coming on called *Do You Remember Love?* with Joanne Woodward. It's about an English professor who has Alzheimer's. I told Mom to watch it."

On the night of the movie, Fan, Mom, and I were in our respective homes with our remote controls ready. We had done so much amateur research on the subject of this crazy disease that we actually looked forward to anything out of the ordinary. Besides, Joanne Woodward is one of our favorites.

I made sure Kate went to bed early. I closed up the front of the house, and Zab and I curled up in the warmth of our bedroom, fireplace ablaze at the foot of our bed. As we watched the movie, tears welled up, then fell over my bottom lids as Joanne Woodward brought my mother to life on my very own television screen.

Zab said, "Pretty real, huh?" I just nodded and sniffed.

The final credits barely began to roll when the phone rang.

"That's it," Fan's voice was on the other end of the line.

"Yes," I said, "that's it. What now?"

"I think it's time we brought in somebody trained in this sort of thing. A neurologist maybe?"

"OK, I'll call Mom. It's time," I said. As soon as I hung up the phone, it rang again. I knew before I answered it who was on the other end.

"Hi, Mom, what did you think?"

"Scared," she said in a steady, even tone. "What do we do now?"

"It's time to see a specialist," I said. "We're still just guessing at this thing. I'm sure Dr. Walker can recommend a good neurologist."

"There's only one in Hammond." Mom was already ahead of us. "I guess we'll start there."

Journal Entry
November 30, 1985

In November of 1985, I was told that I was in the early stages of Alzheimer's disease. I have been told and read that the disease causes a gradual loss of memory and intellectual skills. It's said that it also causes a premature senility.

Since 1981, I have been under a doctor's care for circulation. I have had a few dizzy spells and almost fainted one time. I was under the care of a neurologist who ordered an

EEG and a CAT scan, but I was told it was normal. Soon after that I had various bouts with depression. My G.P., Dr. Walker, sent me to a counselor, but I don't think that helped much. I also saw a psychologist.

On October 5, 1985, I went to Dr. Walker for a checkup because I had not been feeling well, was forgetful and dizzy at times. He had me take a series of tests to be sure what I was feeling was caused by something in the body. The tests showed no physical problems other than my spastic colon, which I have had most of my adult life. On November 6, 1985, Dr. Walker referred me to a neurologist. My grown daughter, Kim, who had been very concerned with some of my actions lately, went with me.

The three of us talked at length, in a very relaxed manner. I presume he was putting me at ease. Then he tested my reflexes with various devices. He then gave me some mental exercises; he flexed my arms, legs, back, hands, and did various things that he seemed to think were normal. He gave me a list of words which I was to repeat. I was then told to finish a sketch he had made of 1/2 a diamond and a half of a building, etc. I was unable to do any of these. I was concentrating so hard my face became extremely hot. I never could do it. I could only recall one word on the list he had just read, and I was unable to finish one side of a simple drawing of a house, or a simple division problem.

In later reports to me, he said that a new CAT Scan showed a slowing down since the CAT Scan in 1981, whatever that means. I don't know. At any rate, he believes that I do have Alzheimer's disease. I have read that there is no way to say a person definitely has the disease until an autopsy is performed. If that is so, I'll never know for sure that this is what is causing me to have these symptoms. I have thoughts that come into my head and before I can really catch them they disappear. It's hard to explain. (I'm sure many words are misspelled even though I've checked many of them with the dictionary.) I can't help but notice that I have not kept consistently writing on the same line as I go from one thought to another.

It is all the more depressing that I can't write or think straight because I have spent much time writing both as an occupation and as a vocation. I worked for the Enterprise, the weekly newspaper in Ponchatoula, for many years, under four different editors. I also hated giving up substituting at Ponchatoula High School after twenty years.

During that time, I believe I taught every subject offered at the school. I was very fond of the kids as well as the principal and the faculty.

At this point of my life, I am able to do most things normally. I can hold a normal conversation, although many times a certain word will not come to me. One example is the day I was talking to my son and I said that Alzheimer's was the gradual loss of memory and intellectual skills. I got to the word "intellectual" and the word would not come to me. I thought about that word all evening. When I woke up the next morning, it was still on my mind. Then I said it immediately.

Some time ago, before I had ever been to a doctor about this condition, I tried to use my typewriter and I was shocked when the letters I typed were all wrong. Unknowingly, I had put my hands on the wrong home keys. I tried over and over to type a sentence and none of them made sense. The same type of thing happened when I tried to use my sewing machine. I could not remember how to use the machine. I had to change the thread and could not thread the machine properly. I even re-read the instructions and I still couldn't do it right.

I am still driving, but not at night. I don't have any problem with driving the car, but finding the places I'm looking for sometimes causes a problem. On that same kind of thing, some time I will be in the mall and get confused about where certain stores are and how to get to them. In the house, the most annoying thing is that I will put away kitchen things, for instance, and I can't find them when I need them. Usually, I've put the articles in the wrong place. This is such a contrast to my former philosophy of having a place for everything and everything in its right place.

All of this is very annoying, but I am handling it, so far. I find I can think clearer when I am alone or with one person at a time. Sometimes when there is a group of people around I get confused about things. Sometimes, I am completely normal for a given period of time. In fact, Kim told me a few days ago that she had seen no signs of confusion in the last couple of weeks.

Lou Howes

January 1986

Mom was actually relieved in November to find out that she had something with a *name*. She had been waking up daily with the fear that she was slowly going insane. Of course, that fear and Alzheimer's disease were too synonymous for me, but Mom was not as depressed as I was, or at least she did not appear to be in front of me. She saw a disease that could be researched and maybe, one day, be treatable or even curable. The optimism that runs rampant in my family again came through. Mom saw hope and tried to make us see hope as well.

I was not as chipper. I didn't want to believe the neurologist when he said Mom had Alzheimer's, even though Fan, Mom, and I had already suspected it. It's just that he was so complacent about it, as if he had to humor Mom because she was so sure that she had it. It was almost as if he were a mechanic fixing Mom's car, greasing only the squeaks that Mom pointed out and ignoring the fact that the engine was falling apart.

Three days before that diagnosis, I had spent the entire afternoon fixing Mom's bank statements from January to October. She had been complaining that she was having trouble reconciling each month's balance. At first, I thought that it was just Mom being her meticulous self about finding every penny. She had always known the eventual destination of every cent of Pop's paycheck. She had to; sometimes he only pulled in $300 a month. I brought the statements home and soon discovered the source of her frustration. Many of the checks were not recorded, especially in the month of June. In March, most of the checks were recorded twice, one immediately following the other. I realized that not only did these errors flow throughout the checkbook, but that Mom didn't even catch them when she tried to balance the statement each month.

Through the Christmas season, Mom and I hadn't had much of an opportunity to talk about the diagnosis. Ironically, she was in a great mood most of December, except for the afternoon of torture she spent trying to write Christmas cards. In January, we were back to normal, getting ready for Pop's birthday party. Our family never lets a birthday go by without cake, ice cream, presents, picture taking, and a loud round of "Happy Birthday to You." It would be impossible to estimate the number of photos Mom has of puffy cheeks blowing out birthday candles.

On the afternoon of the party, Kate was kneeling in a chair at Mom's kitchen table drawing what she called her "people" on tiny pieces of paper. She then lined up each drawing around the five points of the white Formica star to form a family. I sat next to her mixing horseradish, ketchup, and tabasco to create a sauce for the fried oysters, while Mom was at the sink cutting up shallots for oyster stew.

"Aren't you a bit young to be getting senile?" I asked Mom.

"Just because you get old doesn't mean you automatically get senile," she said. "You used to say 'seline,' remember?"

"Yes, I know, and I used to say that this was the 'rape of the neck,'" I said as I touched the back of my neck. I didn't want Mom to change the subject. "About getting senile, please?"

"Well, scientists now know that senility is not a normal part of aging. It's a specific brain disease, and it's usually Alzheimer's," she answered matter-of-factly.

"You sound like a textbook."

"Hey, this is going to be a great adventure. Lighten up! Alzheimer's doesn't just happen to everyone, only about four million other po' old souls."

"Oh, great," I smirked, "that's encouraging."

"What else goes with these green onions?" Mom stopped chopping and looked at me.

"You're making oyster stew, remember?"

"Right." Mom walked across the kitchen to the refrigerator, opened the door and stared inside. "What did I come over here to get? That's the damnedest thing about this disease. What was I doing?"

"Making oyster stew." I put the tabasco in the pantry and walked to the fridge to stand beside Mom. "If we both look really hard, maybe it'll come back to you." I leaned over with an exaggerated frown of concentration, my head almost entirely inside the refrigerator.

"Get out of here, you goose," Mom laughed and popped me on the butt. "That's all I need. Whatever happened to good ol' pity? I wouldn't mind being pampered once in a while."

"Oh, Mom," I smiled, "Good ol' pity is out. Guilt is in."

"I'll take care of you, Mom," Kate had climbed

down from the chair and was hugging Mom around the legs.

"That's my sweetheart," Mom said reaching down to swing Kate to the countertop. "See? Kate still loves me."

"Kate loves everybody," I said. Then Mom picked up Kate's family of drawings. I could see the surprise in her eyes. "They're something, huh." I leaned over and kissed Kate on the top of her short Buster Brown haircut.

Mom looked up at Kate. "You really are something, kid." Kate just smiled and placed her people back on the star.

"I'm taking Art Theory and Criticism this semester. Thursday nights." I sat down in Pop's chair across from Kate. "I guess I'll take it for graduate credit. I've been wanting to make this plunge into graduate school for a while now, but I don't even know where I'm going in the studio. One thing I do know, though, posters are long gone."

"There's nothing wrong with doing posters," Mom said. "Don't be so hard on yourself."

"No, I want something else, but for the life of me, I can't figure out what."

"Hey," a deep voice rumbled in as the back door shut.

I stood up for a hug. "Happy Birthday, Pop."

"Ready for some raw ones?"

"Not me!"

Mom and I exchanged glances of disgust as Pop opened the oysters and let the juice drain off in long strings before placing them on the platter.

Journal Entry
March 10, 1986

Dr. Walker has taken an interest in my actions since I was diagnosed, and he asked me various questions. My mind went blank when he asked what medicines I was taking. I had left my list at home and couldn't think of a thing. When I got home, I started to cry and couldn't stop. I even got in the shower to calm down, but I couldn't stop crying. Finally Bert made me get out and dry off and dress. He was very kind and I finally calmed down. We spent the following week at the camp. I was still very depressed about the way I felt and how easily I broke into tears.

I am at the camp with Bert and all is calm, so I sat down and wrote a letter to take to Dr. Walker when we returned. I told him about the tears and the depression I felt. I explained to him how I couldn't remember any medicine when he had asked me. He kept my papers that I had written and told me to keep writing. I also told him about the fact that I have sudden jerks or pulls of my arms. For example, I'll be reading the paper and my arm will jerk suddenly and almost pull the paper out of my hand. Another weird thing is this: I will be sitting or standing and I have this illusion that someone is standing behind me. It's so strong I turn to say something. Now, that's weird!

Bert and I plan to stay the week here. I almost didn't come because of my mother being alone but my kids said they would check on her. It is peaceful here and I have been in good shape with the exception of asking the same question twice every now and then. That irritates Bert and when he fusses about it I go into the darn tears and can't stop. I think I just get mad at myself. Dr. Walker had given me a depression medicine, but it's hard to know what to tell him. I seem to be fine until the outburst of tears I just wrote about.

Maybe I should stay down the river all the time. I guess we will when Bigmama is gone.

Recently, I have been doing an annoying thing. I will go into a room to clean, for example, and then I'll leave to go to another room for some reason. Instead of going back to the room I am cleaning, I forget all about that and start doing something in the first room. Later I realize I never did finish the job I began. That's not a major thing but it is aggravating.

March 31, 1986

It is the day after Easter Sunday. Bert and I got up early to start cooking, some small thing happened, can't remember exactly what, but I started crying. I was cooking and crying all at the same time. I had forgotten to get something I needed for dinner; I guess that's what triggered it. I finally calmed down and finished cooking the meal. It is really a confusion sometimes in the kitchen. I can stand there for three or four minutes just trying to remember where a certain thing is, things that have been in the same place in my kitchen for years.

Bert gets mad at me when I ask him something and he

answers me, then, about ten minutes later I ask him the same thing, completely forgetting that I had asked him before. I know that is aggravating. Luckily, he only fusses when the kids aren't around.

I went to church on Sunday, took Bigmama and brought her home without anything unusual. I find I cannot keep my place in the hymnal anymore. The printing is small and I get confused trying to keep up with which stanza we are on. I don't know, maybe a lot of these things are just aging and are normal, but it sure seems like it has hit me all at once. I've lost interest in so many things I used to enjoy doing. I really have no involvement at all. I guess I have spent most of my life in some kind of volunteer activity and now I miss it. However, I don't think I could handle much of anything and would probably screw up what I was trying to do. I've already experienced that in my own personal activities. I guess it is just as well, because since Bert has been retired we come to the river a lot and I wouldn't want to be tied up with something when he wanted me to go with him.

I talked to Dr. Walker about my depression and tears. He has me on a medicine for depression and told me to keep a record of my feelings and see if it helped. Well, I have done

that and since I started writing down everything, I haven't really had any bad crying spells and things have been doing pretty good. At this writing, Bert and I are at the camp for a week. I have found a nice young lady to check on Bigmama so I feel freer.

May 27, 1986

It is early in the morning. I woke up earlier than usual and Bert is still in bed. I mention this in the record of my feelings mainly because I am always much clearer in my mind when everything is calm. As for my memory: I am getting worse, I guess. I seem to ask the same questions more often and get confused. I guess what they call "short term memory" is my biggest problem. For instance, I will talk to someone and ask, "What time are we going?" Five minutes, or less, later I have no memory of what time I was told. Those are the kinds of things that Bert hates.

I really can't blame him for getting aggravated when I do that. He is very good to me and has taken on almost all of the household affairs that require a clear mind. It upset me very much, at first, when he took over all the stuff I had been handling all of our married life. I felt left out I guess. If you spend most of your life being a very reliable person, it isn't easy to realize you have lost most of your intellect—including your spelling. There are so many silly things that confuse you: like paying for something and counting the change.

Yesterday, we celebrated my daughter-in-law's birthday. I have always made a cake for each of the "kids" (little and big). I started getting everything together and just couldn't face trying. Bert took over, I read the directions and he made the cake. He did a darn good job, too. We had a good time at her party and I was relaxed and enjoyed it. Right now, the good things in my life exceed the bad things.

One of the most aggravating facets of this stupid disease is tears. When I foul something up, down they come; when Bert gets outdone with me, down come the tears, when I think about the future and what it will bring, down come the tears.

I try very hard to keep most of my feelings between me and Bert. There is no sense in making everybody miserable. Right now, at the camp, at 8:30 a.m.—all is tranquil. I'd like to stay here all the time! It is quiet and tranquil here on the Tangipahoa River. Circulation, that is the cause of all of this. If your blood does not circulate well, you do not do anything

well. My circulation must be lousy. I can hold my head up to look at something and if I stay that way very long I get very dizzy and unstable. I tried to paint a high wall and had to stop. I'm finding out more and more what this disease does to you. Not only a loss of memory, but an inability to do things that you have always done well.

June 14, 1986

I have not been keeping up with this journal as I should. For a long time, I have always been happy to keep my grandchildren whenever asked to, and we get along fine. I spend a lot of time with them and take them to the movies. This year they each had a week with us as usual. However, it was not the same. Maybe it's just that I'm getting older, in addition to the Alzheimer's, but I lost my patience a lot. I could really feel the pressure on my nerves. I guess this is the last year I will do this.

I wonder what changes will come in a year. I do not have much trouble in a conversation when it is one-on-one, but if there are more people talking in the room I usually just sit back and watch and listen. I know this is not very significant, but it is an "about face" from my normal habits. So many *changes have occurred in my daily life. It seems that changes come very often and it surprises me when I realize I'm a different person. This terrible writing and spelling is a prime example of the change. I was always a neat writer—NO MORE!*

When Dr. Walker first took my case, he suggested that I walk at least a mile a day. I have been doing this almost every day and really enjoy it.

Lou Howes

July 1986

The family is still adjusting to Mom's seven-month-old diagnosis, and Mom is trying to adjust to her new head. Pop's ingenuity has made life easier for her, though. He keeps a few dollars in her wallet to make her feel more secure and has changed out the telephones to an instant dial system in which Mom only has to press one of our names to make a call. He bought Mom a digital watch to replace hers with the traditional hands, even though he knows it will not improve her fading concept of the passage of time. At least, Pop thinks, she will feel more comfortable know-

ing she can still read time.

Now that school is out for the summer, I can stop by during the day to visit. Because we live in a typically safe small town like Ponchatoula, Mom and Pop have never gotten in the habit of locking doors. Kate and I always feel free to walk in unannounced and roam through the house until we find one of them.

"Hey, what are you doing?" I asked as we found Mom sitting on the floor in Ricky's old bedroom going through some papers in a drawer. There were remnants of ten years of Scouting, newspaper articles, camp uniforms, and fifth-grade reports on China.

"You startled me," Mom said when she heard us come in. "I thought you were just one of those ghosts that stand behind me. Hey, sweetie." She reached over and kissed Kate on the cheek.

Ricky's twin bed was another "Pop creation." It towered three feet from the carpeted floor, held in place by drawers and drawers of enviable storage. At the foot of the bed, shelves displayed Ricky's childhood collection of plastic and glass horses, while the wall held two calendar paintings of horses mounted on wood that Fan and I had decoupaged for one of his birthdays. I swung Kate to the high bed and placed Fan's old doll house beside her.

"What are you doing with all of this stuff?" I asked as I sat down on the other twin bed, this one placed uncreatively on the floor by the front windows.

"I'm throwing most of it away," she said.

"What? Mom, don't throw that stuff away. That's some neat junk." I had always been a pack rat like Bigmama. Mom, however, held little sentimental value for anything old.

"I don't want someone to have to go through all this after I'm gone." She tossed one of Fan's English IV notebooks into the garbage can. I immediately retrieved it.

"Mom, you've got *lots* of time left. Good grief! Why don't you just let us go through our own stuff, and you go through yours. I want to check everything before it gets to the garbage man; I don't trust you."

"Oh, I haven't thrown everything away." She smiled. "Look what I found." She handed me a faded manila envelope containing a stack of newspaper clip-pings, each entitled "In Our Community."

"Your old feature story." I was pleased. "I haven't read these in ages. Not all of these people are dead either, but they are pretty old."

"Yes, I thought about taking them to the new editor at the *Enterprise*. He just might want to run them again," she said.

"I'll take them for you," I said. "What's this?"

"You can have it," Mom handed me what looked like yellowed white fabric carefully folded and placed inside a plastic bag. I unwrapped a crepe de chine dress stiffly creased from age.

"What is this?" I asked again.

"My wedding dress," she said, not even looking up at me.

"Mom," Kate spoke up from above, "can I wear it?"

"Sure, honey," Mom said.

"No, Kate," I intervened. "It's really old, and the material is ripe. I'm afraid it might tear. Let's just keep it in this bag." I refolded it gently and returned it to its plastic home, while Mom continued to root through musty-smelling papers and trinkets. I remembered this room was red once. We each could pick the color of our sheetrock walls, and Ricky chose red. Luckily, Pop had long ago painted over the red, but Ricky's handwriting remained on the facing between the two front windows. The writing was a list of dogs we had owned and the day each died. One, Petie, had a broken heart drawn beside the date. All of Ricky's childhood memories were still here: his horses, his Scout badges, his lifesaving certificate.

"Have you seen Bigmama yet today?" Mom interrupted my thoughts.

"No, I thought I'd take Kate over in a little bit. Mom, have you told her about your Alzheimer's?"

"No, it would just worry her."

"Then how are you going to tell her she has to move to Florida?" I asked. Mom's sisters, Betty and Tricia, still live next door to each other in Melbourne. They are planning to move Bigmama there permanently since Mom cannot take care of her anymore.

"I'll tell her soon enough," Mom said.

Bigmama reared her four children alone after Bigdaddy left her during the Great Depression in 1933.

She never remarried because she is a devout Catholic that would sooner boil in oil than commit a mortal sin. We heard that Bigdaddy had finally died last December in Jackson, Mississippi, at the ripe old age of eighty-nine. We, of course, teased Bigmama right away, telling her that it was all right for her to marry again. She just said, "Aw, go on."

Before he divorced her, though, Bigdaddy bought a faded white house and had it moved on family land by the railroad tracks in Arcola. It was placed on two-feet-high brick piers just a piece up the gravel road from Bigmama's sister. Mom, a full-fledged tomboy, became fast friends with her first cousin, who told her that if she could kiss her elbow, she would turn into a boy. Mom practiced daily but couldn't make the transformation. She lived in pants, though, much to Bigmama's embarrassment, except at school and church.

"Girls couldn't do anything!" Mom used to tell me. "You had to sit pretty or you'd get a spanking. You had to watch every move you made."

The Great Depression made it hard for Bigmama and her brood to live comfortably. Mom's memories were of six rooms and a path to the outhouse, potted meat and cod liver oil on a daily basis, and iron-filled tap water that left an orange ring in the footed porcelain bathtub.

I watched Mom get up from Ricky's bedroom floor and stretch past my height. She closed each drawer neatly and picked up the trash cans as Kate and I followed her into the living room. Mom still wore pants in the winter and shorts in the summer and did very little to hide her obvious tomboyish looks, of which she was still proud.

Bigmama moved to Florida on June 25, Mom and Pop's forty-first wedding anniversary. Mom had told her about the Alzheimer's, and Bigmama seemed to have known about it, to have sensed it coming. Bigmama also understood that she had to leave. I hated to see her go.

I scheduled a second-opinion appointment for Mom with a neurologist at Ochsner's Clinic in New Orleans for July 18. Pop drove with us to the city, and Mom was interested in the possibility of a different diagnosis.

August 1986

Bigmama hadn't been gone five weeks before Kate and I flew to Melbourne to visit her. We knew before asking that Zab wouldn't want to go, not because he didn't miss Bigmama, but because he doesn't like to travel for any reason. When Kate asked her daddy to go with us this time, he just said, "I've done that, punkin. You go, and I'll pick you up at the airport on Monday." Six days later, just as he had promised, Zab was waiting for us at the other end of the terminal. When Kate saw Zab, she ran to meet him.

"How was Mickey Mouse?" Zab asked after all the kissing and hugging were over.

"He's too big, Daddy. I was scared." Kate frowned as Zab carried her to the baggage terminal.

"That's OK. Was Bigmama glad to see you?" he asked me.

"Oh, yeah. Betty and Tricia were lucky enough to rent her an apartment right across the street from them, so it's like she's right next door."

"Daddy, I swam in Uncle Hank's pool."

"You really swam? That's great," Zab said, then

turned to me. "Did she really?"

"More like dog-paddlin'," I answered, "but she could stay afloat. Tricia and Hank even let her get in the hot tub."

Zab arranged the luggage neatly in the trunk as I strapped Kate into her carseat. We still had an hour's ride from New Orleans before we hit that welcome sight of the streets of Ponchatoula. Now I know what Zab meant when he said that the best part of a trip is the coming home.

"Has Mom heard about her tests at Ochsner's?" I asked as we pulled onto the interstate.

Zab shook his head no.

"I can't believe that. It's taking forever, and I'm sure Mom's anxious about it. If we haven't heard by the end of this week, I'm going to call them. How's she doing?"

"Same. You haven't been gone that long." Zab smiled as he glanced back at Kate. He silently pointed to the back seat. I turned around to see Kate's head drooped to her shoulder as she snoozed quietly in the sunshine.

"Kate posed for me last night. She sat so still that I was able to get four sketches done before she got restless. Getting back to Mom, did you get to see much of them?"

"Just a couple of times. They went down the river right after you left. I think Ryan went with them."

"I wish Fan and Ricky would accept the fact that Mom can't babysit anymore. Chad stayed almost two weeks in June. They know Mom can't drive the kids to the show or anywhere else, for that matter, and you know Pop's not going to take them."

"Pop said he doesn't mind, said Mom enjoys having them around."

"Oh, Mom told me that she loves to see them, just not be responsible for them, especially for more than a couple of days."

"I'm sure your daddy will tell them when it's time to stop."

After a week, Mom still had not heard from Ochsner's, so I called to schedule an appointment. I drove Mom and Pop to New Orleans, and we sat in the waiting room for more than an hour before we overheard a nurse ask the receptionist for Mom's file. She said that the doctor wanted to read the psychiatrist's report before he saw us. After another half hour, they called us in for a conference. I was already outdone with the fact that I had to call them instead of vice versa; but the long wait and the fact that he was just now getting around to reading the test results really began to raise my blood pressure. His abrupt tone of voice didn't help matters much either.

"This report confirms the fact that you probably have Alzheimer's disease, Mrs. Howes."

"So what's next?" I asked him before Mom or Pop could say anything.

"Nothing. There's no cure."

"What about drug testing? It must be going on somewhere."

"Well, not here at Ochsner's or anywhere else in the United States, for that matter," he paused, "except at the National Institutes of Health in Bethesda, Maryland."

"That's enough. What do we have to do?" I asked. Mom and Pop were letting me go on, so I assumed they

approved.

"Well, one physician from here has had his mother accepted there. It's all experimental, but they do pay your expenses."

"Just tell us what we have to do."

"I would suggest you call N.I.H. first. Ask for the Division of Stroke and Neurological Diseases. Tell them you wish to check into their current experimental testing program."

When we got back in the car, I finally asked Pop and Mom what they thought. "Was that OK? I was determined not to be wishy-washy after the way we'd been treated so far."

Mom said, "That was great, honey. You did fine. Call those people and let us know what you find out."

I turned toward the back seat to catch a glimpse of Pop. He nodded his head once and smiled at me.

Journal Entry
August 23, 1986

There was very little accomplished that day at our appointment at Ochsner's. The doctor asked a lot of ques-

tions, and I had a series of tests with a woman psychiatrist. Pictures: she had me identify pictures of all kinds of things. I did pretty well on that, but she never said a word, nor could I say anything. She had a test on matching two similar objects—this was very hard. One was hands of the clock in different places on the paper and I was to match them. Also, some vague faces in black and white which I was to match. I think I really did bad on those.

So, I had to return August 15th to get the results of the tests. Well, what he said, loud and clear, was that I positively have Alzheimer's disease. He talked so gruff and so fast, as if he thought we were going to dispute him. He emphasized that there is a tangle of nerves in my brain which will get worse as time goes by. Then I will lose a lot more of my ability to remember. The picture he described was not a very pretty one.

However, he did tell us that there were some experimental things being done and they would welcome volunteers for the work. Kim called the National Institutes of Health in Bethesda, Maryland and they asked her to get all my records. If we are accepted, Bert and I will go to Maryland (they pay your way). Hopefully, Bert can hang out at Beth's, my niece in Fairfax, Virginia, when he can't be with me.

To best understand what this disease can cause, let me tell you some of the things that have happened to me in the last three years. My short-term memory has gotten very bad. I have trouble remembering anything I don't write down. I continually am asking someone a question and then repeat the question, never remembering that I just asked it. In normal conversation I lose words and names. They just will not come to my mind. It is embarrassing, really. I have trouble following instructions for recipes and medicines, especially medicines with varied dosages at various times. In church, I have found myself not able to keep up with my hymnals or prayers. I can't keep up with the music. Sometimes it seems to be my eyes, but I don't think so. I've recently seen an optomologist and he said I was fine. Anyway, it is annoying, maybe it's just my inability to concentrate for any length of time on one thing.

One thing I believe I hate the most is hiding things from myself. I will put something away in the kitchen and never put it in its original place. Then I have to look everywhere to find it. I have a hard enough time remembering where things are that I have known for years. Then when I put them in a wrong place, that's worse. I think what I hate the most is a loss of intellect. My handwriting is horrible; my spelling is worse. I have Liquid-Papered this diary to death with my proofreading. Sometimes I repeat what I have said and don't even know it.

October 1, 1986

As of this writing, we have been in touch with the lady doctor who seems to be in charge of my case, Dr. Moral Mouradian, in Bethesda. Kim talked to her yesterday. She said that at the moment they were short of beds, so she would have her secretary set up a time and inform us. I presume she will send us plane tickets; they are paying for us both. The next step will be our trip to Bethesda. Kim made some notes: they will do an evaluation on me, run tests, C.A.T. Scan, and a Lumbar puncture. If I do qualify for the experiment, I will stay there several weeks on the drug program.

Lou Howes

October 1986

"I wish I were going with you tomorrow, Mom. This is so exciting." I walked around the side of her bed to the built-in chest of drawers and pulled out six bras, six step-ins (Mom's word for panties), and six pairs of socks. The bed was already filled with six neatly folded shirts and pants, as well as two pairs of pajamas and a robe.

"Then come on. Pop would be delighted if you took his place."

"I'd get fired if I took off two weeks to go play in Bethesda. That's the beauty of retirement. You're both free birds. Besides, I told you, next Wednesday, Zab and I are going to Chicago." I stooped down to open the big suitcase on the carpeted floor.

"That's right. For one day. I still think that's ridiculous." Mom placed her makeup inside a shower cap for safekeeping.

"I do too, but when you go with Zab, you take what you can get. We'll be flying out at 7:30 in the morning and be home in bed by 9:30 that night. Zab has a business meeting at noon, and I'm just going to saturate myself with art all day, everything from Seurat at the Art Institute to Picasso's big baboon outside. I'm looking forward to it in spite of the fact that it's so short."

"Is Kate going with you?"

"No, Zab's mom is going to pick her up at the day care after school, and they'll bum around together till we get home. Kate did ask that we bring her a gray Pound Puppy. When I wanted to know why it had to be gray, she said, 'Because I want to name it Gravy.'"

"Then she should ask for a brown one."

"No, Mom, she wants to name it Gray-Vee. Get it?"

"What a kid!"

I had just begun packing Mom's clothes into the bottom of the suitcase when Pop walked in.

"Here," he said handing me a roll of string.

"What's this for?"

"To tie up the pants and shirts that go together, so Mom will know what matches."

"You never stop thinking, do you?" I took the string and started wrapping each matching set. Pop didn't answer, just went back to the boathouse to get in one last day of tinkering before he had to leave. Mom sat quietly on the edge of the bed, her mind off in the distance somewhere. Her glasses seemed to hide the thoughts that were slowly tangling inside her brain. She seemed to be lost within them.

"Hey!" I startled her, "you can't forget this." I threw a new book covered with soft red fabric across the bed. The book's pages were empty, waiting for Mom to write "The Bethesda Story." As a news reporter, she had always turned to writing to express her thoughts and to record her research on any given topic. The journal she has kept since 1972 is filled with matter-of-fact dates and events, a typical reporter's rundown of each year of our lives. The diagnosis of Alzheimer's last November, however, called for a more personal view of her life. She left the old journal and moved on to a stenographer's notebook to record her feelings and her constantly changing symptoms. Her journal then became her therapy as well as her account of the disease, and I think she felt better because of it.

Two days ago, we celebrated Mom's sixty-second birthday. One of her gifts was this bound red book, empty of words, but filled with eager anticipation. Mom reached across the bed and opened to the inscription on the first page. She read it aloud: "We love you, Mom! Go for it! Love, Kim, Zab, and Kate," then said, "I always wanted to write the great American novel."

"Well, now you can write the great American journal instead."

Journal Entry
October 29–November 1, 1986

The Bethesda Story—Getting to Bethesda turned out to be a slapstick comedy. We had been sent Eastern airline tickets from New Orleans to Washington, D.C. However, the plane we were to take had trouble so we were rerouted to Pittsburg via U.S. Air. When we got to Pittsburg the plane to Washington had trouble so we were rerouted to Baltimore. From there we took a bus to Washington National Airport. We picked up our luggage, which, by the grace of God, was going around and around in the terminal. Then we waited for about an hour until the shuttle came and took us to the first step of our stay at the National Institutes of Health. We met Dr. Mouradian and I was put in Room 213, a semi-private room. Since I did not have a roommate, they let Bert stay there with me until he got a room at a boarding house.

Dr. Mouradian is a charming lady. She is very pretty and speaks with a slight accent. Very quietly, I would guess she is in her early 30's. She has been asking me many questions about myself. Not only medical, but about all facets of my life. She has already decided that I am intelligent—her word, not mine!

Here at the hospital every patient is assigned a nurse—called a Primary Nurse. Mine is a pretty, tall gal named Carol. I have a therapist, a young lady who does the psychological tests, and there are two men neurologists. This is my third day, and I am now officially on the drug program. I have had two days of medicine and no sign of any ill effects.

Some of the tests were like these: "I'm going to give you this list of words and I want you to remember them. I'll ask you about these later." Then, another such as a frame of designs of all shapes that I looked at for about two minutes and then she would have me match them with the ones like it. Anyway, after two days of this, I was exhausted, mentally and physically. We must have done that for two or three hours at a time. I'll never know what they concluded.

November 3, 1986

I have just returned from a half hour walk with the recreation lady at the hospital. It was nippy and felt great. The hills were a bit hard on my knees but we made it. My walk, or anywhere I go, has to be scheduled for the time in between my tests. I am still having to lie down for ten minutes and have my blood pressure taken; then stand up for five minutes and have it taken again.

All this, I presume, has to do with the results of the testing with the new medicine I have been taking. The nurse said this will go on for a long time. I asked Dr. Mouradian what the drugs were doing. She said that the four red capsules were to improve my memory, and the others were to avoid side effects.

I am taking all the tests again which I had taken before I had the medicine. I honestly felt like I did better on the tests. I know my head was clearer the whole time I was taking the tests. A group of men asked to try out some of their testing material and lab work on me. I spent almost all afternoon working with them, more of the stuff like before. I was listening through earphones and identifying where the sounds were coming from. Also, a figure would flash on the screen and I was to say which side of the machine had sent it. They said I did the test well, like getting all the sounds right. I do believe my head is getting clearer. The people I worked with there said they couldn't believe I had Alzheimer's.

Bert kept some notes on various tests that he and I had. I took a Lumbar Puncture. I had been told not to stand up after I got it because when my head is up I could get a very bad headache, called an LP headache. I did not get up the whole day. That night I got up to go to the bathroom; I forgot about the LP. But when I stood up I surely remembered. It felt like my head blew off. Carol was on night duty and got me back to bed. Carol said, "If you stand up it hurts; if you lie down, it stops hurting." That may sound easy but it also means lying down to eat, to use a bed pan, and everything. I got a pain in the neck trying to eat in a lying down position. It also can get messy. However it wasn't too bad. Dr. Mouradian said that some people get the LP and some do not. They don't know why. I just happen to be one who got it. I also had an EEG and a Pet Scan.

This time we were taken to St. Elizabeth Hospital in Washington, D.C. They had two machines that Dr. Mouradian did not have. There they took a 133x NON, a localized Cerebral Blood Flow study. When I first walked down the hall I was asked to pretend to kick a football, throw a baseball, use a tennis racket, and throw a football. I was told later that they did that to stimulate my body.

Two young ladies were in charge. They asked Bert if he would like to take the test also, and he did. They had a different machine than I had before. I didn't mind the test, but each time I was tested I was blind-folded, and they put a cup in my mouth. They really didn't want me to move or talk. We took a number of different tests, but of course, we didn't know much about them. They didn't tell us that St. Elizabeth was an insane asylum.

One thing that I failed to record in my journal was that Dr. Mouradian asked Bert if he would like to enter the family and come into the hospital as a "Well Person." He would be taking all the tests that I took and she could use the results as a comparison to me as an Alzheimer patient.

He and I both had a lumbar puncture. I had the LP headache but it wasn't as bad as the first time. It didn't last as long. Bert had a mild LP headache. Bert took an MRI test and I took one later. They sat me down in a big metal container and whatever was going on made a loud noise, over and over. I decided to count the loud noises just to have something to do. There were 65 loud KA-PLUNKS! They made four rounds.

There were some odd things that happened to me at two different times that were very unusual. About four o'clock a.m. I woke up and immediately my mouth filled with water. It was the oddest sensation. I reported it, but nobody knew why it happened. The second thing was strange. It seemed to me that I was in a dark high bed and when Carol came to my room she seemed to be coming from a high place. I guess it was only the darkness and the pain, but it was really weird. It was only momentary, then I realized where I was.

Lou Howes

December 1986

Mom and Pop's first trip to the National Institutes of Health took up the greater part of November. When they came home, Mom told me about the variety of mental exercises the therapist had given her to stimulate her memory. Within a few days after their return from Bethesda, Kate and I found Mom sitting on the side of her king-size bed, looking up at the multitude of family pictures on her wall, reciting the alphabet.

"Who are you talking to?" I asked as we hopped onto the bed behind her. Kate gave Mom a hello kiss.

"Hey, sweetheart," Mom grinned at Kate. "My therapist told me to talk to myself. It's good for my brain. A-B-C-D-E-F-G."

"You learned your ABC's at Bethesda?" I asked sarcastically.

"No, they told me to do this to keep from forgetting so fast," she said. "Next, I name everybody on this wall. See? There's Fan and Kim and Ricky." She sounded sing-songy like our first TV teacher, Miss Sherrie on "Romper Room," looking through her magic mirror at the end of each show.

"And there's Fan and Bren's three: Chris, Chad, and Cary—all C's. And Ricky and Gwen's two: Jan and Ryan." Mom paused. I saw her catch a quick glimpse of Kate then turn back toward the picture wall with an exaggerated frown on her face.

"Hmm . . . I know I'm missing somebody. Oh, who is that pretty little girl? She looks so familiar."

"Mom, that's me," Kate said.

"I know it is," Mom laughed. "I was just teasing you." Kate seemed relieved. She was never quite sure anymore when Mom was serious.

"Don't forget those two old people," I said as I pointed to Mom and Pop's wedding picture.

"Old?" Mom protested. "I was only twenty, and Pop was twenty-three. Both 5'9" and 125 pounds wringing wet!"

"Tell Kate about your wedding cake," I said as I kicked off my shoes.

"It slid sideways in the back seat of the car," she said. "Bigmama had to make an extra cake to stick in the hole at the bottom. Nobody even noticed."

"Did you eat it?" Kate asked.

"Sure, it tasted fine. Just a little lopsided."

"Mom," Kate had a quick thought. "Can I be your teacher?"

"OK, what do you want me to do?" Mom was always a great playmate when it came to her grandchildren.

"Uh, let's see." Kate thought a long time. "What

other things did you do in Bethesda?"

"Well, let me think," Mom said. "You could call out some numbers or letters and see if I can repeat them."

"Good. I'll make out a test for you," Kate said as she scrambled for a notebook and pencil, then sat on the floor at the foot of Mom's bed.

"Ooh, I hope I make an A," Mom said as she winked at me.

Journal Entry
January 11, 1987

I am very displeased with my writing in this journal. The front fly itself is a mess. I had my friend help me transfer the material I had written earlier on paper into my journal. She read the material to me and I wrote it in the journal. Sometimes I was ashamed of it. Perhaps I need some more of Dr. "Moral's Magic," my name for the drugs I took in Bethesda.

This is the first time I have sat down to write since I left NIH on November 7th. I came home to my family getting ready for Thanksgiving. We had no trouble with the plane this time and the family was there to meet us. It took a long time for us to get back to our old lifestyle after almost a month at NIH. However, we miss everybody there. We felt part of a large family. The whole crew was kind and friendly, and Bert and I were happy to be a part of the important adventure.

By the way, I had an unusual thing happen. I was dressing in my room and suddenly I thought I saw swirls of red water on my hands. I started to dry it but it evaporated quickly. There was absolutely no wetness that I could feel in the whole procedure. Now that is weird!

There comes a time when you have to accept the fact that you really have Alzheimer's disease. You have read a lot about it and you know what is ahead for you. You become angry and frustrated, and the tears come against your will. You begin to feel sorry for yourself and think, "Why me, Lord?" You are outraged that this should be happening to you! I went through all that and when I finally calmed down, I decided that there were two things that were going to keep me going. The most important of all was to keep my trust in the Lord. The other thing was to keep my sense of humor and use it for a weapon.

When I can't find something that I have put in the wrong place, I blame it on Al. When I say the same thing or ask the same question twice in a short time, I blame it on Al. When I start to say a word and it won't come to my head, I blame Al. Al took it! When I tried to make change for a purchase and couldn't, it was Al's fault. The line, "Al did it" has become a joke at my house.

My son, Ricky, gave me a sweatshirt for Christmas. On the front, it said, "I remembered." On the back it said "I forgot. Al took it".

Who is Al? Al is Mrs. Zheimer's son, Al Zheimer. I know it's corny, but it beats dwelling on the sad side of the story.

Yesterday, we got a telephone call from Marge Galespie, the coordinator, in Bethesda. She wanted us to come to N.I.H. again from January 26–31. I am looking forward to it. The time I have spent in Bethesda has been a good time, give or take a needle or two. While I'm there I don't even think about Alzheimer's. I'm kept too busy taking tests to dwell on my misfortune. Bert and I both are always ready for whatever they want us to do.

Lou Howes

January 1987

Pop and Mom apparently had a great time in Bethesda. Pop even volunteered to be what they called a normal patient and took a bunch of the same tests Mom was taking. He wouldn't even let them pay him. He said he felt sorry for them if they thought he was normal. The doctors must have enjoyed them. They just called them back Wednesday for the second time. Pop would never say, but I think he was actually looking forward to it. He brought along one of his tablets of dollar bills. He stacks together fifty crisp one-dollar bills, real money, then paints one of the edges with rubbery, red glue, the stuff the printing shops use to make tablets. When he sees somebody really gullible, he pulls out this tablet and says something like, "You've been so nice. Here, have one of these." Then, he tears off one and hands it to them. They just stare at that dollar, thinking it's counterfeit.

Journal Entry
February 11, 1987

When we got to NIH, we were warmly greeted by the

staff, and I felt like I was coming back to my "home away from home." Dr. Isabella Heuser will be testing each of us physically and asking us a lot of questions concerning our life history, sickness, diseases, etc. It seemed that she wanted to know everything about us before she does the tests.

The doctor and her crew started getting all of their equipment together and attached an IV to both Bert's arm and mine, which stayed there throughout the procedure. We could lie down as much as we wanted and could walk around holding the tube of our IV. We were tethered, so to speak, and could walk only as far away as the tube extended. There was an apparatus on wheels which we held onto as we walked.

At intervals, we were given neurological tests, and a page of questions that we had to answer. The questions were all to do with our feelings, emotional and physical: Are you afraid of crowds? Do you think every one is against you? Have you lost your interest in sex? Do you hear voices that no one else does? Are you feeling listless? Are you uneasy with the opposite sex? Do you feel anxious when talking to people? Bert had to do this also. I could not keep my answers and questions straight so I had Carol, my nurse, read them

to me and put the answers on the sheet. It was a confusing experience.

We had blood flow tests during the day and night, 36 hours. I failed to tell about the horrid night I had. In the first place, the equipment used for the blood flow tests constantly gave out noises, very loud noises. I had to keep still in bed in order for the IV in my arm to stay straight and not disconnect. That created a great strain. I lay on my back and woke up with extreme pain all over my body. It felt like a hot poker. I didn't know whether or not I was allowed to move, so I called to whoever was behind the curtain and told them about my pain. They gave me some Tylenol. Eventually, after moving around a little, I felt better. Later that night my shoulder got a cramp in it, and I rang for the nurse who gave me more Tylenol. Soon the pain eased.

I found it very thoughtful of Dr. Isabella's associate to come over and ask about the pain in my back and shoulder, and to thank us for our participation in their studies. Just for the record, Dr. Isabella is a tall pretty red head with hair to her waist. She has a German accent and sometimes we couldn't understand her. On the other hand, she asked us how to say certain English words.

The next day, Bert and I each took more psychological tests. I was with a girl whose accent was so strong I couldn't understand all she said. These tests were done with a computer, and I found them much harder to understand. It was the first time during all the tests that I felt so confused and was unable to perform the tasks. It suddenly hit me that I was losing my ability to handle complicated instructions. I came face to face with the realization that my condition was getting worse.

Lou Howes

February 1987

Within a week after my parents returned from their trip to Bethesda, Kate, Mom, and I flew to Melbourne, Florida, to see Bigmama. She had not been doing well, and Betty and Tricia had had to place her in a nursing home for round-the-clock care. I knew it was in the middle of the school year, but I was afraid Mom might not get to see her mother again before she died, not to mention me not getting to talk to her one last time. Kate and her new Chicago Pound Puppy, Gravy, came along for the ride. The hour-long drive with Betty and Tricia to the Merritt Island nursing home gave me plenty of time to ask details and allow my sensitive five year old to adjust to what she was about to see. Mom already knew more than we did because she and Pop had just been here in September for Bigmama's ninetieth birthday.

"How long has Bigmama been in this place?" I began. From where I sat in the back seat of the car, I could see little strands of gray peek through the back of Tricia's auburn hair. I always thought she should have been a blond because she looked like a brown-eyed Doris Day with a double chin. She even sang like Doris Day, only louder.

"Oh, honey, let me see." Tricia turned on the blinker as we came to the next stop sign. "I guess since November. I know through Christmas. She was in the hospital four or five weeks, and we'd take turns sitting with her."

"Five weeks," Betty echoed from the front seat.

"I *said* five weeks." Tricia didn't take her eyes off the road. "She was really out of it. Just too much diarrhea."

"She went in the hospital because she had diarrhea?" I turned to Mom next to me, but she didn't answer.

"Ooh, yeah, all the time," Betty said. "Lou knows. Remember helping me mop up?"

"Oh yeah," Mom nodded as her eyes reflected memories of their September trip.

"All the relatives left. I guess it was about the beginning of October," Betty continued. "I went over to the apartment to get her ready for bed. She was half-conscious as if she were asleep with her eyes open. She was jerking too, like she was having a chill or something. I called Tricia, 911, everybody, and we took her to the emergency room. After they started an I.V., she perked up ready to go, but she stayed five weeks."

"Did she ever go back to the apartment?"

Betty shook her head no as she straightened the ends of her short hair that touched the collar of her blouse. Betty was indeed the pretty one, even more so now than my memories of her from childhood. Tall and slim, she seemed to be in total control of her body, passing on to me the latest info on healthy eating and vitamin supplements. She never appeared to be in any pain, in spite of the fact that in the early Seventies, she found out that she had an unusual disease called Scleroderma. Ironically, it made her even more attractive because it tightened the skin on her entire body, like a slow face lift. Unfortunately, arthritis came with the package, along with the knowledge that one day the disease would cause the rest of her body to constrict, including the esophagus. In the meantime, though, Betty hasn't let it stop her; she has stayed active with the Sweet Adelines, a touring singing group, and volunteers for Meals on Wheels and the church bazaar.

Tricia is another disease-of-the-week movie star. She and Hank were involved in the Melbourne community long before Betty moved there, volunteering for every new project, teaching arts and crafts at the nursing home and chairing the annual St. Patrick's Day dance. Yet, not to be outdone by her two older sisters, Tricia has developed her own rare neurological disease called Tic Douloureux, which required extensive surgery on her jaw and facial muscles.

What a group, these three sisters, I thought to

myself as we pulled into the parking lot of the Merritt Island nursing home. They had weird things happening to their fragile bodies, yet none of them allowed something as trivial as disease to disturb their daily lives. Their older brother, Dodo, however, was still flying high and healthy at sixty-five, but, at the same time, grumbling about life's little injustices.

Mom held Kate's hand as the lobby doors opened. A pleasant-looking gentleman sat by the door, nodding to each of us as we entered, his hand resting on the smooth curve of his cane. A small sofa to our left cradled a petite lady wearing a dress as salty as her hair. She didn't seem to notice us, just continued to count out loud from one to ten.

Betty led the way down the hall until we reached Bigmama's room. The darkness inside was broken only by a light coming from a crack in a partially opened bathroom door. As my sun-drenched eyes slowly adjusted to the dark, I spotted a splash of white hair on a white pillowcase and a white thermal blanket leading to my fingertips on the foot of the bed. Bigmama looked different. Her soft locks of short hair were pulled back into a tiny bun on the top of her head, and her glasses were on the side table patiently waiting for her to wake up. She wore a creamy pink nightgown with a collar trimmed in crumpled white lace. The rails on the side of the bed made Bigmama look small and mortal.

Betty opened the mini-blinds on the opposite side of the room. I could then see a long tube rising from the edge of Bigmama's blanket to a hanging bag above her head. The walls were lined with drawings from great-grandchildren and "Get Well" cards with yellow roses on the front. The side table held a small arrangement of silk flowers, its puffy shape interrupted only by a card on a plastic stick stuck into styrofoam underneath.

"Mama?" Tricia said loudly. "You've got company. Lou and Kim are here. Kate too."

Bigmama slowly opened her eyes into a tiny squint. "Where are my glasses?"

"Here, Mama." Tricia wiped them on her sweater before placing them on Bigmama's face. "They're missing a stem," Tricia whispered to me, "but she doesn't seem to care."

"Hi, Mama, how are you doin'?" Mom leaned down to kiss Bigmama on the cheek. "It's Lou."

"Lou? Well, I'll be," Bigmama smiled up at Mom then spied Kate and me still at the foot of the bed. "Kim? You too?"

"Yes, ma'am." I walked around to give her a kiss. "And Kate came with us." I turned to motion to Kate to come closer.

"Hey, baby," Bigmama put out her hand as I lifted Kate to a nearby chair. Kate reached over to hug Bigmama, then showed her Gravy. "So this is Gravy?"

Kate nodded and smiled.

"What have they done with your hair today?" Betty said patting the uncharacteristic bun. "A big gal that bathes her just loves to fix Mama's hair. She slicks it down with setting lotion. Sometimes it's in a barrette or a bow. Mama seems to like all the attention, and they just love her."

"What's this for?" Kate asked referring to the tube.

Tricia walked toward the closet, folding an extra blanket she had found on the chair. "That's Bigmama's supper. That's where all her food comes from."

Kate looked at the bag, then looked at me, expecting me to dispute Tricia's claim.

"She's right, sweetie," I said. "This tube goes right into Bigmama's stomach. Isn't that something? She doesn't even have to sit up to eat."

"Really?"

"Really." I let Kate down so that Mom could sit down, but she pulled Mom over to another chair by the window, then crawled up into her lap. Mom pulled a book from Kate's satchel, and Kate began to read the words quietly. As Tricia and Betty talked softly in the bathroom restocking the cabinet, I realized I had Bigmama all to myself. I sat down in the chair next to her and pulled out my sketchbook and pencil. Bigmama had leaned on her side toward me, grasping the railing with her left hand.

"Tell me," she began as I drew my favorite model, "how's Lou been doing with her Alzheimer's?"

"You don't forget a thing, do you, Bigmama?" I smiled at her as my pencil raced across the pad. "She's fine. Still testing drugs in Bethesda."

"That's good," she said. "It gives her something to do. Something to look forward to."

"Do you like it here?"

"The people are really sweet to me. It's not so bad. My sister used to take care of Papa like this, so I guess this is only right. After my mama died, he did what he could, but it was hard. I think everyone resented me being Papa's favorite, but I couldn't help that. If Mama's baby hadn't died the year before I was born, he wouldn't have worried about me so much. I guess he thought he was going to lose me too, and—" Bigmama took a deep breath, let out a long sigh and continued. "My sister didn't last much longer than Papa, just a couple of months. She had bronchial problems, what with having to go back and forth from the kitchen to the big house taking care of Papa."

Bigmama grew quiet for a moment, her eyes fixed on the wall above my head. I darkened the shadow between her cheek and the pillow before moving on to outline the contours of her arthritic hand that clutched the railing.

"Now, my little sister wouldn't have died if she hadn't been so stubborn," she said.

"Your *other* little sister?"

"Yes, such a shame. She was a nurse, too, and still refused to go to the hospital to have that baby. Just too much pride, I guess."

"And the baby?" I looked into Bigmama's deep eyes, cloudy with age.

"It died, too."

"What are you two jabbering about over there?" Tricia said in a big voice that broke through our conversation.

"Bigmama's sisters," I said as I turned to a new page in my sketchbook and leaned over to kiss Bigmama's forehead. Kate had moved to the floor where she was coloring a drawing she had made in the car on the way here. I nestled in the chair above her and drew the scene before me, three daughters gathered around their mother's bed.

Betty noticed my drawing as she collected the coats to leave. "Tricia, come look at this!"

"Kim, you really got my double chin. Look at that!" Tricia laughed as she showed Mom my drawing.

"Look at those sagging boobs! My word! It's hell to get old."

"You're not old," Kate said, and Tricia hugged her tight as she handed back my sketchbook.

Before we left, I leaned close to Bigmama's face and whispered, "We have to go now, but we'll be back tomorrow for one more visit. We can continue our talk then, OK?"

"OK, angel. Take good care of Lou, will you?" and her bent fingers touched my cheek.

The next day, I was eager to get to the nursing home to see Bigmama. She had been so happy to see us yesterday that I knew another visit would do her heart good. When we entered her room, however, I soon realized why she was in there in the first place. The staff had her frail body sitting upright in a chair next to the bed, and she was confused and irritable.

"Get me out of here. What's going on here? Where am I?" Bigmama's forehead had wrenched into a scowl and her eyes were wide open.

Betty turned to me and said softly, "Sometimes she's like this, a mixture of medicine and poor nutri-

tion. She's just wearing down."

"Take me home. Get me out of here," Bigmama glared at Betty when she came closer.

"Where's home, Mama?" Betty pulled the blanket up over her lap.

"Arcola, of course. Where do you think?"

I took Kate out of the room and into the lobby. The lady we had heard counting yesterday was back on the same sofa, but this time saying, "Little girl, little girl, little girl." I didn't know what to do, still shaken by my last view of Bigmama in that chair, so Kate and I walked outside to the concrete lot. There, I felt protected between the parked cars, surrounded by emotionless machines, hunks of metal that couldn't cry when their relatives were sent to the scrap heap. I felt the sun warm the tears on my cheeks as I rooted through my purse for a Kleenex, and Kate put her arms around my legs in a quiet hug.

March 1987

Ricky and I have gradually grown apart since his marriage to Gwen fourteen years ago. They live about three hundred feet from our house, but we only see them at family birthdays and Christmas. Gwen is the only sister-in-law I've ever had because Zab's two older brothers decided to remain single. I've always liked her. She has a great sense of humor and laughs when we tease her about being so short.

Ricky is an adult now, even though he hasn't changed much since he was a kid, fist fighting with me in the front yard. He still goes hunting every chance he gets, still fidgets, and is still immersed in sales of some kind. Big money has become very important to him. When Ricky was about two or three, Pop would reward him with fifty-cent pieces and silver dollars if he would sleep all night in his own bed and not crawl into theirs. Ricky called it big money and was fascinated by the coins. Apparently, money still fascinates him, especially now that he has entered the world of insurance. He has met with me a couple of times trying to talk me into investing in some sure-fire method of instant cash.

Since I'm not that interested in money, I'm afraid I have been one of Ricky's more hopeless customers, so

he pursues other prospects. If he has a personal problem, he usually calls Fan. Fan won't invest any money with him either, but she is still the Queen Bee, and he respects her advice on his personal life. Her marriage is more of his ideal, one in which the wife takes care of her husband's needs, just like Mom took care of Pop's.

Anyway, tonight Ricky and I were riding home from Fan's house in Morgan City, a community built on the edge of southeast Louisiana and surrounded by swamp. Since Ricky and I are the godparents of Fan's oldest son, Chris, he invited us to be his sponsors in confirmation, a Catholic ritual that prepares adolescents to face adulthood. I rode down after school with Mom and Pop, but they decided to spend the night, so I hitched a ride back to Ponchatoula that evening with Ricky. The light from the car dash reflected his little-boy face that looked out of place on a man over six feet tall; he looked much younger than his thirty-three years. His face didn't show a wrinkle, and he resembled early pictures of Pop, even though Ricky's light brown hair was full on top, unlike our bald-headed daddy. From where I sat on the passenger's side, I could see

Ricky's left hand where the two fingers that had been connected at birth were free of each other. He wore a wedding ring, even though Mom had predicted otherwise. His tics were still apparent, too, as he cleared his throat, sniffed loudly, and stretched his neck as if he were restrained by a tight collar. Mom had had Ricky tested at the university clinic when he was in high school, and a doctor suggested he might grow out of that fidgeting. However, in the dim light enclosing us, I realized the doctor may have underestimated the longevity of the stage.

As the car followed the winding road along the levee, we chatted about the evening's ceremony, how grown-up Chris had acted, how proud of him we were. We didn't talk about Alzheimer's or Mom or Pop. I wasn't even sure if Ricky knew I had just been to Florida to see Bigmama.

"Mom and Kate and I went to see Bigmama a couple of weeks ago."

"I guess I knew that." His eyes didn't leave the road.

"Mom did pretty well on the plane. We sat in the front seat, so there weren't a lot of distractions."

"That's good."

"Bigmama was glad to see us. She's been in the nursing home for about three months now." I was hoping he would have asked about her before I mentioned her condition, but he didn't. "She's really thin, being fed by a tube and all, but she has her good days, too."

"That's good," he said again. It seemed like several miles before we said anything else. Ricky looked preoccupied with the way the asphalt road curved in the darkness. We passed very few cars. Suddenly, he took a deep breath, and looked over at me.

"Kim, I think Gwen's been seeing someone else."

"What?"

"She moved out last week."

"This is news to me." I just stared at him, but his expression was serious.

"It's been over for a while," he sighed. "We just decided to stay together because a divorce wouldn't look right."

"Wouldn't look right?" I was afraid to ask why that was important to them, so I continued on a different course. "Where is Gwen now?"

"She and Ryan are at her mother's. She wants to move to Houston at the end of school to live close to her sister."

"And Jan?"

"She's still with me." Ricky could see the shocked look still on my face. "Oh, Kim, you know Gwen's family. If the marriage gets tough, those daughters just leave."

"No, Ricky, Gwen is totally different from her sisters. This can't be something that just happened overnight. What brought all this on?"

Ricky made a sweeping move to wipe his eyes, then he laughed nervously. "Your little brother has not always been a good boy himself," and he left it at that.

As the car crossed over a bayou, we could see a statue of Mary surrounded by lights in the shape of a rosary. The image doubled as it left its reflection on the surface of the shimmering water in front of it. The shrine was sheltered by cypress and weeping willow trees, both having foliage that seemed to drip in the night air. If their tears weren't long enough, Spanish moss hung from their branches and allowed a sprinkle of rain to trickle down its gray tendrils and land in quiet circles in the muddy water below. The view broke our conversation into unfinished bits and pieces until we finally reached Ponchatoula and home.

April 1987

I haven't seen much of Ricky since we rode home together from Morgan City a month ago. This weekend, however, it will be difficult for him to stay cloistered since it's time for the Strawberry Festival again. The two-day event attracts more than 100,000 people to Ponchatoula each year, along with their cars, their ice chests, and their wallets. Because the grounds are located in Memorial Park, a half-block north of my house, a half-block east of Ricky's, and a half-block south of Mom's, we plan little more than setting up lawn chairs in the front yard for forty-eight hours of people watching.

Every festival, Fan and her husband, Bren, bring their kids and sometimes a sack of live crawfish. This year, I was looking forward to a long, uninterrupted gab session with my sister. The two-hour-plus drive from her home limits the frequency of her visits, but she does manage to get to Ponchatoula about once every two months. When Fan comes, Pop is grateful for the reprieve from the kitchen. By now, Mom has forgotten not only how to follow a recipe, but also how to work the appliances. Pop has taken over the cooking, and my worries of Mom leaving on the gas burners can be set aside for a while. In fact, Pop has taken over all the household chores. For the first forty years of their marriage, Mom waited on him hand and foot, treating him like the lord of the manor. Since Alzheimer's came along, however, they have had to swap places. Pop now cooks, cleans, buys groceries, and does the laundry. In the last couple of years, Pop has had the advantage of having Emma, a lady who used to babysit for us and iron for Mom, who could now be his housekeeper one afternoon a week. Other than that, he handles everything from balancing the checkbook to making up the bed.

My biggest surprise came the night he invited Zab, Kate, and me for supper, and *he* served *us*, in spite of the fact that one of his daughters was in the house. I told him then how proud I was of the way he was taking care of Mom.

Pop said, "I just want to know one thing: since she took care of me for forty years, does that mean I have to take care of her for forty more years?" I knew he didn't expect an answer when he just looked at me and grinned.

Today, however, Pop could sit back and relax because his kids were waiting on him again. We were celebrating the Strawberry Festival by boiling the crawfish in his back yard. I could eat five pounds easily if I'd let myself. Bren said I'd fill up faster if I would suck the juicy fat out of the heads, but the thought of their brains traveling with it was too much for my wild imagination to bear. The lobster-tasting meat in the tails of these little mud-bugs was enough delicacy for me.

Boiling crawfish was always easier on Pop's carport. Bren and Chris filled the washtub with water from a nearby hose while Chad helped Pop pour in the fifty pounds of live, agitated crawfish. A few fell to the ground and raised their claws in defense as they tried to quietly back away. Chad and Chris were too fast for them, though, grabbing them from the rear and pitching them into the water. Zab poured in a couple of boxes of salt to make the crawfish belch out their last meal before being transferred to the boiling pot. Pop had welded his own propane burner complete with rack to hold the pot. His come-along, Pop's word for his winch, was rigged up on a limb of the oak tree beside the carport and could be used to raise the sack, lift the boiling basket from the pot, or just hoist up Chad by his belt loops.

While waiting for the crawfish to purge, Fan and I went to get the fixins ready, fixins being anything that would be thrown in the spicy water to boil with the crawfish. Our five-year-old daughters, Cary and Kate, were busy playing school in our old bedroom with Mom as their eager student. I pulled a bag of onions onto the kitchen table and positioned myself in Pop's chair, paring knife ready. Fan stood at the sink washing the corn and potatoes, her light brown hair falling down her back to her shoulder blades. I had just begun peeling the transparent outer skin of my first onion when Fan turned off the water and dried her hands. She reached in the cabinet above the exhaust fan and took out a box of matches.

"Here, hold one of these in your teeth," she said. "The sulphur will soak up the onion fumes, and you won't cry."

"OK." I placed the wooden end of a match in my front teeth.

Fan went back to the porcelain sink and began stacking the clean corn on a tray. "Have you seen this year's poster?"

"No, I'm just glad I didn't do it."

"I've seen it, but I like your old ones better."

"You should. They're all over your kitchen." I smiled at her through my match. "Did I tell you I've decided to start my M.F.A. at L.S.U. next year?"

"What's an M.F.A.?"

"Master of Fine Arts. It's the art world's version of a doctorate in studio art."

"What brought this on?" Fan put the tray of corn on the table and sat across from me.

"A couple of things," I said. Those couple of things

were hard to explain to Fan, my math teacher sister whose taste in art was restricted to photo realism. I wanted her to understand that I wanted to produce conceptual art—art with an emotional impact, art that she might not like. I wanted to tell her how unhappy I was to be viewed as a graphic artist, even though she was proud of me for it. I wanted to justify to her this feeling of urgency that I had, the one that plagued me whenever I thought of how much more Mom had wanted to do with her life, but couldn't.

"And?" Fan looked up at me with blue eyes in such a way that for a minute I thought I was looking at myself in the mirror.

"Well," I began, "I'll be able to teach on the university level, and there's so much out there I have left to learn. I've been wanting to get my M.F.A. for as long as I can remember. Just kept putting it off, I guess. I sent off for the application months ago; the deadline isn't until April 15."

"What will you do about school?"

"You mean Ponchatoula High? I'm going to take a sabbatical for a year to get a good start on it. It should

only take me three years to finish."

"Sounds to me like it's all set?"

"Yeah, all set." I wrapped the onion pieces in a paper towel and pushed them toward the white star on the table. "You know what we should make? Puffs. I haven't had those in ages. Remember, you and Ricky and I used to fill them with Mom's figs?"

Fan nodded, smiling, then paused for a minute. I knew exactly what she was going to say next. She looked squarely into my eyes and sighed. "Speaking of Ricky."

"I know. I know." I stretched back in my chair until my arms hit the window behind me.

"He said it's all Gwen's fault."

"You don't believe that, do you?" I leaned forward again. "It usually takes two."

"Well, I'm staying out of it," Fan said. "It's their business, and I'm not getting involved." She stood up and walked back to the sink and the window above it that overlooked the carport. Leaning on the edge of the porcelain, she quietly watched Bren help Chris drain the salty water from the crawfish and dump them into the boiling water. Their normally dull brown shells turned bright red. "I do feel partly responsible, though."

"You? Why?"

"Ricky always told Gwen, 'Why can't you treat me like Fan treats Bren?' He thinks that's the way all marriages work."

"It works for you and Bren."

"I'm happy." Her voice sounded defensive.

"Well, it's definitely not your fault, Fan. Ricky's just looking for somebody else to blame. He can work things out. Besides, we have enough to worry about with Mom." I joined Fan at the sink and washed the onion peelings down the disposal. "She's getting worse right under Ricky's nose. Her depth perception is all screwed up. When she takes her walk, she sees a crack in the sidewalk and thinks it's a step up or down when it's really flat. You should see her try to hang up the telephone or pour a glass of milk. It goes everywhere!"

"I can too pour my own milk."

I turned around to see Mom walking into the kitchen carrying a navy blue blouse on a hanger. She looked at Fan and me out of the corner of her eye and grinned. "I just can't hit the glass."

We all three laughed. "At least you haven't lost your sense of humor, Mom," I told her.

"That's the worst part about this stupid disease," she said. "Before, people laughed; now, they think I'm just crazy. They think it's the disease."

"We know better, Mom," Fan said. "Whatcha got?"

"I'm just going through my clothes for Bethesda."

"Our mom, a famous television star!" Fan smiled and hugged her around the shoulders.

Mom and Pop had been invited again to fly to the National Institutes of Health, this time, for two reasons: to test a new drug, SMS, and to participate in the filming of "The Health Century," a nine-part series that would air nationally on PBS in October. Mom jumped at the chance, but Pop said he'd pass. Mom and I had already gone shopping for a new outfit, but I had not been able to talk her into a dress. The old tomboy insisted on pants.

"Come show us what you've got laid out, Mom," Fan said as the three of us walked to the bedroom.

On her bed, Mom had a mound of partially folded

clothes spread in no apparent order, some still on hangers. Both of her closet doors were wide open to reveal shuffled shoes divorced from their partners. Several of her clothes drawers gaped open at various levels, letting socks flow at will. Fan and I automatically began folding the clothes and organizing them on the bed. Fan picked up a pair of light blue pants and examined the waistband.

"What's this?"

I walked over to see what she meant and saw a big black dot marked on the inside of the waist.

"Oh, Pop put that on there so that I could tell the front from the back," Mom said.

"He's something else," Fan said as she checked each of the other pants for the same telltale dot. "He's done them all." She handed them to me and sat down on the carpet by the edge of the closet. "Which shoes are you going to wear on TV, Mom?"

"I don't know. I guess my blue sandals."

"Mom," I said, "those old things? They're so old-fashioned; they even have wedge heels!"

"Nobody's going to see my shoes . . . my pants

either, for that matter."

"Too late to change her now, Kim." Fan smiled up at me from the floor.

Journal Entry
April 14, 1987

The coordinator of affairs at NIH called Bert a couple of weeks ago and told him that they wanted us to come to Bethesda to participate in a TV special about Alzheimer's Disease. She wanted us both to do it, but Bert said no. Later he did do a portion because I did it. It was hectic the next morning trying to get dressed and ready for the TV stuff. These days, I tend to fall apart under stress, but we finally got dressed and got a cab to NIH. I realized I hadn't brought half of my makeup and got all upset. But a couple of the young nurses made me all up and brushed my hair; they are so cute and sweet to me.

For a while it was "hurry up and wait" as the TV crews got everything ready. Then, the part I participated in was a mock Pet Scan. Then I was interviewed by Dr. Thomas Chase's neurologists and they asked various questions about Alzheimer's like how I knew I had it and what does it do: all the questions everyone wants to know about the disease. I felt pretty good about my part. There wasn't too much to do, just talking. They told us it would be shown on Public Television some time in October.

The main reason for us to go to NIH this time was to participate in a new drug, SMS, that has been approved by the Food and Drug Dept. I am to take the drug and then there will be tests and tests and tests. Dr. Moral and Dr. Isabella came in and told me that the test has started. I will have a delayed breakfast and they will give me the first injection of the medicine. I am to report anything that happens from now on, even though it may not seem to have anything to do with the test.

On Monday, I was cold all night long, so I put on more clothes. I was sneezing and my nose was leaking all the time. The heat would not come out of the radiator, just cold air. I finally put on my sweatsuit and went to bed. I sneezed all the next day and had a drippy nose constantly. That morning I woke up very depressed. I was even crying and I didn't even know why. I reported it to the doctors, but they didn't know if it was a side effect of the drug or what. However, I was all right the next day but never did know why I had that. The

doctors were upset because I just don't do things like that. I try to be congenial and smile. I have always felt that way around here.

Bert went to the seashore yesterday, but I could not go because I have been taking the medicine every day. Dr. Moral was afraid of some side effects occurring while I was there. Friday, Kim called. She told me Ryan had his First Communion and she got him a present from me. I talked to Kate and she wants us to come home soon because she misses us. We talked to Gwen and Ryan who called to tell us about his First Communion, too. He was so proud of it.

On Saturday, I took an LP. After that, I had to stay on my back until night. It was not bad to get the puncture itself, but I must keep my head down at all times to avoid the LP headache which is one enormous pain in the head. I had to lie down from the time I got it until Sunday morning. By that time I had a horrible backache. I am writing this on Sunday morning, and this is the first time I have been able to stand up. To make it worse, I was in bed at night and reached for some water, and spilled it all over my gown. The nurse who answered my ring was Ralf, the black male nurse. Here I am with Ralf taking off the wet gown and putting me in a hos-

pital gown and on the bedpan. Anyway I did not get the LP headache.

Oh yes, to complicate this, I had to use the bedpan for all my urine. This was constant because they push liquids in you all evening to wash out the system, I guess, after the puncture. Anyway, it was a bad night. I ended up in tears of frustration, and I had a sweet, old-fashioned nurse help me get back to bed. I finally calmed down and went to bed. I still couldn't sleep because my rib cage was so sore from being in bed all day. Later, a nurse came with some aspirin, and I went on to sleep finally. When I woke up this morning, I was caged in and couldn't get out. It seems I woke up and stood up in my sleep.

On Tuesday, my roommate was changed to another room. I don't know if they were planning to do this today because of the Blood Flow work that will be in here tomorrow, or because the nurses said something to them. When my roommate got up and put on the TV as usual this morning, she couldn't get any sound. And I kinda let her gripe about it and then showed her, for the 100th time, how to turn up the volume on her hand set. I didn't go over and do it for her because I really was hoping she couldn't get it on. I pointed

at it on her control and after a while she left the room. The next thing I knew she had been changed to another double room. She hardly said a word to me while she was getting her stuff together. It was just as well because we will be doing a Blood Flow test all night long.

I'm writing this on my last night here. Yesterday, Dr. Isabella gave us a Blood Flow like we had the last time we were here. We lie on the bed and she puts an IV in our arm and draws blood over an eight hour period. However, when she put the first needle in, my arm began to pain. I stayed there about five minutes and the pain became worse. So I rang the call button and she came. She was unable at first to know why but then she found that the needle had slipped into a wrong vein.

Lou Howes

Sat, April 26 at NIH — 1987

Dear, darling son,

We have just come back from doing the laundry,
isn't that exciting? actually It is a real dead day, they
slow down here on The week end,

It was good to talk two my "favorite sons" I
sure miss you
and Ryan, and Jan & Kim etc etc etc,
+ Kate + Jan
I have been having a lot of tests and I am now taking
Dr. Moral's medicine, the brand new one that may
be available to the people who have AZ.

I have an injection of the drug in
burning at the needle + she expects that.

my arm every morning and I am to tell them if I
have any side afects. The only thing I have had were a burning at the
needle sit. which the expected, and a
flush face
The big Al has stolen my hand-writing and
spelling so hang in there. also he pushes my pen
off the line every once in a while.

Please share this with Kim + Jan, if possible. It's too messy
to write another one now. Tell them to save this letter
and when I have been on the medicine for awhile
I will write again + hope it is better.
Loads of love, Mom + Pop

June 1987

In Louisiana, I know spring is gradually changing to summer only when the air gets muggier. In the summer, the humidity gets so heavy on my back that I have to lift the shoulder seams of my shirt in order to peel clinging cotton from skin. Air conditioners are my friends, from noisy window units to God-sent central air. Romantic tourists think that the humidity adds to the tropical atmosphere of the state. I just think it makes it hot. Well, it was summer all over again now. I thought that just because Mom's Alzheimer's was slow, the days would pass just as slowly. During her third trip to Bethesda in May, I was encouraged to see her handwriting improve. Yet, within weeks after her return, the drug wore off, bringing back the film of black that clouded her brain. I truly wished I could have been with her when her mind was clear.

It seemed the edges of my family were slowly dissolving with the rising humidity. Childhood memories were fading, dampened by the reality of divorce, illness, denial. My black-and-white reasoning was trying to blend on a palette in my mind to create muggy grays—grays that swallowed all the senses like swamp "water," mud that hid the bodies of white egrets shot by clumsy sportsmen. Bigmama . . . my last memory of her at the nursing home in Florida left an uncomfortable twist in my stomach. She was still there, still being tube fed, quietly fading into herself. Grandpa, Pop's father . . . last Sunday, he entered the hospital, fighting fluid around his heart. I have visited him every day, as though I have to take his daughter-in-law's place as his caregiver. Mom cannot get there alone, much less make decisions about his care. It won't be long before he'll have to go into a nursing home himself.

Now, I discover that the L.S.U. School of Art has turned me down for their M.F.A. program because they moved the deadline for submission up one month, but failed to change the deadline date on the application forms. They didn't even look at my slides. I've made an appointment with the director for June 24 to ask him to reconsider my application.

Last of all, Gwen moved to Houston at the end of May, taking Jan and Ryan with her for a few weeks.

The dissolution of Ricky's marriage has not been pleasant for anyone. The kids have begun what I assume will be a summer ritual: a few weeks here, a few weeks there.

Journal Entry
July 1, 1987

Bert and I left Bathesda May 14, and had a good flight home. I had been on the drug, SMS, from April 17 to the time we came home. There were some very positive signs of my clear head when we got home. The Drug seemed to have helped me for awhile. However, I gradually seem to be returning to the clutches of Alzeimerrs. My short term memory is very bad. Dr. Moradian told us that It is no longer a just an ocasional lost thought, but almost always when I ask a question, I catch my self askeng it again.. Very embarising! I started this with the thought of using liquid paper for the errors, but it seems that I will just spell as I can and let it go. It is so depressing.

And the words *that won't come out of my mouth! it makes you wan't to never try to talk to with anyone. Then there are times when I talk normaly in any conver easally. I* still take my long walk every day. I always go on the same places. I haven't gotten lost yet. one or two times I hove made a wrong turm, but it doesn't take me but a moment to look around at the houses and ather things for me to know where I am. Every body in this small town knows who I am, so I couldn't get too for before some one whold help me.

I have high hopes for the new drug, THA, Now I read that it hasn't gone through enoung testing to put it on the market. Our next trip to Bathesda will be to test the new drug.I sure need it. Of course, the longer it doesn't get on the market, the worse I will get, and may reach a point that I couldm't help them in the program.

Lou Howes

July 1987

I sat in the bow of Zab's skiff and crossed my legs around Kate's skinny body, stuffed tightly inside her yellow life preserver. My calves were her seat belt as the boat tilted with each new bend in the river, the brown water racing in a blur past my fingertips. I could feel Zab behind me in the stern controlling the throttle, his sunglasses a one-way mirror of the swampy banks. We rode in the wake of Pop's boat, which took the curves ahead of us. I could see Mom in the passenger seat next to Pop, her visor catching the sunlight as it flickered through the open flap of the canvas tarp above her head. Both boats slowed to idle whenever we came upon bass fishermen drifting along with the current. I waved out of habit whether I knew them or not, and they waved back in between casts, their flies landing just the right distance from floating lily pads.

In some places along the bank, I could see through the trees to the open swamp. It looked like a van Gogh landscape with chunks of creamy paint for weeds and heavy brush strokes for grass capped with yellow wildflowers. Van Gogh's landscapes are solid underfoot. His foliage grows on firm ground. This swamp, however, was deceptive. It looked as if I could run across it, but I knew it was mushy underneath, a swarm of tangled roots, cypress knees, and mud. Hunters have been known to lose their way for days in these swamps, gradually driven insane by hypothermia, mosquitoes, and the search for hard ground.

Both of our boats pulled up to the camp where Fan and Bren were waiting for us. Cary was already in her bathing suit and life jacket waiting for Kate to get there to swim, but Chris and Chad had taken off in the flat to the lake. I tied the lines in a halfhitch as Pop helped Mom step out onto the wharf. After we all carried in the groceries and luggage, Fan and I separated to the kitchen while Bren and Zab crashed on the porch talking about the burnt-out building Zab was planning to renovate for an office of his own. Pop started piddlin' around, turning on the pump and the gas and lighting the pilot light in the stove. From where Fan and I stood in the kitchen, we could see Mom checking out the walkway on the side of the camp.

When Mom was first diagnosed with Alzheimer's, her doctor suggested that she begin walking a mile a day to keep her body active. Mom set out a specific ten-block route in the neighborhood to which she adhered faithfully, give or take a Louisiana rain or two. Pop even built her double planks around the camp so that Mom could get in her walk when they came down here.

"What's he doing now?" Fan asked me. Pop was placing clam shells on the banister on the front porch.

"Forty times around the camp equals one of Mom's miles. He's putting up forty shells." As I spoke, Mom walked around for her first lap, took one of the bright white shells off the banister, and tossed it back into the front yard. She smiled at Pop as she walked past him for lap number two.

"What next?" Fan shook her head.

"Hey, come sit down. I have all good news to tell you."

"Shoot." Fan pulled up a rolling chair across the table from me.

"I never get to see you anymore," I began. "So much has happened, I don't know where to start."

"Start with L.S.U."

"Let me see. Last time we talked, I was supposed to meet with the director to get the School of Art to reconsider my application. Remember I had been sent the wrong date? Well, he apologized for the screwup, told me he would talk to the painting faculty, do what

he could. He didn't promise anything, though."

"Then what?"

"He must have done something. A few days later, I received a letter from the Graduate School saying that I had been accepted into the M.F.A. program in the School of Art. Isn't that something?"

"That's great," Fan said pulling her long hair up into a ponytail. "So are you going to take a sabbatical?"

I nodded and looked out over the slow-moving river trying to remember all of the things I had been saving up to tell Fan. "Did you know Kate and I went to see Gwen and Ryan about a week ago?"

"To Houston?"

"Yes, I had been promising Kate a trip, so we flew to Gwen's. She loves her job. She's already found Ryan a Catholic school for next year close to their house. And, get this, Ricky is, I guess you could say, courting her again."

"What do you mean?"

"He's sending Gwen roses and cards, messages on her answer machine, trying to talk her into coming back."

"That's nice. He likes those cards, doesn't he?" Fan grinned at me.

"This courting seems to be taking up a lot of his time. He doesn't stop by to see Mom and Pop unless he needs something."

Fan looked at me with one of her famous "Now, Kim" looks, the look that meant I had just said something of which she did not approve. I shrugged my shoulders and smiled at her sheepishly like a puppy that had just missed the edge of her newspaper.

I walked to the back of the camp to get towels for the girls who were still expecting to swim. Through the back door, I could see Mom walking on one of her last laps around the camp. As the shadow of the aluminum awning grayed her silhouette, it seemed that she became one with the open swamp behind her. She still looked the same on the surface, that young bride that could strike a match with one shot from a .22. Yet, now there were memories inside that head, tangling as slowly as the roots of the cypress trees, decomposing as deceptively as the muck underneath the surface of the swamp.

September 1987

"Mommy, what was that smell in there?" Kate looked up at me from the bottom of the ramp.

"That was urine. Most nursing homes smell like that because some residents have to wear a diaper."

"Like a baby?"

"Just like a baby."

"Was Grandpa wearing one?"

"No, I don't think so." I held the door open with one hand and grasped Mom's arm with the other. "This is a ramp, Mom, going down."

Mom edged her foot forward a little before making a first step. Kate took the door from me and waited for Mom and me to get through. I saw her catch a glimpse of a hunchbacked woman slowly hobbling toward us on her walker. Kate held the door for her, too, then caught up with us at the car.

"Do you think Grandpa liked my drawing, Mom?"

Mom turned around slightly in the passenger seat, even though she could not see Kate with her blind left eye. "He sang to you, didn't he?" Mom said, then repeating Grandpa's song, "K-K-K-Katie, beautiful

Katie. You're the only w-w-w-one that I adore."

"He sang that to you when he first saw you in the crib more than five years ago." I smiled at her as she closed the back door.

"When the m-moon shines over the c-cow shed, I'll be waiting at the k-k-k-kitchen door." Mom's last note trailed off into a whistle.

"I think Grandpa's much happier in this place than he was in the last nursing home," I said as I backed up the car and headed it in the direction of the mall. "There just seems to be more people here that he knows. Old farmers ready to be put out to pasture, I guess."

"When I get that way, don't even think twice before sticking me in there," Mom said. "I won't know any different."

"Isn't it a little early to be worrying about that?" I asked.

"I just wanted you to know it's OK with me."

"Speaking of nursing homes, I think Bigmama's in a nice one."

"I know." Mom turned toward the window as we approached the mall entrance.

"Are you and Pop still going to see her next week?"

"Yes, with Dodo and Olive."

Kate spoke up from the back seat, "How old will Bigmama be, Mom?"

"Baby, I can't even remember my own birthday, much less hers."

"She'll be ninety-one, peanut; and Mom, you're going to be sixty-three in October, just in case you're interested. While you two are off gallivantin' in Florida, I've got another battle to fight with L.S.U."

"Tell me again," Mom began.

"Remember the letter that said I was in? Well, I had been accepted into the School of Art, but not by the art faculty. Someone in the School of Journalism had signed the consent form. How it got over there, nobody knows."

"So now what?"

"Zab said I should take it to the dean of the Graduate School, but I don't know. The graduate coordinator told me that my hours this semester would count toward my M.F.A., and I could reapply for the spring semester. It's just that I'm starting a semester later than I had planned, that's all."

"I can't keep all this straight," Mom said as I turned off the car.

"It's confusing for me, too, Mom, but I'm determined to get that degree."

As we walked through the mall, I tried to avoid the red displays because the bright color hurts Mom's eyes. Today, with Kate by her side, however, she didn't seem to notice. The escalators and stairs were also out of the question because of Mom's screwed-up depth perception, so we relied on the mall's one elevator and its abundance of handicapped ramps. As we turned around the corner from Penney's, I spotted one of Mom's old friends heading straight toward us.

"OK, Mom, here comes Miss Gloria," I said beginning my usual coaching. "Remember? She cuts your hair, and y'all used to party together all the time."

"Yes, yes."

Gloria walked up to Mom with a big smile on her bright face and beamed. "Hey, Lou, it's Gloria Griggs. How's life treating you?"

I could kiss her for saying her name.

"Sure, Gloria, I know you." Mom reached out to give her a hug. "We don't get to party much anymore, do we?"

"No, Lou, we're just getting too old."

They both laughed as we walked on in opposite directions.

"Uh-huh," Mom murmured to herself. "Gloria . . . yeah, we used to dance all night. Had a ball!"

"That's right, Mom. I still remember standing inside the hall closet when you thought we were in bed. I could pet Miss Gloria's fur coat and listen to the big bands at the same time. That was ages ago."

"Heavens, could we cut a rug!" Mom said.

At that moment, we looked up to face a former teacher friend of Mom's standing right in front of us. I had not seen her coming in time to brief Mom, and I knew Mom would never remember her name. They hadn't seen each other in years.

The lady touched Mom on the shoulder but turned to me and said, "How's your mother?"

Mom replied before I could say anything, "Why

don't you ask her; she's standing right here."

"Oh, well, Lou, I didn't think you'd remember me," she stuttered, placing a plump hand to her flushed cheek.

"Of course I remember you. How've you been?"

"Just fine. We sure miss you at school," the lady added and hurried her good-byes.

After she had gone, I turned to Mom. "You did great!"

"I did? Good. Now, who in the hell was that?"

"You're such a good fake, Mom." We all laughed. "That was a lady who taught at Ponchatoula High when you subbed for so long, remember?"

"I can't remember anybody's name anymore, not even my own. Who are you?"

"Very funny," I said sarcastically.

Mom laughed. "That's the worst part about this old Alzheimer's. Nobody knows when I'm just goofing off."

"I know you remember your own name."

"Howes, as in How's ya doin'," Mom said.

"Have you ever thought about it? Pop's name sounds like Bird House instead of Bert Howes," I protested.

"Oh, you're making that up," Mom smiled, then stopped walking. "OK, then, why do you stick Howes in your name now?"

"You mean on my paintings?"

"Yeah, Mommy, you put Kim Howes Zabbia on the bottom," Kate said.

"That's easy. The Zabbias didn't give me any talent. Mom and Pop did, and they can have all the blame when I fail, too."

"Thanks a lot," Mom smiled.

By this time, we had reached the end of the mall walkway and were shortcutting through Sears to reach the car. We hadn't accomplished much more than chatter and certainly had not done any damage to our checking accounts.

"Hey, don't forget about your TV show when you get back from Florida," I told Mom as we got into the car.

"Isn't it cruel to say 'don't forget' to a person with Alzheimer's?" Mom said dramatically.

"Poor Pitiful Pearl! OK, I'll remind you."

"That's better. What good is having Alzheimer's if I can't milk it a little bit?" Mom grinned.

Journal Entry
October 10, 1987

With the increased trouble that I have when I try to talk sometimes it could be, if they waited too long, I won't be able to get those stuborn words to come from my brain to make a statement. "I find that particular side of Alzheimer's Disease is very annoying. I did enjoy the TV Program which we saw here on Tuesday, Oct. 6 on one channel and again on Wed. on another channel. Also, my kids recorded it on VCR. I was pleased with it. All my friends said I looked so relaxed. I told them that that's because of the great relaxed people we work with at NIH.

Right now one of my most anoying aspect of this disease is the tears of depression. when you think you have everay thing under control, up comes something that you have done wrong, or forgotten to do, or, down comes the tears. No matter how much you tell yourself it allrught, or just the dease, it still brings the darn tears coming to your eyes. I do my best to stop them but they still come. I can look at this terrible joournal, the spelling, the writieng etc. and it can make you so depressed. Everybody here has plenty to do and I feel that I can't add one thing to what is being said or done. day by day I try very hard to keep all this attude from showing or to even think about it. I have such a suporrtive family that I keep pretty content most of the time. in fact I worry about them more than I do about myself.

Lou Howes

October 1987

On October 5, the "Health Century" segment on aging and Alzheimer's disease aired on PBS, and we were right there glued to the tube. We saw Mom on a moving belt getting ready for a scan of her brain. Of course, since Mom was lying down, the camera caught a head-to-toes view of her new outfit, including those tacky shoes. All Mom would say was, "I don't want to hear a word." In the question-and-answer segment, Mom appeared relaxed and self-assured. Pop, on the other hand, was nervous, though he didn't even realize he was being filmed. He answered the questions in his deep Southern accent, "We noticed it maybe three years ago. Then it got bad enough for us to stop her dri-vin'. I drove uptown one day, and she's supposed to bring the car behind me fo', five blocks, and I looked in the rearview mirror and I noticed her way on the curb the whole time. That's 'bout when she quit."

"I thought they did great," Zab told me. "You wouldn't know to look at your mom that your dad had to go in the voting booth with her last Saturday."

Journal Entry
November 4, 1987

I found that finding everything I could about the dis-aease made me more aware of what was hapening to me nown and what I am facing for the future. It isn't a very pret-ty story. However, there is more promising news about the new drug, THA. I have read all of the news that I could find in the newspaper and TV. If the powers to be can get the drug through the Food and drug ass. and clear it to go on the market I was to to NIH as soon as the time is right (we had heard that it would be awaible after Christmas, but Marge called to teell us of the change and about the delay in aproval. of the use at this time.

It sounds so good, but all we can do now is to Pray and wait. My memory is getting worse. I try so hard to keep up with the Date and the Time of day. It realy doesn't matter because I very seldom do anything alone, but I try hard to keep up with a fairly normal idea of what is going on. Even the calendar confuses me some time. I know I would be bet-ter off by just let other people do the things that I don't do well any more, but something in me says, "Hang in there and keep on working with what I have left." I just hope that I can test the THA drug soon. and that it will have a good affect on me. At least it gives me something to look farward to.

Lou Howes

November 1987

I was in Morgan City visiting with Fan when I heard the news that Bigmama had died. The body would be flown to Louisiana for the funeral. Within the four days before the services, most of the cousins arrived, saddened by the reason but happy to have an excuse to get the family together again. Even though I enjoyed seeing my relatives, I felt aloof, my mind flee-ing back to memories of Bigmama. I guess everyone else felt that way, too. On the surface, we all knew Bigmama would die one day. Inside, we hoped she never would.

At the funeral, I walked immediately to the open casket. She was actually there, robed in a long lavender dress that Betty had made for her to wear to a grandchild's wedding. The crystal rosary that used to clunk against the pew in church was draped silently across her fingers. Her left hand bore a small yellow band, her wedding ring that had been stored in the bottom of a jewelry box for more than fifty years. As my eyes finally reached Bigmama's face, I noticed that something was different. She didn't look the same. Her glasses had both stems and were pink shell-rimmed glasses that didn't look at all like Bigmama's. In fact, her face looked cold. I had never touched a dead body before, but today, I watched my fingers reach over the edge of the casket and lightly stroke the back of her hand. I wanted to be reassured that her warmth was truly gone, not just flickering inside. I was right. Her hand felt as cold as her face had looked. It was hard, like the hands of a statue, a hollow shell that had at one time housed a warm soul. Bigmama wasn't there at all, and I felt relieved.

The funeral Mass was held at St. Helena's in Amite, the Catholic church closest to Arcola. When the prayers began, I could almost hear Bigmama's voice one syllable behind everyone else's. During the Mass, my oldest cousin, Beth, spoke, reminiscing of her days as a little girl reading books at Bigmama's library and washing dishes at the kitchen sink, water coming from the pump handle attached to the side. Then Tricia's son Nat spoke, reminding us of our childhood vacations in Arcola, going to the store for candy bars and playing at the river by the gravel pit.

My mind mixed their words with my own memories of Bigmama's small, porcelain kitchen table and the high chair that had served all four of her kids and each of her thirteen grandchildren in turn. I remember sitting in that chair at that very same table and watching Bigmama mix yucky powdered milk and spread pink deviled ham on a slice of bread. By the time I became a regular visitor, World War II had been over for about fifteen years, but Bigmama ate as meagerly as if she were still using ration stamps.

That big white house in Arcola was not the poor run-down structure I had heard Mom talk about. To me, it was a wondrous place filled with stories of their childhood, tales of every event that had ever occurred inside those poorly insulated walls. Bigmama would tell me who slept where, whose tea set was whose, and who hated to dust the bottom rungs of the dining room table. I could look out of Bigmama's bedroom window through her spindly rose bushes and actually see a ten-year-old tomboy, Lou, perched in an oak tree spitting down on her little sister, Tricia. I could see a pretty Betty, her eyes cast down, walking shyly beside an imaginary knight in shining armor. I could see Dodo throwing rocks at the trains as they passed only a gravel road away from their front yard. In the afternoons, I could sprawl out on the daybed on Bigmama's back porch and flip through crusty picture albums that had been pack-ratted away, their yellowed pages crumbling in my fingertips. I could relive as many of this house's early days as my imagination would allow.

A box of Kleenex poking in my lap brought me back to the funeral at hand. My cousin Tammie wanted me to know that Fan was about to sing. The entire family joined in, with Bigmama's four children singing the loudest. Uncle Dodo put his arm around Mom's shoulders and pulled her close. From where I sat behind them, I felt they were sharing a moment that no one else could understand. There was pain in my uncle's eyes as he looked down at his younger sister, a pain, I thought, about more than the mutual loss of their mother.

We all went to the little Arcola cemetery where Bigmama's grave had been dug beside those of the rest of her family. Bigmama was the last of her four sisters and two brothers to die. Her designated spot, the first one off the road, had been waiting for her for a long time. We were quiet as the priest read the last passage, but no one seemed to want to leave when the graveside service was over. It was as if we hadn't quite done enough. We knew we needed to drive to the old house for one last look.

Cousins on top of cousins piled into three cars and headed for the house as our parents drove on back to

Ponchatoula. I could feel the mood shifting from quiet mourning to smiles and giggles as the caravan turned up the familiar gravel road beside the railroad tracks. Through the bushes, we could see the worn path to Bigmama's driveway and the big oak tree that still had a pirate's plank for a root. Since Bigmama moved to Ponchatoula in 1968, no one had lived in this big old house for any length of time. The front door was locked, but I rubbed the dust from the glass panels and could see the worn spots on the floor where Bigmama's favorite chair used to rest. I could smell the same musty insides through the crack by the lock. As we walked to the back, we noticed that the wooden steps leading to the back porch had rotted out, as had the walls of the washhouse that had held the wringer machine. There was still a circle of dirt where Bigmama's dog, Blip, used to sleep under the tree by the dining room window, but the grass had long ago grown over the clay tennis court scraped in the front yard. As we walked to our cars, I heard the crunching gravel that once offered me priceless fossils in the days when I thought it would be exciting to be a paleontologist. The only fossil left now was Bigmama's house with its peeling white paint and musty smell. My eyes tried to soak up as much of it as I could before the cars and the cousins pulled me out of its sight.

The next few days were filled with cousin visits, cousin chats, and cousin dinners. Bigmama's great-grandchildren, too, were becoming as close as their parents, even though many did not go to the funeral. Kate was one who chose to stay away, preferring instead to spend that day in her kindergarten class. She didn't seem to mind not having a chance a say good-bye to Bigmama.

Eventually, the relatives flew out to their respective homes, and it seemed our life would get back to normal. I was again able to meet Kate after school, walk with her the one block home, and listen to the highlights of her day. On this particular day, Kate entered the house ahead of me and threw her books on the dining room table. From where I stood at the back door, I heard her say, "Hey!" as if she were greeting someone in the kitchen. When I reached the kitchen, Kate was standing in the middle of the floor alone.

"Who were you talking to?" I asked.

"Bigmama," she said matter-of-factly.

"Wait. Come here." I sat down in the chair by the kitchen desk and asked her what she meant.

She smiled at me and said, "It was Bigmama. When I came in, I saw her standing right there."

"By the sink?"

"Yes, ma'am."

"What was she doing?"

"Just looking around. She had her hands out on the sink."

"How do you know it was Bigmama?"

"Because it looked just like her. She had white hair and her white shawl on." Kate crawled up in my lap and put her arms around my neck.

"Were you scared?"

"No, it was Bigmama, Mommy."

"Did she see you?"

"When I said 'Hey,' she looked at me with a little smile, then disappeared, just like those Star Trek men. I walked around the counter to see if she was still there, but she was gone."

I hugged Kate tightly and heard my words crackle. "The next time you see her, would you say 'Hey' for me, too?"

Journal Entry
January 7, 1988

Christmas was I should say, not the same this year. I guess I mean I was not the same. I could not get into the spirit. Kim helped me to select my presents and I could not have done it alone with out her also Bert helped me with the selections and did all the wrapping and also address my Christmas cards. This may be the last year for cards, but I do like to send to others and recieve from others. I enjoyed our annual getting togeather with our kids and their families. The main change is in my dear Dear Husband. He has helped in every way since "Al" came along. He helps me do so many things that I can't handle very well any more. he was not a man to do too much in the kitchen. All this has changed now he cooks better than I ever did. It first, when he took over most of the cooking, and started changing almosst every thing I had cook before, he cooked it another way.

I finally decedied that it had to be done by someone and

I couldn'nt do it right anymore. We have now just worked togeather. Bert did what he wanted and I helped when I could. The one thing I did get *to do every day is to clean up afterward. Most of the things get put back where they belong. The rest, we find later.*

I am constantly finding something that I have done all my life and now find it to be hard to do correctly. Exsampall: wash a load of closes and dry them. That isn't hard but the next step is to fold those clothes and put them in their right placee in the drawsers.

Also, there is the kitchen. you have all eaten and now we dry the silver and put it in the right place. I think all of life is repeating the same stask over and over and over. I'm sure nobody ever thinks of it in this way, but it seems to be another of Al's tricks The spelling and writing are downright depressing as are the lost of words in converssation the loss of words are pitifull.

Lou Howes

January 1988

Since Bigmama's death two months ago, life in the Howes family has been a confounded sequence of events. In this short period, so much happened that we felt like Alzheimer's had become contagious. I know I was confused.

For one thing, Ricky's wife, Gwen, did move back from Houston, but they divorced December 7 because Ricky had found someone else in the meantime. In an effort to keep Christmas from being too different for Mom, I invited Gwen to our annual get-together. She was still a part of the family as far as I could tell, not being familiar with the unwritten rules of divorce. I was already unhappy that Fan had requested to have the traditional event a week before Christmas and not on the exact day. I had been trying to make the season resemble the past so that Mom could handle it. Her Alzheimer's was gradually forcing her familiar surroundings to look foreign; I didn't think it was wise to make any unnecessary changes now. Nevertheless, when Ricky brought along his new girlfriend to our Christmas exchange, the word awkward could not even come close to describing the afternoon. So much for tradition.

On Christmas Eve, I visited my eighty-nine-year-old Grandpa in the nursing home for what turned out to be the last time. He was very tired and miserable, and I knew he wouldn't be with us much longer. The day after Christmas, Pop called to tell me Grandpa had died. From December 1984 to December 1987, I had lost all four grandparents.

My cousin Dougie called last week to invite us to the Covington Mardi Gras parade, but also asked me to bring along any literature I might have on Alzheimer's disease. I caustically thanked him for being so sensitive to Mom's condition, especially since the last time we talked about the subject, he laughingly said, "Hey! I hear Aunt Lou's going insane!" But this time, he was serious; he was worried about his dad. He said Uncle Dodo had been acting strangely at work, forgetting appointments and such. Dougie thought his father might be showing the first signs of Alzheimer's.

Recent changes in my family would have been enough to keep a normal person on the edge of giddy insanity. However, I never have made the claim that I was normal. Besides, I had my own battle to fight with the School of Art at L.S.U. In October, I had been assured by three professors that there would be openings in the M.F.A. program in the spring and that they would recommend that I be allowed to fill one of them. I submitted a new application to the head of the painting faculty whose responsibility it was to present it to them for a vote.

His words were cautious, "The only negative comment I've heard is that if we take you now, you'd be filling one of the spots for next fall, too, and what if somebody really good came along? You wouldn't be competing against them. I do plan to recommend that they accept you, though."

Apparently, all of these recommendations went unheeded. On the same day that Bigmama died, the painting faculty voted not to accept any new graduate students for the spring semester. My level of tolerance was growing thin, not to mention Zab's. We didn't understand how a university could send a letter congratulating a student on being accepted into its Graduate School, and then say, "We don't want you," once she arrived. We finally decided that someone with higher authority than the School of Art needed to hear my story, so we visited the acting dean of the Graduate School.

After reading the letter and hearing my story, the dean apologized for L.S.U. He told me he would talk to the School of Art, telling me, "It's our mistake, not theirs." I told him that I didn't think they would be too happy to have my admission forced on them, but he said that he planned to meet with them himself to explain the mixup.

Within another week, I received a letter confirming all that the dean had promised, including another apology for any confusion or inconvenience that I experienced. Accompanying the letter was a handwritten note from the dean asking if he could place copies of the various correspondence in my file at his office. It seemed I was finally going to be part of the M.F.A. program at L.S.U. after all.

Journal Entry
February 26, 1988

I have been telling myself to perk up and stop getting depressed when everything is lousy and I can't spell well, or see well, or remember over and over again. There is so much that goes around in my head that I want to put down. really what I need is a little "Comic Releif" So, here is my poroduction. the title is "watching Lou dress."

Now don't get the wrong idea, this is not an X rated show. In fact, it is not an R rated show. I would have to label it a family afair.

It begin with the hard part, the, the decision! What will I wear? From long engraved habit, everything must match! This sometimes means frustration. I always wear pants, so that helps. However, now we, must find out how cold it is outside. I don't know why I do this. It is always warm and always cold, no matter what the thermomeyter says.

Allright, now comes the time to get dressed. All of these clothes have a front and a back, OK? Now we proceed to find out which one is the front, and which one is back. about this time, I husband comes in to see how I am doing. He gives me a tip on finding the right side. By this time I am completely confused. However, I do manage to get the dressing fairly complete and normal and decent. Now, that is just the every day dressing. getting ready for a special affair is another story.

May 5, 1988

We have heard from NIH that they want us to come to NIH for some testing. We are to come for a few days for some testing. This testing will be with a stronger version of the "SMS" drug. I never got to be tested with "THA" as it was pulled from the market for severe liver damage. We will leave May 25. I will be happy to see everybody again although I can't say that about an LP. I know they are inevitable. I know one thing. I'll never do as well as I did before on all of the testing. I think, or Bert said that they want to give me all the tests that I took when I was there and then compare them to ones taken in Bethesda before. When we first were called for the short trip to NIH, I told Bert that I would bet they can find someone will need to use me for a test of some kind. I don't care. I hope to get to see Dr. Moral and alll of the crew. I took ally of my pictures that I had taken when I was ther before and I am trying to relearn their names again and hope it works. We will be leaving here.

May 25–28, 1988

For the first tests we went back to, we stayed in a motel, then we caught the NIH shuttel to go to the hospital. I had many tests with this crew. I couldn't keep up with the names, but I knew some were Pet Scans, and NHR, blood tests and urin spemen. It ended with me taking a test that I have had before and I sure do not like it. (EEG) They put some scom kind of greasy stuff in your hair and then some other stuff in your hair. Then there were a lot of other mecannucal noises—loud, very loud! The messy stuf made my hair a sticky mess and later turned to hard cah to chalk. which was very hard to get out of your hair I had no way to really wash it. I there after we went back to Motel and washed my hair. I found stuff in my hair for a week off and on.

After we finished that job, we were oficially on our regual routine for testing the next Drug. It seems that they have found that the Drug, SMS, that I tested the last time we were her here at NIH has been made more strong and they have had some good results. So, I hope it will not run into any trouble. I had my first injection and everything went well.

To back up a bit, I had a few, The first day I took some Psy. tests. It was some of the best I have had before, but a lot of them were new. One of them were to look at pictures and tell about the I was to say everything I could say about the picture. The girl was so surprised that I knew all of them and so much about them. She said I really knew I was a teacher to do that. however I was not very good in a lot of them. I just couldn't rememeber a lot of things I still can do well on the number tests tests.

June 6, 1988

First injection of the SMS. Now every morning they have us on a strict diet while taking the Drug. Every morning, there is a Blood Flow where they take drug I ly on the bed my back and the Dr. draws blood at intervals. I really don't understand what's going on. The only thing that is uncomfortball was a dry, dry mouth. However, there was somebody always around wyth some water.

June 19, 1988

They threw a bumer at me yesterday. The people with Dr. Isabella wanted Bert in the same room as they were so, They movened all the furniture from our rum to Isabella's room so they would all be in area. It was so confusing! I had to learn where everything was in the room. It was the same size, but a different arranged. and, of course I was confused trying to put the right things where they belong, etc. With Bert's help, I got it all done in time for the next day's proceures. I don't know if I said anything about "this". All work, machines and all is done in my bedroom. They just put all the machines, etc. on the bead. They have a neat system. While I am lying on the bed, I don't feel as if I the room until I look around and see my things.

Of couce, when I got up and walked around I could orientate myself. Most of the time I am on my back so that Limenedited. I had a Lumbard puncture (a spinal tap", and I stayed quiet for a long time so I had no pain at all during the time I was there. Dr. Iszablella' work is to complex to try to describe.

Took blood from Bert every 15 min. for 24 hours. They gave him a shot of a drug. He had to stay in bed 28 hours. He stayed awake in his chair half of the time and then slept half of the time It was very complicated. A young neurologist was wunorkng with the group. Dr. Baronte. He was a nice looking, and pleasant young man with a Italian accenent. he was hear from Italy and had a strong accent. I worked with him on setting up all of the SMS procedr. Every morning he would take bood from me and give me the SAS. They sure took a good bit of blood. But it was used in whatevr the hold *proceany was. I was constantly takey tests so I guess they had that way of seeing if it was doing good.*

Today is Saturday, so it is quiet Bert and I both have a Heplioc. These are a small apratus on the arm that allows them to take blood at intervals and to insert the Drug into the arm. That way, they don't hae to stick you each time.

Dr. Baronte left to go back to Italy yesterday morning. he was gone when we woke up.

June 28, 1988

We came back from Bethesda.

I was in good condition. I been on the new medicine for some time When we left Bert asked Dr. Maradian about the results of all the drug procedure. She told us that out of 10 tests 6 of the tests were better and 4 were weorse.

I felt that I was much clearer in my thinking and reaction, and wrriting skill.

However, that has all worked off, I guess because I can tell the diference in me and I am basicaly back to "square I".

The drug gradualy worked out of my system. My handwriting and spelled is a mess again.

Lou Howes

September 1988

More often these days, Mom has been showing signs of confusion. Of course, our lives are usually hurricanes of activity that would set back even the most organized among us. Nevertheless, even a relaxed pace has created unusual behavior. Mom's sister Betty came in for a visit in July. The three of us and Kate spent time in both Morgan City with Fan and Pensacola with Tricia's daughter, Janie, an occupational therapist. During both visits, Mom wanted to come home early and didn't understand why we couldn't leave on the spot. Her mood swings changed from pessimistic complaining to hearty laughter, making each hour as unpredictable as the one before it. Either she was too cold and the room was too dark or everything was just hunkydory.

We've all managed to live with Mom's mood swings up to this point. Most of the time, she doesn't even know they are happening to her, so we don't take her unorthodox responses personally. The one symptom that is growing worse is Mom's ability to read and write. Losing the ability to think was Mom's greatest fear, but losing the ability to write was her greatest sorrow. She fought to continue keeping a journal, since stopping meant an end to the old newspaper reporter's chance to communicate with an outside source through her favorite medium, the pen. Mom was reaching the point at which the letters failed to form words on the page. Mom was forgetting how to read.

She had been complaining about her eyes, saying that the words were jumping around and that she couldn't follow text from one line to the next. Pop and I tried one of Bigmama's old magnifying glasses, but enlarging the letters didn't help. I had read somewhere that a yellow transparency placed over writing would enable old eyes to read better—something about clearing up the contrast. That didn't work either.

Even as much as a year ago, she was having trouble writing legibly in her journal. During the "Health Century" interview, she said, "I can't write in my diary. I have to write on a piece of paper. Then I have to have somebody read that to me so I can put it in my diary. I don't have but one little brain that works at a time, I think."

That somebody was Mom's good friend, Dot Perrin, whom we've referred to as Aunt Dot since we were kids. Aunt Dot told me that she used her left hand to cover any written words on the journal page while her right forefinger pointed to the first empty line. In this way, Mom would know where to write. Mom then told Aunt Dot what she wanted to write, and Aunt Dot would repeat it one word at a time while Mom wrote. When that became too slow and tedious for Mom, she tried dictating her notes into a small cassette tape recorder, but quickly became frustrated with the buttons and refused to allow someone else to be around to help.

Mom's last journal, in which their fourth trip to Bethesda was recorded, consisted of a legal pad and torn-out sheets of notebook paper. It ended unevenly, since her handwriting had deteriorated to the point at which it was difficult for her to complete a sentence. Words trailed off the page, and spelling took on a whole new language. Mom had once been an avid proofreader, correcting her mistakes obsessively, whitening the text with bottle after bottle of Liquid

Paper. Eventually, she replaced the correction fluid with frustrated scratch-outs.

Mom's journals, as well as her letters to us, are interesting works of art in themselves. They describe her symptoms not only literally, but also visually. Her penmanship shows a progressive inability to stay on the ruled line, while at the same time her words are describing this symptom. In one of her letters home last year, she wrote, "The big Al has stolen my handwriting and spelling so hang in there. Also he pushes my pen off the line every once in a while." As Mom wrote the last sentence, the word "every" drooped under the line on which she was writing.

Finally, Mom became so embarrassed by her poor penmanship and incorrect usage that she asked Betty, during her visit, to copy her notes legibly, but word for word, into a bound book. After Betty left, Mom relied on me. I didn't realize at the time that I would be transcribing her final written paragraphs.

Journal Entry
June 1988
(Copied by Kim)

Changes since I came home from the last trip to Bethesda term—my short memory is very bad. I have forgotten if I have eaten or dressed, or eaten. Sometimes forgotten if I have same time it is on the table when we are eating meals.

I know why. I have stopped talking less. This is a complete change in my talking. I have always been able to carry on a conversation on a one to one level or with a group. Probably too vocal.

I cannot decide on anything. Bert gets so outdone with me, and then I cry and he gets mad again. I really try to stop the cycle, but it is hard. It is a vicious cycle. I get depressed because I can't do things right and there are the tears again. Then Bert is angry again. What a mess!

I have heard that a disease goes for the most vulnerable part of your body. I know that my eyes are getting worse. I am not able to see because, sitting here, my eyes are watering and I have to keep drying them to see.

August–September 1988
(Copied by Kim)

I have a problem in my writing and my reading. I am trying to see if it will be easier to read if it was a dark black pen.

It is hard. I have realized that I cannot read my own writing. I thought that if I could not read it, nobody else could read it.

I really don't have to write. I could live the rest of my life not writing, but I would be very sad.

I wish that you could know, when I have something else comes up, if it is normal old age and arthritis or it is the result of "Al."

I doubt that there is very much difference. Whichever it is, it is very depressing. Whatever it is, it is rotten. I fear there is very little difference. I cannot write anymore, It is just a lot of words that don't make sense to me.

I am sorry that we did not hear anymore from Bethesda. Dr. Moral said she would let us know the results of the last time I was there.

I had heard that she and Isabella had been sent somewhere else. I tried to get Bert to call Marge Galespy, the gal that seems to be the coordinator. She would know what the last results were. But he said they might not still working on our case. I guess there is no reason for me to do anything but pray.

I wish I had more to do to keep me busy. I really miss not being able to read. I could always pass the time and read. Most of the things I could read and write right.

Lou Howes

October 1988

Mom continued to be on my mind, even as the new school year began and I reported back to Ponchatoula High School. My year's sabbatical proved to be the perfect remedy for burn-out since I was excited about coming back. I guess teaching is what I was meant to do. Even though I consider myself to be a creative teacher, I never really considered this profession to be the end-all, the ultimate in my life. I saw my art as the loftier of the two, the one with the prestige, the one that took skill.

Teaching was so much a part of me that I didn't think about appreciating it, yet because of that, I realized that I could never have pushed it away for very long. I even found it difficult to escape into a book; a little voice inside me would say, "Write that down. Add it to that unit you did last semester." I'd read the newspaper and see the name of one of my kids in the news, one of the fifteen hundred or so I've taught since 1974. My dreams for them were so much greater than they had for themselves.

Anyway, I was back at it again, planning a new unit that I called "Autobiography Boxes"—a dumb title, I thought, for a really in-depth unit, one in which my advanced students could explore their own lives, their own conflicts. This unit gave them a chance to use their art as therapy as well as personal expression. It has been difficult for me to grade them, however, without thoughts of Mom's conflict coming into my head. I stood by the counter in the art room with my grade book in hand, staring down at one student's finished product, one that moved me to swallow hard. The outside of the box was beautifully decorated with lacy cloth surrounding a family photograph of happy people. Inside the box, there were dead flowers and the same photo ripped in half.

I wondered how many of my students could see the inside of my own box, the other side of Miss Zab. I wondered how many knew that my mother had Alzheimer's disease, that I checked on her every day, that I was still trying to commute to L.S.U., and that I had a daughter and a husband and another life. I hoped they didn't know, in a way. I wanted them to think that I lived only for them, for their success. After all, I had become an expert at clicking on my teacher face at 7:30 in the morning and clicking it off when the final bell rang in the afternoon. I had been taught to juggle, to handle a multiple existence, to be pulled in several directions at once. Maybe my teaching was my therapy. Maybe I couldn't live without them, the students that shot my ego to the ceiling while allowing me to mold their thoughts and force them to look inside themselves. Maybe I needed to see one more face light up when it finally caught on to a concept. Maybe they might not notice that I needed them as much as I thought they needed me.

November 1988

It wasn't until this past summer that Mom started getting lost on her regular walk home. Even though she had memorized her route, she would get turned around when she was distracted. Mom knew she lived in a small town, for every time she took her walk, someone would drive by and ask her if she wanted a ride. That was fine at first, but before long, the friendly interruption would cause Mom to lose track of the streets and not know which way was home. One day, she told me that a young man drove her home. She told him she had Alzheimer's and was lost. Mom couldn't remember his name, but she said that she saw him drive to work every morning. Later that week, Pop bought her an engraved Medical Alert bracelet.

Emma, Mom's housekeeper for years, recalled a similar incident that happened about the same time. Her daughter was driving, and they came to the corner of North Seventh and Beech Streets. Emma saw Mom walking in the middle of Seventh Street, in front of my house, turning circles in the street, crying. A man in a car was screaming at her, "Get out of the road, you stupid woman!" Emma got out of the car, yelled at the man, "You don't even know her." Then, taking her by the hand, Emma walked Mom home.

Mom finally stopped taking her walks alone when she found herself lost in Memorial Park. What Ponchatoula calls a "park" is one square city block with few trees, a couple of baseball diamonds, and some playground equipment. If I stand in the middle of the block, I can see all four streets that surround the park that is located exactly halfway between Mom's house and mine. It's impossible for a person without Alzheimer's to get lost in the park because it's an open block divided into four quarters by a running sidewalk.

It was this simple network of sidewalks, however, that twisted Mom's sense of direction. On one particular day, one wrong turn resulted in a seemingly endless trek around the park. Mom knew she was not on her memorized route, but she could not figure out how to escape this self-made maze. It was not as if she were a zombie, aimlessly walking in all directions; Mom knew she was lost. She also knew she was in her own neighborhood, the same neighborhood that had protected her for the last forty years. She just kept taking the wrong turn when the sidewalk reached its end, pushing her to the point of hysteria.

Later, when Mom recalled the incident, she could not remember how she finally reached her own home. Zab's friend, who lives across the street, filled in the missing memory. He said that he and his daughter had been watching Mom walk aimlessly in the park, both of them wondering what was wrong. Then they saw her sink to the ground. (Mom had not remembered falling.) He then took his truck to the park to help. Even though his daughter was not quite three years old at the time, she still has a vivid memory of her and her daddy rescuing Miss Lou and getting her home.

February 1989

In the last few months, I've noticed Mom's confusion coming to the surface even during Mass. Fortunately, Mass has changed very little in the last twenty years, and knowing when to stand, sit, kneel, or genuflect is ingrained in Mom's Catholic psyche by now. I don't think even Alzheimer's disease would mess with Catholicism.

As we sat down for the homily, I felt a sudden tug and turned around in time to see the lady sitting behind Mom reach up to tuck Mom's tag into her collar and pat her gently on the shoulder. When I smiled at the lady to thank her, I felt a lump growing in my throat. Now, I usually don't cry when it comes to Mom's dilemma, but it seems that, sometimes during Mass, I feel my eyes bubble up and my throat get so knotted that I can barely sing. Mom has always had tons of friends, both young and old, and I know it hurts them to see her this way. To the older crowd, she was the great joke-teller, the life of the canasta party, the one they could count on to energize a dull get-together. To the younger set, she was "Mama Lou" and the favorite substitute at the high school. She was just that kind of mom, the kind to whom all my friends could turn for advice. This morning, though, I needed a little advice myself from another source. I looked up at the crucifix over the altar and whispered, "OK, God, do your stuff. Clear my head, if you don't mind."

As I studied the deeply carved curves in the statue's

hair, I thought of the series of fabric paintings I completed last semester at L.S.U. Instead of paint, fabric had formed the muscular structure of larger-than-life human figures, preening men displaying their love of self. I felt almost sacrilegious thinking about my satirical paintings of male vanity at the same time I was studying the flowing lines of that body hanging on the cross.

Anyway, my Graduate Review Committee must have thought so, too, for they put me on School of Art probation for a semester. One professor on the committee asked me if I had done the paintings intentionally to repulse him, while another compared them to the sensation of entering a room in which someone was screaming a string of profanity; all she wanted to do was leave. So much for free expression, mine as well as theirs.

Even though I didn't think so at the time, the committee actually did me a favor. Upon receiving my probation notice, I went immediately to my studio and released my anger in paint. Using my fingers in slashing crosshatches, I painted with more emotion than I

had ever felt before. It was an exhilarating forty-five minutes, a feverish slinging of acrylic onto paper stapled to my studio wall. When it was over, I stepped back to see two angry faces peering out from the surface, two red faces scourged by vermillion green and titanium white. I thought the red on my fingertips was the rich red of alizarin crimson, but it was blood from cuts made by the hardened peaks of thick, fast-drying acrylic.

I shifted in my pew as the drone from the sermon continued to echo against the church rafters. My mind had definitely drifted away from Mom, and my eyes were now dry. I studied the backs of the heads in front of me, then the heads in front of them, then the heads in front of them, until I had studied all the heads between me and the first pew. I became fascinated by the repetition of the wooden rows, the varying spaces between strangers and families. I closed one eye so that the entire scene in front of me would flatten into a two-dimensional space. My right forefinger and thumb began to measure the depth of the intervals between each row, and I discovered that the distance of each interval was half the distance of the one behind it. I knew this was it. This was my new subject matter.

Later in the week, I returned to the church to sketch the pews from various viewpoints, from the choir loft, looking down, from a humbling angle on the floor, looking up. Being in this empty environment that usually houses a multitude gave me an eerie feeling, as if I were not supposed to be there. To compound the quiet, the clay in my pencil made noisy scratches as it scored across my waiting sketchbook. The overwhelming feelings of loneliness that bounced from the walls had to have come from within me. I should have found solace in this place alone, yet it was drawing from me emotions that I did not yet understand, emotions that I hoped would come through in my paintings.

May 1989

Pop has made a complete turnaround. If someone would have asked me five years ago who would take care of Mom, my answer certainly would not have been Pop. I guess he just loves her. He acts as if it's no big deal, as if caring for Mom is what he is supposed to do.

Mom's sisters have pitched in, too. Tricia and her husband, Hank, came in a couple of months ago for a week-long visit, and Pop had her cooking every night and mending holes in his pants pockets. Betty will be here soon for her fiftieth class reunion, so that will give him a break, too.

Fan comes to Ponchatoula once every two months. I wish she would come in more often, at least once a month, but she lives two hours away and has three kids pulling her in three different directions. Ricky, on the other hand, lives close enough to help, but seems preoccupied with his new wife. His teenage daughter Jan lives with them as well. His son, Ryan, still lives with Gwen in Houston.

Mom and Pop can easily blame Alzheimer's for the fact that they seldom get down the river to the camp anymore. It's not the distance; the Tangipahoa River runs only about eight miles from their home, and the camp can be reached by boat within an hour. Mom still enjoys the drive, but only if she is warm enough and if she can ride in the big boat. Her lack of depth perception makes her afraid of falling when Pop helps her in and out of the boat, and it takes Pop a week to talk Mom into going in the first place. She feels safe in her surroundings at home and is insecure about spending the night anywhere else. When Pop finally convinces Mom to go with him to the camp, she does manage to adjust to the camp environment. However, when Pop is ready to go home, he has to begin his persuasion tactics all over again. The frustration of it all makes a weekend trip hardly worth it, even though in the eyes of a younger Mom and Pop, weekends were always reserved for going down the river.

When they bought the camp from Pop's parents around 1960, we began to practically live down there. Pop had already constructed a fifteen-foot wooden boat with a cabin, which we christened the Miss Fay Ann after Fan, and the camp was named Kamp Kim after me. As for Ricky, we named the two flats King Richard I and King Richard II. A little five-horsepower outboard hooked to the back of one of the flats was enough for him to pull Fan and me up and down the

river on the surfboard for hours. Our days down the river were filled with swimming, waterskiing, or just walking the lakeshore looking for cow bones and driftwood. Our nights smelled of kerosene lanterns and buzzed with the soft sound of crickets scratching their legs together. We would play Parcheesi into the night and wake up to take a cold morning shower right outside the back porch door. I remember thinking that I could never marry a man who did not love to go down the river as much as I did. He would have to have a boat, any kind of boat, and he would have to want to go down during the cold of a winter's night. That's the best time, when the only people down the river are the faithful ones, the ones that hang on after all the tourists go home, the ones that love the river even when the cypress trees age the shore with their gray-haired, mossy limbs.

The Miss Fay Ann and both King Richards are long gone now, replaced several times over by the shine of a white Fiberglass hull or an inboard-outboard motor. Yet, Kamp Kim is still standing, always there on the banks of the Tangipahoa, waiting quietly for the day when Mom and Pop will need her again.

June 1989

My Aunt Betty came in just as she had promised and stayed with Mom for twelve days. She looked the same to me, maybe younger if anything. Her dusty white skin seemed tighter than it had before, almost like white pantyhose stretched over five unhappy toes. Her Scleroderma had progressed, I guessed, but not because Betty told us anything about it. It was just something she lived with, she said, nothing for us to worry about.

Kate and I went over early on the Saturday morning after Betty arrived. We found her and Mom in the bedroom getting Mom dressed for the day.

"OK, Lou, do you want to wear these navy pants today?"

Mom, who was sitting in her pajamas on the edge of the bed, looked toward the closet but not at anything in particular.

"Doesn't matter to me," she said, then turned our way when she heard us come in. "Hey, looky here."

Kate hugged Mom first, then went for Betty's waist.

"Whoa, Kate, my Lord! You've grown so tall. What are you eating, sweetie? I love your short little haircut." Kate just smiled.

"She's 4'4" and still going strong. What are you two girls doing in here?" I asked as I sat beside Mom on the bed. She reached over and put her hand on my knee.

"Betty's trying to dress me. Always has tried to dress me."

"Oh, I know better than to get you all dolled up," Betty laughed. "I remember, pants or shorts, and that's it." She walked to Mom's chest-of-drawers and began rooting through one of them looking for underwear. "Where are your bras, Lou?"

"Mom wears undershirts now," I said. "They're warmer and don't have that ornery clasp in the back."

"Kim's been wearing them for years. I wish she would've told me about them sooner." Mom smiled at me.

"At least you have something to hold up, Mom.

With me, nobody can tell the difference, so why bother."

"Mama," Kate blushed.

Betty smiled at Kate and just shook her head. "Your mama's so bad."

"Betty, I've been trying to prepare Mom for the Hendry family reunion in July." I opened Mom's closet to get her a short-sleeved shirt.

"You're all going, I hope."

Mom spoke without noticing that I was unbuttoning her pajama top to replace it with the shirt. "I don't know."

"We'll have a great time," Betty said. "It's at Janie's house, Lou."

"Where's that?" Mom looked at me.

"In Pensacola, Florida, Mom, only five hours from here. Janie is Tricia's daughter, remember?"

"How will we get there? Where will we stay?"

"Don't worry, Mom, we're going to drive. We'll have plenty of cars there in case you want to come back early."

"I don't know." She stood up to pull up her navy pants, then sat down again so that I could put on her shoes and socks. "I can still tie my own shoes."

"Have at it, then. They're your shoes." I scooted back on the floor and watched Mom tie two perfect bows. I wondered at the time why has she retained this particular skill? How can she still tie her shoes when she can't even find the food on her plate?

"Where will we sleep?" she asked me as she began walking into the living room toward her favorite chair.

"I've rented one hotel room so that if you change your mind at the last minute, you don't have to go. There are two big beds in one room for you and Pop and Zab and me," I explained as I settled onto the ottoman beside her.

"And me," Kate protested.

"Of course, you, Kate. I'm sorry."

"Lou, you'll have a great time." Betty walked over and kissed her on the top of the head. "What's this?" She pointed to a yellow strip of tape over the telephone receiver that matched a yellow strip on the table underneath it."

"Oh, Pop and I put that there so that Mom could

hang up the phone after it rings. If she lines up the two yellow stripes, she knows she's hung up the phone."

"Yep," Mom grinned, "before that, I could only answer one call a day."

"She's right; the rest of the day, the phone would be off the hook."

Betty just smiled and joined Kate on the sofa. She reached the side table and found a pack of pictures to share.

"Are you ready for your class reunion?" I asked her.

"I guess so. I brought a dress I'd like you to see. If you don't think it will do, I can go to the mall this week to buy another."

"I'm sure it's fine. I don't think there are any standards for fiftieth class reunions, unless it's biggest beer gut or baldest head. Fan's twentieth is next month. I know she'll be in for that."

"She'll come in before then, won't she? That's a whole month away."

"Well, she's coming in tomorrow for Mother's Day, but her visits are not as often as I'd like. I usually don't know when she's coming. If I knew ahead of time, I could make some plans of my own."

"Have you ever asked her to come in?"

"Hmm, no," I shrugged. "I just assumed she'd come when she could."

"Maybe she doesn't realize how much she's needed," Betty said.

"Maybe so."

The next day, after dinner at my house, I thought I might take Betty's advice, but no time seemed the best time to bring it up. Ricky and his wife had gone to Mississippi to see her mother, but Fan and Bren came in and stayed for a long afternoon. Eventually, Bren and the kids walked two blocks to the Disher's house to visit his parents, and Fan stayed behind to pack up. I followed her out to the car and waited till she opened the trunk.

"Listen, I've been thinking," I began slowly, not completely sure of what I was going to say next. "Do you think, maybe, you might be able to take one Saturday a month, you know, to come help Pop with Mom?"

"I never know what our schedules are, what with

three kids and Bren's golf games, and coming over here means two hours over, spend the night, and two hours back the next day."

"I know, I just thought maybe if you set aside one Saturday a month, I could make plans ahead of time."

"I can't tell which Saturdays I'll be free. Kim, you don't have to go over there every day, every Saturday."

"Somebody does. That's the only break Pop gets. Don't you feel just a little guilty?"

"Don't throw guilt at me!" She stopped packing the trunk and glared at me. "Mom and Pop used guilt on us all of our lives and I'm not going to let guilt control me now."

"OK, OK." I waited a moment. "Then will you just do it for me?"

Fan shut the trunk. "I can do this. If I know I'm going to be able to come in, I'll call you a few days before. I don't know how often that will be. It may not be once a month, but that's the best I can do."

"I'll take it. Thanks," and I hugged her close.

She gave me an exasperated smile and opened the door on the driver's side. "Ricky could help, too. He lives right here."

"I don't have much patience with him."

"You won't know unless you ask."

"He'd do it if you asked him to. Hint, hint," I smiled at her through the car window.

"We'll see." Fan waved as she backed out of the driveway and headed for the Disher's house to pick up the rest of her brood.

On Monday, I went back to my teaching as usual, content in knowing that Fan was going to try to come in more often, and Betty was keeping Mom company all week. I could relax for a change and concentrate on these last two weeks of the school year. My calm lasted only until 3:00 that afternoon, however, when I discovered that Mom had fallen on the sidewalk and fractured her elbow earlier that day.

Betty had taken Mom for a long-awaited walk on her old route around the neighborhood. As they reached the sidewalk, coincidentally in front of my house, Mom stepped off the edge, turned her ankle, and landed in my driveway. Someone passing called for the city emergency unit because Mom could not get up. She was in pain, totally confused, and hysterical.

I know a fractured elbow must be serious pain, but Alzheimer's has made Mom more sensitive than usual. It's as if her skin is thinner, and her nerves scream when they are touched. She has such a low tolerance for pain now that even a hug can hurt her. To compound the discomfort, Alzheimer's prevents Mom from concentrating on more than one thought at a time. When she has a pain, not only is it greater than it is for the average person, but it also occupies her every thought.

A month has gone by since then. Mom's fractured elbow has actually accelerated her confusion because her mind focuses on any discomfort it causes. Her arm is still in a sling, and her activities are even more confined than they were with just Alzheimer's playing its part. Fan called to let me know she would be in this weekend for her class reunion and Father's Day, so Kate, Zab, and I have decided to take off Sunday and ride up the Natchez Trace for the day. I typed a list of activities that Mom could and couldn't do and sent them to both Fan and Ricky to make them aware of

her daily needs. It included such menial tasks as "cannot entertain herself except with television" and "cannot bathe herself." Fan already knows most of the items on the list. Ricky, however, needs to do a little homework.

October 1989

The family reunion went off as planned, complete with a cautious Mom in attendance. Janie's high ceilings echoed the laughter, and flashbulbs cut white holes in eyes as cameras and camcorders appeared from every purse and satchel. Ice chests brimming with beer and wine jammed Janie's utility room, as her two big loppyeared dogs chose wisely to hide outside under the porch floorboards. This time around, we chipped in to have the meals catered, in spite of which Janie spent a large portion of her time warming deep-dish casseroles and laying out platter after platter of turkey, ham, and roast beef.

The reunion kept the family talking for weeks after that fourth of July. My memory was not so much of the cousins, but of the two nights in the bed next to Mom

113

and Pop in the motel. After two sleepless nights, I understood Pop's frustrations first hand and admired his stamina. When I asked him how he had managed this far, he just smiled and said, "I have AIDS, one in each ear." Of course, I thought, he just removed his hearing aids before he went to sleep.

I didn't have that luxury during the reunion, in addition to the fact that I'm usually a light sleeper anyway. Mom woke up almost every hour, scared and crying. I know it is common for people in a motel to wake up confused, not knowing where they are, but every hour? Mom would sit straight up in bed alarmed, then change moods to frustrated agitation. When I asked her what was wrong, she'd just say she needed a drink of water or a trip to the bathroom. When she finally did go back to sleep each time, she mumbled indistinguishable words as if she were enacting her dreams.

Two days after we arrived home from the reunion, Mom and Pop flew to Bethesda for a brief two weeks of drug testing. This time, however, I knew better than to expect a journal to return home with her. It's been a year now since Mom has written a sentence, much less recorded any symptoms in her journal. Her handwriting has been reduced to scribbling with readable letters popping in and out of the flowing curves of hopeful cursive script. It was as if Mom had come from an ancient culture, one that relied on oral storytellers to pass on the heroic adventures of their forefathers. It was as if she were turning to me to help her record her emotions, to communicate, somehow, for her mute fingers.

We have been one, Mom and I, since that afternoon in her kitchen five years ago, joined in purpose on either side of that stubborn turquoise table with the white Formica star. We began our adventure that day, the day she misdiagnosed herself with a magazine article on depression. We set out together that day, even though it took us a year to realize that our journey was in Al's hands. Al plotted our course along the river of Mom's mind, knowing all the while that this journey, this voyage, would take us back to the beginning of her existence, back to the bright light of her birth, even back to the womb.

I knew it was now up to me to interpret this emotional voyage. I wanted to explore it through my art, but I wasn't sure how to begin. The lonely figures in empty church pews still populated my work, but in the last few weeks, they have begun to physically resemble Mom. Maybe this is the answer. I decided to sit out this semester from L.S.U. The break would give me more time to spend with Mom and the chance to explore this new possibility.

"Hey, you promised to pose for me today." I found Mom in the kitchen on a warm Saturday afternoon. She was leaning on the table wiping it with a towel.

"I forgot, but that's OK. Where's Pop?"

"I don't know. I just got here." As I walked over to Mom, who called herself finished with the only task Pop still gives her to do, I noticed that she had only wiped half of the table. "Good job, Mom, you can still do some things, huh? Here, I'll put it up for you." I took the towel and made a quick pass at the remainder of the table, then threw the towel toward the sink. Placing my sketchbook on my old chair at the table, I opened the cabinet door to get a couple of glasses. "Want a Coke before we start?"

"Sure," she said, sitting in her own chair.

"Pop must be in the boathouse, wouldn't you think?" I asked. I popped the flip top on the can and poured Coke into her glass before sitting down across from her.

"Gives him something to do."

"Hand me my sketchbook, Mom, please. It's on the chair beside you."

"Where?"

"Right there on the chair beside you." I pointed over the table to the seat of the chair.

"Here?"

"Yes, ma'am," I said but walked around to retrieve it myself. "Thanks. It's tough trying to find something, isn't it?"

"Ooh, yes, I reach here and it's not here. It's there," she smiled. "I should write that down, but I can't write."

"Sure, you can. When was the last time you tried?"

"I don't know."

"Well, now's as good a time as any. You have to keep practicing, or you'll forget it. Here's a sheet of paper." I pushed it across the kitchen table and placed a felt-tip pen in her right hand.

"OK, what to write?" she asked.

"Write your name," I said, hoping she would remember her own name.

"I don't know. I'll try." She placed the pen correctly in her fingers and began making circles in the air above the paper.

"Here's the paper down here," I said as I gently pulled down her hand to the table and the waiting page.

"Here?" she asked. "OK, what to write?"

"Your name, Mom. Write your name."

"OK, let's see. L," she began and her fingers created some curved lines that eventually turned into a lower-case L. "O," she continued, "and U. How's that?"

"That's great, Mom," I said. Somewhere in the midst of the continuous curves, there were indeed the three letters of her first name. "Now, what about Howes?"

"Oh, I don't know," she said, moving the pen back to the paper anyway. "Let's see." Mom's fingers were white as they pressed tightly around the point. She began the curves again, not realizing that the pen had run off the edge and was making black marks on the Formica table. In earlier years, she would have whipped out the Comet immediately and scrubbed them clean. Today, however, she didn't notice.

"Wait, Mom, let's get back on the paper."

"OK, now, what was I writing?"

"Your last name," I said. "Write Howes, H-O-W-E-S."

"OK," Mom leaned over the table top, totally concentrating on the task at hand. She slowly wrote some cursive letters on the paper, then pushed them across the table to me. "How's that?"

As I turned the paper to me to read, I could see that the word Howes was not there, but several other words were. In the midst of the scribbling, I could decipher a small "I love yoow."

"Perfect, Mom." I swallowed hard. "You did great!"

November 1989

Yesterday, I took Mom to the mall in Hammond to shop for the Christmas presents she used to buy alone.

It was just four years ago that Mom was doing the same thing for Bigmama, only Bigmama's list was simpler: tree ornaments for everybody. Mom, however, wanted her gifts to be just as unique as they had been in the past.

"How about ornaments?"

"No, no."

"What about clothes? I can get sizes and . . ."

"I never give clothes."

"What then?"

"I don't know."

Mom has been physically wearing down lately. The arthritis she inherited from Bigmama is moving from her knees to her back. She's beginning to hunch her shoulders a bit, making her body appear more decrepit than her mind at this point. Together, we must have been an odd pair. I held Mom's hand and led her through the larger aisles, telling her aloud what I saw. Clerks shied away from asking us if we needed any help. Old acquaintances avoided us, afraid of not knowing what to say, afraid of an awkward moment. Since Mom can no longer distinguish people at a dis-

tance, she was unaware that anyone walked the other way. Besides, it didn't matter; she had other things on her mind.

"Where did all this red come from?"

"It's Christmas, Mom. Red and green everywhere."

"It hurts my eyes."

"I know. I'm trying to avoid as much red as I can, but it's everywhere you look."

"That's for sure."

Mom soon became too frustrated to finish, so I took her home. We could always try this again on a better day. Besides, Fan was coming in next week to continue this shopping mission with Mom. She makes practical decisions more quickly than I do, so I knew that even one afternoon would dent Mom's extensive list.

I plan to take advantage of the time to get more work done. Over the last two months, my paintings have become life-size portraits of Mom. She never hesitates to pose for me, excited about the idea of her plight in paint, but I have much work to do without Mom sitting in the studio. I have taken a zillion photos of her anyway, knowing I couldn't always wait for Mom to have a good day. The empty pews of last semester have changed to rows and rows of seats in a lonely stadium or theater. In several pieces, Mom just sits alone staring into nowhere. Sometimes, faces or silhouettes emerge among the shadows.

One painting, in particular, has pushed to a more narrative angle. It is set in the old high school stadium, the same one in which Mom used to jot down notes about a Friday night football game before reporting to her typewriter at the newspaper office. In the painting, Mom is stepping off the ledge into the darkness while Fan and Ricky look on. Ricky is close enough to Mom to help, but instead, chooses to lean casually on the railing and grin at the viewer. Fan wants to help but is separated from the others by the railing itself. In the black void below Mom's faltering step, a shadowy figure waits to catch her as she falls.

Because of their detailed complexity, these paintings have been tedious to finish. The drawing stage takes many hours, and I lose motivation before the paint is even dry. I just don't feel any satisfaction from creating this work. Maybe it's the subject matter that's giving me an uncomfortable uneasiness in the pit of my stomach. Maybe it's just the fact that I'm on the outside of Mom trying to look in rather than vice versa. Either way, something's not working.

I'd like to assume that God is aware of all that's going on down here. I know Mom talks to him enough. Well, he apparently caught the tail end of my request for more sibling participation in Mom's care. When I asked, I didn't expect him to literally move Fan's entire family from one home to another, but I guess he had his own reasons. Last month, Fan's husband, Bren, received the final word that Texaco was transferring all its engineers to its New Orleans branch next summer. They weren't too thrilled at the thought of leaving Morgan City after fifteen years, but they realized they had no other choice. Fan and her family are even considering moving to Mandeville, which is only thirty minutes from here and a thirty-minute commute to New Orleans for Bren.

Of course, God has yet to light any matches under Ricky's rear. My brother already lives close enough to

Bert Howes and Lou Hendry Howes, August 1945, one month after their wedding

Pop and Mom down the river, 1977

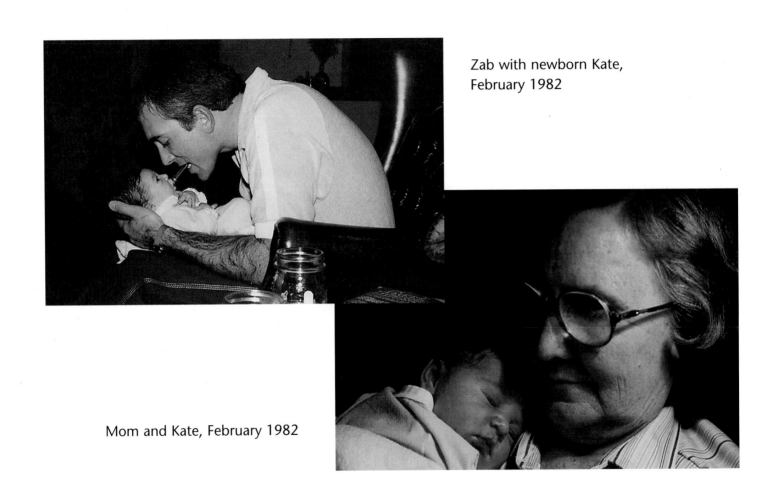

Zab with newborn Kate,
February 1982

Mom and Kate, February 1982

Four generations of
strong women,
April 1982.
Bigmama, 83;
Mom, 57;
Kim, 30;
Kate, 9 weeks.

Family portrait, Christmas 1985,
one month after Lou's diagnosis.
Ricky, Kim, Fan, Pop, and Mom.

Kate giving Mom
memory tests,
October 1987

Lou's writing of "I love yoow," fall 1989

Kate helping Mom down her back steps, 1990.
The yellow tape on the stairs made them clearer.

Kim and Mom at Kim's L.S.U. reception
for her M.F.A. exhibit, March 1992

Kim in her
studio, 1991

Mom and Kim in Kim's studio, May 1992

Stadium I. © 1989, 34" x 46",
collection of the artist.

Stadium IV. © 1989,
33" x 44", collection
of the artist.

Searching for Words. © 1989, 29" x 58", collection of the artist.

Tangled Memories I.
© 1990, 27" x 35", collection
of Dr. and Mrs. Rick Richoux,
New Orleans, Louisiana.

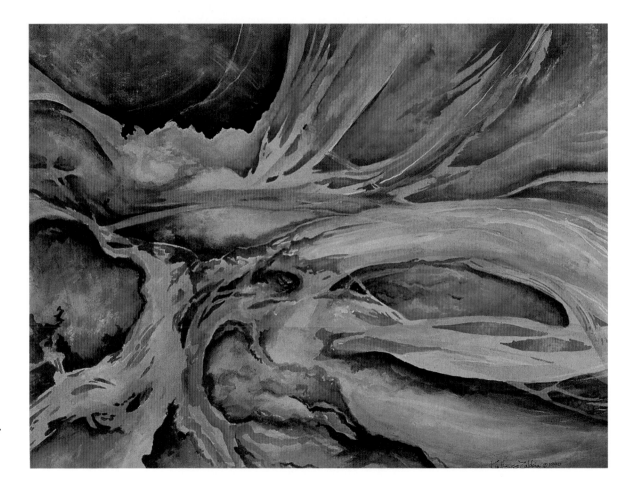

Even the Sky Moves I. © 1990, 26" x 32", collection of Merle and Joe Suhayda, Baton Rouge, Louisiana.

Hallucination I.
© 1990,
26″ x 34″,
collection of
Merle and Joe
Suhayda,
Baton Rouge,
Louisiana.

Lost in the Park I.
© 1990,
27" x 35",
collection of Beth
and Bob Daly,
Fairfax, Virginia.

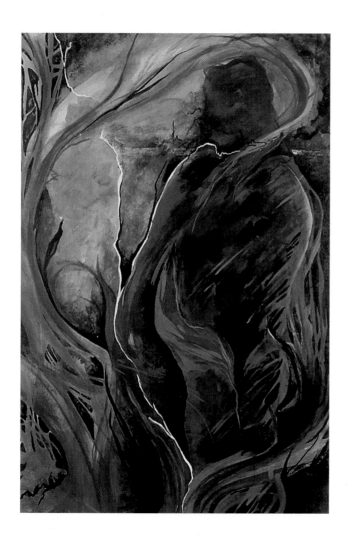

Private War I. © 1990,
25" x 35", collection of
Dr. Louise Baenninger,
Mandeville, Louisiana.

Private War III. © 1990, 17" x 24", collection of Ruth Speirer, New Orleans, Louisiana.

Lost in the Park III.
© 1990, 32" x 44",
collection of
Ruth Hamilton,
Moosejaw,
Saskatchewan,
Canada.

Visions at the Foot of the Bed IV. © 1991, 42" x 50", collection of the artist.

The War Within III.
© 1991, 44″ x 51″,
collection of the artist.

Constricted Messages. © 1991, 50" x 97", collection of the artist.

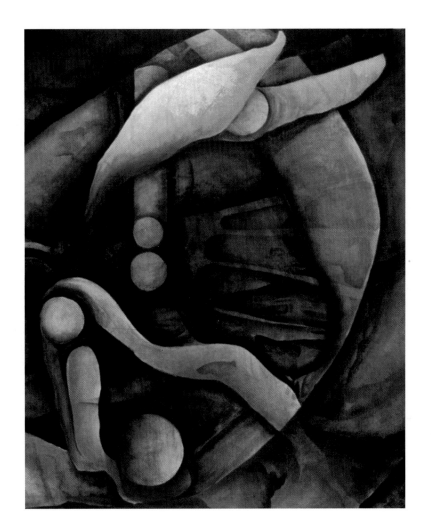

To the Bright Light of Death I.
© 1991, 43" x 51", collection
of Beth and Bob Daly, Fairfax,
Virginia.

To the Bright Light of Death II. © 1991, 42" x 49", collection of Merle and Joe Suhayda, Baton Rouge, Louisiana.

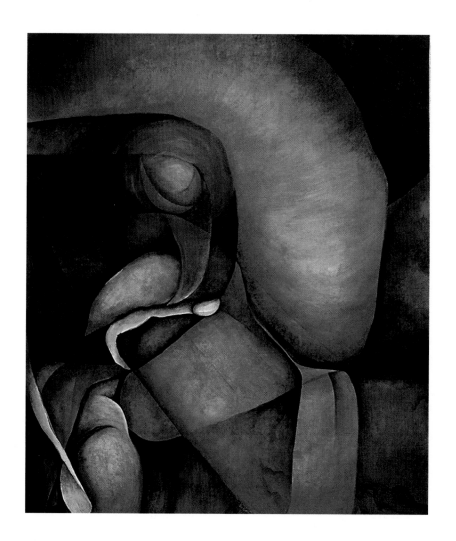

To the Bright Light of Death III.
© 1991, 43" x 51", collection
of the artist.

Nerves Kiss Before They Die II.
© 1991, 40" x 47", collection of
Dr. Alan Stevens, Birmingham,
Alabama.

In Search of Rebirth II.
© 1992, 45" x 50",
collection of Stacy Wilson,
Sulphur, Louisiana.

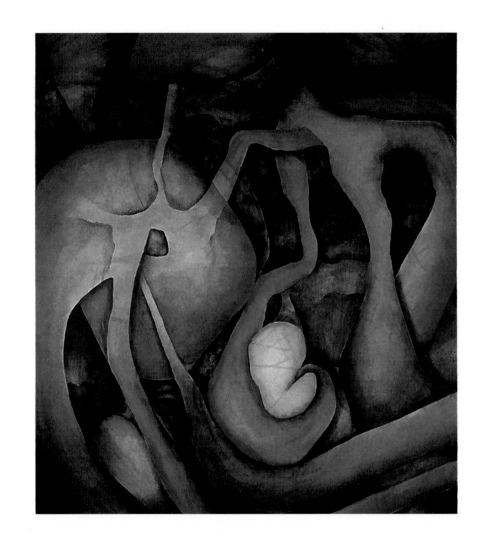

Reaching the Womb I.
© 1992, 44" x 50",
collection of the artist.

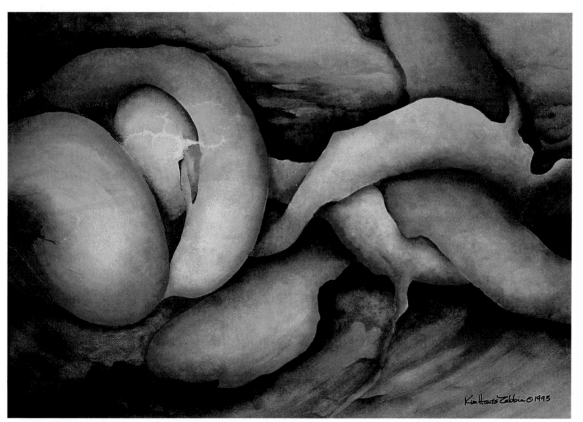

Acceptance I.
© 1993, 20" x 28",
collection of Ellen
Elmes, Jewell Ridge,
Virginia.

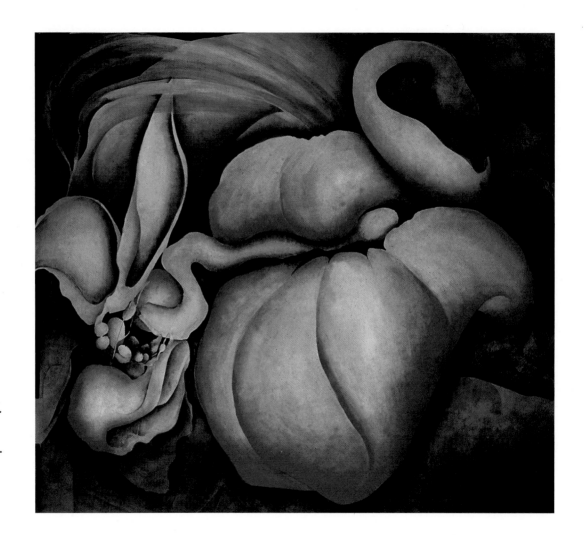

Reaching the Womb III.
© 1994, 38" x 44",
collection of the artist.

To Deny the Inevitable. © 1994, 28" x 48", collection of the artist.

The Ultimate Release, August 27, 1994. © 1994, 48" x 96", collection of the artist.

the situation, so a physical upheaval such as in Fan's case is not necessary. I wonder if there is such a thing as a mental upheaval, but, come to think of it, it's probably his heart that needs the upheaval, not his brain. Last week, Ricky called to set up a different date for our traditional Christmas get-together, a plentiful exchange of gifts and food that always occurs sometime Christmas day. Last year, I begrudgingly agreed to move it to the day after Christmas, but not this year. This year, I've noticed Ricky slowly dissolving contact with Mom and Pop, maybe as a good faith effort to prove to his new wife that his former family is not as important to him as his new family. I don't know.

"It seems you think of Mom and Pop last," I told him. "Why can't they come first for a change?"

"They said they don't care what we do."

"You know that's what they're going to say. They'd still be hurt if no one showed up on Christmas day. They never left their parents alone on a holiday."

"Well, that was them."

"Ricky, look, we may not have too many good Christmases left with Mom. Next year, she may not even know who we are. She needs more and more attention every day."

"Yes," he said quietly, "and I thank God every day that I have a sister who lives close enough to check on them for me."

"What?" I was fuming by this time. "First of all, I don't check on them every day for *you*. I check on them for *me*. I go because Pop can use some relief, because Mom can use some company, because I want to know that they're all right. Not because I want to do you any favors."

"That's true. You've never done anything for me. You never even cooked for me the whole time after Gwen and I split up!"

"Cook for you! Why should I cook for you when I seldom get to cook for my own family? That's beside the point," I said, trying to calm down. "Can't you just take the time to take Mom for a ride or something, anything to relieve Pop for a little while?"

"It takes all my spare time just to keep up with Jan."

"Ricky, we all have kids. You gotta come up with a better one than that. Just promise me one thing: when

Mom dies, don't come crying to me at the funeral saying you wished you could've done more, OK?"

"Now you're telling me that I can't cry at my own mother's funeral!"

"Just forget it. You've missed the point completely."

Obviously, my patience with my brother is exceptionally thin. People who do not know him very well say that he is still going through denial, that he has difficulty accepting the fact that his mother is dying of Alzheimer's disease. People who do know him well know that Ricky is simply self-absorbed. His continuous quest for self-gratification consumes the majority of his time. Ironically, it's because of this quest that he just might be right: he truly does not have enough time.

December 1989

From our bedroom, I could hear Zab closing the French doors and depositing his car keys in their usual home on the dining room buffet. I heard him start down the hall, then detour for a minute to check on Kate. She had been asleep for an hour in her cluttered room off the study. The next sound was a soft click as Zab turned down the thermostat, then appeared at the edge of our bed.

"How's your daddy?" I asked, knowing that the scheduled visiting time for intensive-care patients was only fifteen minutes.

"The doctor thinks he may have had another heart attack."

"Damn. What next?" I said. Both of Zab's parents live only six blocks from us. His dad is eighty now; his mother is seventy-two.

"He'll probably be in the hospital through New Year's," Zab added as he walked around the bed to change his clothes. I folded the newspaper and placed it on the blanket beside me.

"Are we still having Christmas with your Mom tomorrow night?"

"Yes." I could hear him from the bathroom. "She said we'll just do Daddy's presents when he gets out."

"You know, there were three inches of snow in New Orleans yesterday. That's the first time it's snowed since Kate's birthday last year."

Zab walked into the bedroom, but his thoughts were still at the hospital. I watched him quietly crawl into bed beside me and pick up the folded newspaper. As he lay next to me in his white T-shirt, I quietly studied his soon-to-be forty square jaw angle sharply past the bristle of a day's growth. I smiled as my eyes reached his ears, "rubber ears" as Kate called them because her daddy could do anything with them for her sole entertainment. Kate is a photocopy of Zab, from his dark eyes to his dark hair, now slowly graying with each new experience. She looks so much like Zab and nothing like me that strangers have even asked if we were related. I just sarcastically reply that we know who her father is; it's the identity of the mother that's still in question. Kate said that she doesn't mind looking like her daddy as long as he's the only one with the hairy chest.

Zab had finished reading the paper and was about to turn off the lights and turn on the news when he leaned over to me and grinned. "Only two more weeks of freedom, huh?" He had apparently put away worries of his dad for a while.

"Don't rub it in," I moaned. "I dread going back to L.S.U. I've kind of enjoyed not being grilled for a semester."

"Aw, you're already halfway through," he said. "Get tough."

"Sure," I sighed.

At a recent Christmas party, I was asked by a graphic artist I had just met whether I would recommend her pursuing the M.F.A. at L.S.U. as well. My reply was, "Do you have a husband and daughter who will support you no matter what happens?"

"I'm divorced," she said.

"Then forget it."

February 1990

For the last two years, my experiences with the L.S.U. School of Art have been anything but pleasant. I haven't felt welcome from the beginning. It's only been my dogged determination to get this degree that's helped me keep my chin from dragging on the floor. It didn't take long before my insecurity bred paranoia. What's that old punch line? Just because you're paranoid doesn't mean they're *not* out to get you.

Nevertheless, this spring, I found the light at the end of the L.S.U. tunnel: Ann Harding. An accomplished painter in her own right, Ann is an unpretentious and confident teacher whose only concern at this time seems to be making me a better painter. I think Ann is older than I am, but she looks younger than she probably is, her youthful figure hiding her passion for German black bread. Our conversations in my campus studio probed past the technical jargon into the depth of feelings that I had been blocking for so long. On our first encounter, Ann went straight to the heart.

"Tell me about your mother."

I had learned from painful experience not to be too open when addressing any of the faculty members; my words had been twisted before. Yet, with Ann, I immediately felt a kinship.

"Mom was diagnosed with probable Alzheimer's disease when she was sixty-one, about four years ago," I began.

"That's young," Ann said.

"Yes, well, we've been able to trace her symptoms even further back than that. Possibly to three years earlier."

"How did you know? What were the first things you noticed?" She seemed genuinely interested.

"Depression, paranoia, mood swings," I said. "She was treated for depression for a year before we realized there must be something else."

"Tell me about these," she said as she waved at the group of life-size portraits of Mom tacked around the studio walls.

"I'm trying to confront Mom's experience. I don't know if you remember my work from last year; they were paintings of lonely figures in empty environments that usually house many people," I tried to explain. "Well, after analyzing them, I decided I must be trying to paint about Mom and didn't realize it. So I thought that maybe I should place her in those same environments, but I don't know if that's the answer either." I began to feel like I wasn't making any sense at all.

Ann just nodded quietly as if I were, then said, "I like the narrative quality of this one." She pointed to the one of Mom walking off the edge in the stadium while my brother and sister stood nearby.

"This one has to do with family support or the lack of it," I said. "My brother is close enough to help, but won't, and my sister is hindered by the fact that she doesn't live close enough to help as often as I'd like."

"My mother is blind," Ann said out of nowhere. "Isn't that unusual that I'm a painter, and my mother can't even see my work?"

"Maybe that's why your paintings are so rich in color," I said, trying to offer anything.

"I don't know. I've never thought about painting about her blindness," she added.

As she left that first critique session, I thought how different she was from any painting teacher I had ever had. She seemed comfortable with me, as if we were on equal ground, and I felt she respected my opinion. Ann Harding made me feel strong that day, strong enough to believe that my work was valid because I chose to paint it.

"Here, Mom, here's the black chair," I said as I pulled down her hand to feel the arm behind her. My studio at home is well lit and free of anything red.

"OK, now what?" She wasn't quite sure where we were.

"I'm going to paint, Mom. Do you mind keeping me company?"

"Sure, let's go."

"We're already here," I smiled. "You just sit tight. I'll work, and you can keep me company."

My eyes turned from my mother to a painting in progress, half the length of the south wall on which it was taped. On it, I had drawn a detailed portrait of six figures, five of them Mom, gradually turning through the air, each face slowly aging in years. To the left stood the sixth figure, Pop, giving Mom her journal. It misses her hands and floats softly through the air to the next Mom who cannot quite catch it. The third one doesn't even try as her hands fly out searching for words that her lips cannot form. Finally, she gives up, exasperated with her inability to communicate, and, by the fifth figure, complacent of the inevitable future, slow death by Alzheimer's disease.

"Good grief," I said aloud.

"What's the matter?" Mom was still sitting in her black chair.

"This painting is getting too deep for me. It's bordering on the ridiculous!"

"Oh, you know it'll come around," Mom smiled. She was always my strongest cheerleader.

"But look at it! It's so dramatic. Look at these trees in the background. They start off green and alive and then slowly entangle and die just like your brain." My voice sounded like an old Boris Karloff movie. "And the seats in the front turn into tombstones. This isn't it, Mom, this isn't it. I've heard that symbols can kill a painting. Well, this one has bit the dirt."

"How about bit the *dust?*"

"You know what I mean: dead."

Mom just sat there smiling at my frustration. "Well, what do you want?"

I sat down on the carpet in front of her feet so that she could focus on me through her bifocals. Her face brightened as I peered up at her, and she smiled.

"I want to paint what you feel, Mom," I began. "I want to show what you're really going through, to crawl into your skin and step into that brain, to show what it's like to have such an unusual disease as Alzheimer's."

"Well, it is unusual," she added.

"And it's intellectual, at least to me." My eyes glared back at my painting, then moved to the other lonely-Mom-portraits on the adjacent walls. "This painting doesn't show that though; none of these do. Alzheimer's is so surreal, so bizarre. This painting is just too narrative. It's too much of a short story, and I want to paint poetry."

"Then do it," Mom said.

"I don't know how just yet."

In between my subsequent visits with Ann, I met with my chairperson, Robert Warrens, to keep him abreast of my current work. He had been the one who suggested I take off the fall semester if I thought I needed the time to come to terms with my work, and the freedom from L.S.U. stress had been good for me. A tall professor with a full head of hair and a bushy mustache, Bob's small eyes squinted a smile as he entered my campus studio. I took three pages of notes during our thirty-minute discussion, and he had mixed emotions about these recent paintings of Mom.

"You're obsessed with this," he said, referring to the repetition of the environments. "Try to distance yourself more from this situation with your mother. Do not get too dramatic, too moody. All of these are still too illustrative."

Then he paused and walked to the one of Mom searching for words.

"These two figures on the left are great. If you can draw this well, you should do it on all your figures. Why not a bright vivid blue across the sky in the back? It doesn't have to be a night scene to make it more depressing. The idea is depressing enough.

"Become more inventive," he continued. "The repetition of the seats is too much. You're so into that idea, it's robotic. This idea of the play on the sentimental with the disease is against the whole idea of what makes modern art valid. Getting too involved in the sentiment and narration gets you too far away from form and color, just like modern artists' rebellion against nineteenth-century sentimentality."

My fingers were growing weary from writing, but Bob had more.

"Try an ironic play of one against the other. Try brighter colors; these seem to be drained of color. These paintings resemble Andrew Wyeth's style, but he found that distance from the sentimental."

"OK," I sighed. I seldom argued for my artistic self in spite of my newly discovered, Ann Harding–inspired strength.

When Ann and I met for the third time, it was February, and I had become discouraged with my work. My meeting with Bob had left me empty, as if I had been doing all the wrong things. I had felt this insecurity too often before.

"This isn't what I want to do," I broke in as soon as she came in the door. "I'm not enjoying painting this way; it's tedious. The only time I feel alive is at the beginning when I'm in the drawing stages. I've always disliked painting anyway because I feel like it's just coloring in my drawings."

Ann was listening quietly to my ranting, watching my hands fly wildly as I talked too fast. I know I have always put too much emphasis on any teacher's opinion. I had been taught that if I took a class under a particular instructor, I was obligated to respect the opinion of that instructor or not take the class. Yet, now I was expected to be an independent thinker, and I was struggling with it. A friend had tried to get the same idea through my thick skull when I boasted that I had not stopped taking classes since I was in kindergarten because "there's so much out there to learn." She asked me, "When are you going to start trusting your own opinion?"

Ann spoke softly, "Have you ever thought that the reason you don't like to paint is that you're not really painting?"

"I don't understand," I said.

"Why don't you do this," she said. "Pick up your brush first, not your pencil, and stroke paint onto the paper just for the sake of painting. Don't think about your mother. Don't think about Alzheimer's. Just enjoy the act of painting. In the end, you'll be surprised at how much it will relate to Alzheimer's and your mother."

On the hour-long drive home to Ponchatoula, my mind was filled with Ann's words. How was this going to work? I had always planned everything ahead of time. My sixteen years as a high school teacher had drilled me to be prepared for any situation; think it out first; know what will happen before your students do; that extra hour of preparation time will pay off in a managed classroom later.

Back in my home studio, I stared at the white surface of the watercolor paper. I had chosen a smaller sheet for my experiment, still afraid that it wouldn't work out. I had decided to only make one conscious choice: to start with yellow. The fact that I couldn't justify my choice made me think that I might be on the right track. Ann's words were echoing in my head as I picked up my large rounded brush, but I spoke my own words to empty my thoughts.

"I've heard that some people get pregnant after they stop trying." I smiled as I plunged my brush into the watery yellow.

April 1990

I had tried to paint with a clear head and a full heart, allowing only my emotions to control the images that appeared on the paper. Transparent tangles covered the picture plane as faces appeared in unexpected places. Staircases with varied steps were obvious in at least four of the works, and in others, there were cliffs or sudden drop-offs to nowhere. Sidewalks were interrupted by cracks. Silhouettes of shadowy figures loomed in caves, walked toward crevices, or hid behind doorways. One woman's face appeared to be lifted slightly above its natural location on her head, while a man's face peered through her torso. Other figures seemed younger, some huddled into a ball or fetal position.

To me, some of the images still appeared weakly executed. Many of the values needed to be strengthened, especially the darks; yet the paintings had a consistent eeriness to them, a sense of mystery that I knew I wanted to keep. These paintings had taken such a drastic turn since that first splash of yellow back in February.

"Hey, you're not supposed to work during the Strawberry Festival," a soft familiar voice floated into the studio. It was Alan Stevens, an old friend.

"I'm not painting, just picking up the clutter. Come in." I hugged him as he turned around to check out my new work. Alan hadn't changed much since he rolled posters into tubes for me eight Strawberry Festivals ago, except for the fact that his handsome boyish face now towered over me. His older sister Charlotte and I owned a frame shop together until about six years ago. We are still close.

"Zab told me I'd find you in here. He was in the front yard with Kate."

"That's Zab's favorite part of the festival, people watching. I've been in and out, but I don't love it like he does. So, a doctorate in psychology, huh? And, geriatrics no less. Am I right?"

"Yes, I've been working with Alzheimer's patients in a day-care center. I'm trying out new tests to see if their memory improves. All part of my research. How's your mother? I thought you might want to use my tests on her."

"She's still hanging in there, trying to stay on top of things. Tell me about your tests."

"Well, it involves a calendar and repetition of common everyday facts."

"She can't read or write anymore, does that matter?"

"I'm afraid so. We reinforce the concepts orally, but she would be required to write on a calendar. That's OK; it was just a thought." He walked to my easel on the far side of the studio. "How is your work coming along?"

"Considering the amount of time I've had to paint, I'd say great!"

"Are you still teaching?"

"What do you think?"

"I thought so. I don't know how you do it."

"Easy: I don't think about it. Ooh, I'm going to have my first solo show at Nicholls State University in September." I know I lit up like an excited little girl, but this kind of news was hard to hide.

"That's good! They just called out of the blue, or what?"

"No, a friend of mine recommended me to the gallery director in the art department. Get this, his name is Mike Howes."

"Howes, is he related?"

"Closer than you'd think, his dad and Grandpa were brothers. I've only met him once; the only other artist in the family, and I don't even know him. Anyway, I sent him slides of the paintings I had on exhibit at the bank last August, my pew paintings, I call them. I don't think you've seen them."

"Charlotte told me about them. Is that what you'll show?"

"No, I plan to put in all new work. That's what you're looking at now."

"These are really interesting. Tell me about them."

I told Alan about Ann Harding and her advice to try approaching Alzheimer's through the back door.

"You've done all these since February?" he asked.

"Yes, I think they're ten there. My next graduate review is in two weeks, and I'm hoping they'll pass me on to thesis."

"And that means . . ." he prodded.

"That I will be able to proceed with my thesis project of two semesters of work, then graduate."

"I'll bet you're looking forward to that."

"More than you know, Alan."

"These are wonderful paintings," he said, then caught my indecisive look. "They really are, Kim. Have you thought about contacting the people with the New Orleans Alzheimer's Association?"

"Zab mentioned it, but you know how bad I am at selling myself."

"May I call them? I know one lady in particular, Ruth Speirer, who would love to see these." Alan moved around my framing table noticeably keyed up by the thought.

"Sure, just tell her to call me."

"Would you mind if I were to suggest to them that they consider giving you a show?"

"Alan, that's like saying, 'Would you mind taking this million dollars?' Anything you do along those lines is fine with me."

"Then I'll get on it right away."

For Alan Stevens, I knew that meant he would get on it right away. The kid is efficient.

July 1990

The spring semester ended in mixed emotions. My encouragement after meeting with Alan in early April was soon dampened by the L.S.U. School of Art. My Graduate Review Committee voted to not pass me on to thesis, unlike the other graduate students. They loved my "breakthrough" as they called it, but they were not convinced that I could work that way for more than one semester. Even Ann Harding found their attitude difficult to swallow, but she said to keep plugging away, that my work would only improve.

It seems that painting has served as some cathartic release for me. Strangely enough, though, I feel I am releasing not only my pent-up emotions, but also Mom's as well. It's almost as if Mom were living in an Alice-in-Wonderland chaos where sparks of reality mix with flashes of the ridiculous. Sometimes, confusion reigns in her mind as doorknobs move, trees turn into people, and faces appear out of nowhere. One day at my house, she even saw a huge yellow chrysanthemum in a vase and asked who was that young blond-haired girl.

Other times, Mom's thoughts are clear, and we discuss my paintings and this emotional bond between us that has been strengthened by her disease. Mom is excited that she can still communicate somehow through me. I feel I am picking up where her journal left off, give or take a year or two, and she seems to eagerly anticipate our daily visit. Even now, when Mom has a new experience, she has the creative urge to record it, and asks me, "Kim, are you writing all this down?" I answer, "No, Mom, but I'm painting about it." She still has this burning need to reach the outside world, to tell it something that only she knows. I call it the parasite, that feeling that eats away at my insides until I absolutely must stop what I'm doing to create. Luckily, I still have my paintings to feed that parasite. Since Mom lost the ability to write, she only has me.

This summer, my luck has improved. Fan and her family have finally made their move closer to home. They chose to buy a house in Mandeville, where Fan can teach math at the high school and Bren can commute to Texaco in New Orleans. As much as they miss Morgan City, I think they'll adjust easily, especially since their house is located on the seventeenth hole of a rolling golf course.

The highlight of my summer, however, had to be meeting Ruth Speirer. As last year's president of the New Orleans Alzheimer's Association, Ruth Speirer took Alan's suggestion to visit my studio in Ponchatoula and talk to me about this new turn in my work. Alan had described Ruth as a go-getter who could handle anything she set her mind to. I pictured a tall, stern woman with dark hair, sharp angular features and a cold, all-business attitude, but I was dead wrong. Ruth is warm and has rounded cheeks, softened with age and years of caregiving. She spoke in spontaneous, passionate words as she became engrossed in each painting she studied.

Her visit to my studio must have been emotionally draining for her; it was for me. She related several sad incidents of caregivers who had died of exhaustion long before their patients, and she marveled at Pop's spirit and Mom's optimism. I knew my parents were special, but I thought their attitude was typical. Ruth said no, that many caregivers get discouraged quickly because there is no cure and little help.

When Ruth left the studio, she felt exhilarated from her experience with the paintings, yet I felt depressed from listening to her stories of other victims. Nevertheless, the experience must have struck a chord in Ruth's head that made her want to see these paintings get out to the public. She went back to New Orleans that day, excited about arranging an exhibition of the work at DePaul Hospital in November.

August 1990

Emma Hookfin worked for Mom and Pop off and on since she was in her twenties, first as our babysitter, then years later as a housekeeper for them and later for me. When we were younger, we asked Emma about her last name. She said that it came from marrying a Hookfin, then divorcing him but keeping his name. We weren't completely satisfied with that answer, but we left well enough alone.

Emma already had a full-time job as a cook at a bar and grill in Hammond, determined to stay far away from welfare and food stamps. Nevertheless, she stayed on as a housekeeper once a week for Mom and me. After Ricky and Gwen moved to Ponchatoula, Emma cleaned their house as well. Even though Ricky was friendly to her, he treated her as he would have treated any housekeeper that worked for him rather than someone who had joined our close-knit family. Pop did, too. When Ricky married for the second time, Emma went to the wedding, in spite of the fact that she didn't like the way he had treated Gwen. Several months after they were married, Ricky's new wife let Emma go, but Emma said she was glad.

Now, Pop pays Emma to keep Mom company three afternoons a week, as well as cook and clean. She listens to Mom's broken conversations and can usually fill in the lost words because she practically knows the family history. Her own family knows her as the best cake-maker this side of the Tangipahoa River. Emma is always being asked to supply the cake for every birthday, wedding, or after-funeral get-together. She even gave me the recipe for "Better-Than-Sex Cake," but Zab said he didn't think it could be. It came close.

She once told me, "That's fine that my cousins like

my cakes, but I just wish someone would make me one on my birthday."

I said, "Maybe they think you don't want one because you're a diabetic."

"Maybe so, but I'd still like to blow out the candles." Emma's birthday is the day before Ricky's, a week before Christmas.

On one of my daily visits, Mom and I were sharing a candy bar at Mom's kitchen table.

"Emma," she called out. "Want one?"

"Mom," I whispered, "Emma's a diabetic, remember?"

A sweet-lover from way back, Mom sighed, "It's a good thing I have Alzheimer's and not diabetes."

"Yeah, she'd die without her sweets," Emma chimed in. "Her appetite for real food is not that great, though. But, did you know, when we sit down to eat, she never forgets to say grace? She doesn't remember the words to the blessing, just that we're supposed to say it."

When Emma walks beside Mom on their regular route, she holds her hand and warns Mom of any changes in the level of the sidewalk. She looks for the shady streets in the summertime, the ones flanked on either side by giant oaks that shake hands above their heads. In the winter, Emma looks for the sunny spots so that they can stop on the sidewalk and soak up the warmth.

On their walks, Mom feels relaxed with Emma, and even goes so far as to say a cuss word or two in front of her. When we were little, we'd only hear Mom say an occasional "hell" or "damn," and we were well aware that a slip like that on our part meant a mouth washed out with Ivory soap. Mom told me that when she was young, "crap" was her favorite word because that was the cuss word Bigmama hated the most. I guess that's why I used to say "shit" so much because I knew the very sound of it ran chills down Mom's spine. Kate will probably find a word that she knows irritates me just to use when she wants to declare her own independence. So far, the only word that raises the hair on the back of my neck is the word "nigger," but I don't think Kate will ever say that one.

These days, Mom has been venturing so far as to

say "son-of-a-bitch" or "bastard" when she and Emma walk out of earshot of Pop. Emma just laughs, knowing the words are not directed at her, just at some man somewhere, perhaps even at Al.

September 1990

I could hear Zab come in the back door with his usual quiet. It was 8:30 on the morning of my opening reception at Nicholls State, and I knew he would stop by the house to check on me before I left. I also knew without asking that he had just come from Paul's Cafe where he had eaten a small bowl of grits or a biscuit, but only if the biscuits were fresh from the oven. Even if I had not seen him before he left for work at 6:30, I would still know that he was wearing khakis and a long-sleeved, white Lands' End shirt starched so crisply that I could sometimes hear his collar brush across the edge of his jaw.

The reception was not until that night, but I was scheduled to give a lecture at 1:00 that afternoon. Zab helped me pack the car. He would come later after he had picked up Kate from her third-grade class. Even though he wasn't wild about the two-hour trip, he would still be there; he has never missed any event that he knows is important to me.

When I arrived at Nicholls, I went first to the empty gallery to get reacquainted with my paintings. They seemed to have changed in the two weeks since I had seen them last. They were showing me a quiet world of tangled confusion and unsettled emotions. Trees in seemingly innocent landscapes were being transformed into flying women, then dancing figures. Some were rooted to the ground, their arms and faces reaching for the sky. In one, a red vine streaked across subtle faces floating in blue, while a small silhouette hinged uncertainly on the edge of a steep cliff.

Later, I began my lecture by showing the six-minute interview with Mom and Pop that had been televised in 1987 as part of the PBS series "The Health Century." The audience of a hundred or more seemed interested in the video and my subsequent talk, and I was amazed at how many people had turned out. At the reception, I watched their faces as the paintings played with their emotions. I almost wanted to apologize for moving their hearts, alhough I was excited at the mystery of it all. I couldn't understand the power of the works myself, much less explain it to these people.

I was pleased to see my Uncle Dodo and his wife, Olive, that evening studying all the works closely before walking up to me.

"Kim, these are lovely and so much work!"

"Thanks, Aunt Olive, the faculty here seem to be pleased with the show."

"They should be. These colors look great in here. These paintings, they are different from your portraits of Lou, though, or my painting, for that matter." Dodo and Olive had bought one of my pews paintings last year. "Why the change?"

I went into an abbreviated version of the Ann Harding tale.

"Interesting," she said, looking around for Uncle Dodo who had strayed to the punch bowl. "Is anyone coming from home besides Kate and Zab?"

"No, I don't think so. I told Pop it was a two-hour drive, so that settled that for him. It's a school night for Fan, and Ricky's new baby is only a month old."

"That's right. Dodo, here's Kim."

"Hey, hon," he gave me a kiss on the cheek. "How's your mama doing?"

"Fine." I smiled up at him. I always had to smile up at my handsome godfather. He was so tall. He was pushing retirement, but his body showed no outward signs of age, no drooping shoulders, no extended turtle's neck. Uncle Dodo kept his strong Hendry chin tucked in and his long back arched in such a way that he always appeared to be holding his breath. This perfect posture was synonymous with confidence, and he could dominate a room with the same clear voice he had bequeathed to his four children. How could Dougie have seen signs of Alzheimer's in this man? "I just saw Mom this morning. She's doing fine."

"No, really," he said.

"Well," I began slowly, realizing he was serious. "She hasn't been that great, I guess. She's been complaining of her face and hands burning for no reason. Wakes her up at night."

"Really? What else?"

"She's afraid to go out at night. Ricky bought her a

ticket to the symphony when it performed in Hammond, and she refused to go because it was dark. But, other than that, she's about the same."

"Has Bethesda called lately?" Aunt Olive knew that Mom had been waiting to hear again from the National Institutes of Health in Maryland.

"No, in fact, I even called them this summer. I told the nurse that worked with Mom that she was in great shape, that whenever they received any new drugs, Mom was ready to play guinea pig again."

"What did they say?" Uncle Dodo asked.

"The nurse said that many of the associates they've worked with in the past have gone on to live sometimes ten more years. I guess that means, 'Don't call us; we'll call you.'"

Uncle Dodo smiled, but I could see in his eyes that it pained him to think of what his sister was going through. He looked at me for a long time, then reached over and gave me a tight squeeze. "You're a sweetheart" was all he said.

After the reception, I followed Zab's taillights home while Kate snoozed in the back seat. I thought about a teenaged Mom and Dodo and Betty scraping grass from a clay front yard in Arcola to mark off a tennis court while a talkative younger Tricia looked on. I imagined them double-dating when Dodo came home on leave during the war or eating watermelon in rubber swimming caps on the banks of the narrow Tangipahoa that ran not far behind their house. My mind roamed to picture an older Mom sitting on the side of a hospital bed in Bethesda telling Dr. Mouradian the same stories of her growing up in that white house with the steps to the screen porch flanked by jasmine bushes. Mom hated the smell of jasmine. I wondered if she told that to Dr. Mouradian. Mom loved her five trips to the National Institutes of Health, and the staff loved her, but I knew that they weren't going to call anymore. Mom was no longer in the early stages of Alzheimer's, meaning that she had regressed too far to be of any use to them.

November 1990

My exhibit at DePaul Hospital in November opened just as Ruth Speirer had promised, with much fanfare and publicity. Ruth treated me like royalty, introducing me to every psychiatrist and psychologist she could drag to the opening reception. Alan Stevens, too, was ever present, helping Zab and me hang the paintings in spite of a sinus infection he said he was learning to live with. Ruth sold four of the paintings, and I gave a chunk of the money to the New Orleans Alzheimer's Association to help with their program for respite care.

Fan and Bren came down for the reception, as did my cousin Dougie who lives in New Orleans. Even Tricia's daughter Janie and her husband drove in from Pensacola with their baby. Ricky, however, didn't make the reception, nor did he visit the exhibit during the month, in spite of the fact that he had a convention in the city at the same time. He told me later that he forgot the show was up. He has yet to see any of the work.

On November 19, I had to borrow about fifteen of the paintings for two days to take to L.S.U. for what I hoped would be my last graduate review. This time I was positive I would be passed on to thesis. I had been working extremely hard and had two solo exhibits, which gave me the confidence I knew would be necessary to face the committee. When my lonely figure paintings went before the committee three semesters ago, one professor told me that my "paint vandalized the surface." It was then that I realized I had to develop a thick skin or crumble. I chose the skin; I was and still am determined to get this degree. This time, I felt very strongly about my concept, that the paintings explored the emotional bond between me and Mom. I could not necessarily explain how; I just knew I was onto something magical.

One of the members of my committee this semester will be the visiting artist who has also doubled as my graduate seminar instructor. In our class critique of two of my paintings, he was extremely complimentary, an attitude which I hoped would carry over into the review tomorrow. This time, too, I was taking with me the security that my concept was just as valid as any other. I received a phone call from a freelance writer in New York who wants to do an article on my painting experience with Mom for *Omni* magazine. If it's good enough for *Omni*, it should be good enough for L.S.U.

Zab and Kate met me in Baton Rouge for dinner the night before my review. I had just come from hanging the works in a friend's larger studio and felt satisfied as to how they looked. I knew I was ready for the next morning's showdown. My good mood faded a bit, though, after I hugged Kate hello in the restaurant parking lot. Zab was not himself.

"What is it?" I asked before we went inside.

"I wasn't going to tell you before your review, but I figured you'd find out tonight anyway."

"What?" I persisted. Sometimes Zab can take forever to get to the point.

"Your Uncle Dodo," Zab said, "he died last night."

"What?" I couldn't bring myself to believe it. "How? Heart attack?"

"No," Zab looked down at Kate. "Carbon monoxide." He watched Kate's face as I answered.

"Zab, you mean . . ."

"Yeah," he interrupted before I could finish.

"What, Daddy?" Kate asked.

"Uncle Dodo died last night, honey. Nobody knows why."

"When's the funeral?" I was slowly catching on to Zab's protective fatherly tactics.

"Don't worry. It won't be tomorrow."

"Does Mom know? How did she take it?"

"She knows because your daddy called me with the news. I don't know how she took it, though. You'll have to call when you get to Chris's." Zab opened the restaurant door for us.

On the eve of most of my reviews, I have spent the night with my nephew Chris at his typical college-student apartment, which is filled with some of my most unusual artworks. We usually go out, but tonight I was glued to his telephone talking to Mom, then Betty, then Fan, then finally Pop. Mom had not cried, Pop said; she just shook her head.

Most of the family was upset, true, but more dumbfounded than anything. Dodo had always given off an air of confidence, sometimes overconfidence. At sixtynine, he seemed to be on the verge of retirement from his insurance company, leaving more time for him and Olive to travel. However, my first thought was of

Alzheimer's. Maybe Dodo was afraid he would become a victim like his little sister. My thoughts traveled back two years when Dougie had asked me to send any literature that explained Alzheimer's. He and I never did get a chance to discuss it, but I remember asking Aunt Olive what she thought. She disagreed with Dougie's diagnosis, though, saying that the only strange thing her husband was doing lately was letting what seemed to be simple situations turn into crises. In the middle of a casual conversation with a friend, for example, Dodo would blow up for no apparent reason, leaving the friend with the uncomfortable feeling he had unknowingly said something offensive.

The next morning, I arrived at the studio with Uncle Dodo on my mind, not my review. Yet, like most teachers, I had the ability to tune out any personal problems as soon as I entered the classroom door. I greeted the four members who arrived on time as if nothing had happened. I had decided not to tell them about Dodo nor the *Omni* article. They already knew about the two exhibits. The fifth committee member arrived thirty minutes late, but we had not waited for her to begin. After my opening statement, I readied my pad and pen to take notes, and my seminar teacher was the first to speak.

After fifteen nonstop minutes of negative comments, he summarized his surprise attack by saying that he did not believe me when I said that my mother's condition was the inspiration of these works. The rest of the committee jumped on the bandwagon with their own criticisms ranging from "your color lacks the sinister overtones one would associate with disease" to "you need to be exposed to real art more," from "these works seem to ignore a conceptual flow" to descriptions of the paintings as "overly decorative, romanticized, and illustrational." One member objected to the works being neatly matted and framed and said that they looked too finished, even though I had already explained that they had just come from an exhibit in New Orleans.

Needless to say, I left the review with a sunken feeling in my stomach, more of anger than of hurt, and the knowledge that I would again be refused the chance to be passed on to thesis. By the time I returned the paintings to DePaul and drove back to Poncha-toula the same night, I promised myself that I was going to survive these people, that I was going to graduate. When I got home, I received a call from Ruth. The Southwest Alabama Chapter of the Alzheimer's Association had asked her to invite me to show at the Fine Arts Museum of the South in Mobile sometime in the spring.

April 1991

Even though my experiences with L.S.U. had reached soap opera proportions, my life in Poncha-toula was not necessarily standing still. It had just taken a back seat, and a sad back seat at that.

Uncle Dodo's death was depressing enough, but I thought that at least the autopsy might give me a clue as to whether or not he had Alzheimer's. It turned out that the autopsy was a routine quickie for the sole purpose of determining cause of death, not contributing factors such as Alzheimer's. I guess now I'll never know.

Within a month after Dodo's death, Zab's father underwent surgery for stomach cancer. The operation was successful in that they were able to get it all, but his heart gave out two weeks later, on Christmas Eve.

Zab and I then decided that 1991 was going to be a terrific year because the end of 1990 had been the pits.

I began spending more and more time with Mom trying to soak up some of her positive attitude. I even pulled out my camcorder to tape an interview with her for the writer doing the article for *Omni*. During the filming, Mom made a sincere effort to keep up with the questions. She was completely aware of my motives, so she wanted to make sure her answers sounded intelligent.

"I have just recently, yesterday," she said as she watched my face and not the camcorder. "I was thinking about Alzheimer's because we had been talking about it, and it started me again to think about what people don't know about it. Did you know that sometimes in my own house, not our house, people who don't know anything about it. I hate it, but sometimes don't know how, they don't know how to talk to you about it. They don't know it. I've never bothered. I mean they've always asked. If they ask, if they ask, and if they want to know more of it or something, I don't mind talking about it."

"You love to talk about it," I told her, and we both laughed.

"Well, if you've got to have it, you might as well like it. But," she went on, "it's even sometime in the family. They kind of forget that I'm not normal and that 'You did that yesterday' or 'Don't you remember the other day?' You know, things like that, and it's, uh . . . particularly in, um . . . my husband." Mom snickered a little, then said, "You know, he knows all of it, but I really think . . . I really think . . . I really think that he's . . . he hates to . . . to be that way and for me to have to be that way. I think that he happens to be one of . . . one of the people I like best. But he'll say, 'You know how to do that' or 'You're using that for, uh . . . for, uh . . . '"

"For sympathy?" I asked.

"Well, he doesn't sympathize; he fusses," she grinned.

"You know he's never babied you anyway."

"Yeah, I know."

I wanted to cover a lot of information before the end of this interview, so I asked about her journal. "Let's talk about your journal and why you stopped writing in it."

"Well, my journal," Mom paused, then moved forward in her chair. "It's been a long time, huh, since I've written in it?"

"It's been about a year and a half."

"Mainly because they took away my readin', writin', and 'ritmetic," she said with a mock Southern drawl.

"Who's they?"

"Alzheimer's, of course. It's just a little, give it a little, it's all. I've said this all along because it keeps from sounding like," then she continued in a fake crying voice, "I can't write. I can't draw. I can't do this."

"What did you first notice about your writing?" I asked her.

"Well, mainly, the first thing that started was . . . just the fact that my hands did not form. I supposedly have a real, readable, uh . . . "

"Handwriting?"

"Handwriting," she said, "and, uh . . . it's, uh . . . nothing. I can't form it. The first time I found out it was Alzheimer's, I said, 'Well, that doesn't hurt.' Then I realize it's, you can't do it. You can't draw it and you can't, uh . . ."

"Can't write? Can't form the letter?" I wasn't quite sure what she was trying to say.

"Yes, form the letters."

"Can you read it?" I broke in.

"No, for a while I could, but when I started trying to be . . . to use them, I couldn't. I knew what they were. I can, I can look at them even, but I can't. The writing is gone."

"Mom, tell me. How do you feel about the fact that this writer from New York is doing a story about you and my paintings?"

"I am so impressed with anybody that has, is interested in what's going on in my head, in my mind, not my head, but it's all there."

When Kate, Mom, and I flew to Florida in 1987 to see Bigmama, we stayed for four days. Mom did fairly well both there and on the flight home. She could never make that trip today, however. The confusion of an airport terminal would be upsetting. The noisy crowds and planes, babies and buses—typical everyday mass transportation to which we are all accustomed would agitate Mom to tears. Also, since she can no longer work a zipper or button, she could never manage a bathroom on an airplane.

Lately, Mom has been complaining of long rays of light streaming out from behind her eyes as if her sockets held small car headlights. Hallucinations have increasingly interrupted her night's sleep, not to mention Pop's. Mom does her best to remember them for my sake, but I rely on Pop to fill in any lost details. He jokingly complained to me the other day that their house was filled with so many people at night that he couldn't sleep. He woke up to find Mom walking through their empty bedroom, asking him who those people were. She told me later that they were all dressed in white one night; on another evening, they were in regular clothes, but their clothes were sprinkled with white dots. Tears almost always accompany the hallucinations, even though, at this point, Mom can still recognize Pop during the night.

Kate and I arrived one Saturday morning as Mom was just getting out of bed. I helped her to the bathroom and fixed her toothbrush for her. When she came back to the bedroom, I was sitting on the foot of her bed with Kate sprawled out behind me, playing with a deck of Pop's cards. Kate and Pop have been challenging each other to maintain their championship in cassino, and Kate wanted to get in some extra shuffle time without him.

Mom asked the same question she always asks when she and I are together, "Where's Pop?"

"He's out in the boathouse piddlin'," I answered. I usually tell Mom the truth unless he's at the camp down the river without her.

"That's good." She was still standing in front of me at the foot of her bed. She looked down at the carpet by my feet, then her eyes shot up to meet mine. Her voice was excited. "Last night, I have to tell you! I knew you'd want to know this."

"What is it, Mom?"

"I woke up last night. Pop was still asleep. This is so crazy," she said smiling as the memory seemed to take her words inside of her for a while. After a long pause, she began again, "I woke up and saw this . . . this thing here."

She chopped the air with her right hand in a long diagonal line, while her left hand just seemed to waver aimlessly. Her right hand continued to move on this angled track when she tried to continue. "It was big. A beautiful . . . oh, you know."

"Um," I began to feel dumb, trying to figure out this sudden game of charades. "What color was it?"

"Black . . . wood," she said exasperated, then her thumbs came together in front of her waist, and, with palms downward, her fingers began to dance up and down. "You know, keys!"

"A piano!" I yelled as if I had just won the game.

"Yes! A piano!" Mom was really excited then. "A piano, a piano. A *fancy* piano, though. What do you call those kind with the big—" and her right hand went back up in the air to follow its original diagonal path.

"A baby grand?"

"Yes! A baby grand piano, right here; it was so real." Then she looked at me and just as clear as anything, said, "It was so real that I could have played that thing. But I only had a year of lessons when I was a kid." We both laughed. Even Kate sat up when she thought we might be playing a game without her.

"Really?" I said, still smiling. "A baby grand piano?" I shook my head back and forth. "What next? Well, hey, did it just disappear or what?"

"I don't remember," Mom grinned with a gleam in her eyes. "Only God knows; he probably helped me get back to bed."

"Mom, did you know that God really is a man?"

Mom sat down on the bed next to Kate. "OK, why is that?" she asked, waiting for the punchline she knew was not far behind.

"Because if God were a woman, she wouldn't give us a period every month."

Mom and I both laughed again, and for once, Kate understood. "Mama!" she said embarrassed.

Mom leaned over to her granddaughter and said jokingly, "Don't listen to your Mama. She's the crazy one, not me. What're you playin'?"

"I was trying to play solitaire," Kate said, "but I can't. There's only fifty cards; I don't have a full deck."

"That's OK, baby," Mom grinned. "I don't either."

I think it's amazing that Mom can still crack a joke after living with this disease for more than six years. She actually knows she's saying something funny, even though her words don't always come out right. Sometimes, when she does land on the right word, it may have a new pronunciation, such as "apperciate" or "susprise." Mom will just grin and say, "Where did that one come from?" frustrated but still amused with her newly formed vocabulary.

On our way to the mall the next Saturday, Mom seemed relaxed as she watched the blues in the sky float past the windshield. Kate sat in the back seat drawing in her ever-present notebook. As the car jolted over a bump in the asphalt, Mom blurted out, "Yesterday! A food!"

"What, Mom?" I asked.

"An old food," she said. "Hand, hold it."

"A sandwich?" I offered.

"Yes! Old sandwich, used to." She was again searching for that exact word until, "Piano punna!" she yelled.

"Not another piano," I said.

"No, peana punna!"

"Peanut butter?"

"Yes! That's it!" Mom was excited.

"Kate, write that down. That's perfect," I said.

"That's it: peana putta, peana pinna, oh . . ." Mom still couldn't say it.

Kate pitched in from the back. "Peanut butter, Mom, a peanut butter and jelly sandwich." We all laughed.

"See?" Mom said. "When people get old, Kate, they get crazy, and you forget everything. Funny, when we had peana punna . . . there's an old joke . . ."

"About peana punna on the roof of your mouth?" I asked.

"Mama," Kate said, "how do you spell peana punna?"

Mom laughed. "It wouldn't be any fun if I couldn't make a fool out of myself."

May 1991

In spite of an exhaustive letter-writing campaign I had been having with the L.S.U. School of Art, I still made time to paint. The intuitive splashes of yellow and red were developing into a new and exciting vocabulary of form. Light figures in hot colors popped out against cool, dark landscapes, and the spindly tangles of last semester had thickened into large bent knees and fingers. I began to think that because several bizarre images were gradually taking shape, maybe the paintings were trying to reflect Mom's nightly visions. Human bodies with confusing gender relationships floated on planes and clouds. In one painting in particular, the figure was definitely a woman, but her head had been replaced by writhing tangles as her twig-thin fingers tapped at a staircase of piano keys. Biomorphic creatures appeared in several other works: a bird with the body of a woman possibly defending herself against what looked to me to be a bloated, roaring cat; a lion screaming at a relaxed man whose legs were two of the fingers on a hand. Another man or woman was resting in the clouds as his or her legs transformed into claws cutting through the large tangles that embraced it.

On the advice of the Graduate Coordinator, I invited the individual painting faculty members of my Review Committee to my campus studio in the hopes of familiarizing them with my work, or, as he put it, to "reach a common ground of understanding." I had already been working with John Malveto who had been chosen to fill in the vacancy left by my departing seminar teacher. John always speaks softly, but his words are powerful and honest. I knew, however, that any advice I needed from him would have to come in our individual critiques, for he seldom speaks during a graduate review. He made me secure enough about my latest work to invite my chair, Bob Warrens, to my studio. Bob and I had worked together several semesters, and he had always been honest with me—sometimes brutally honest, but always honest. Nevertheless, I respected his opinion, and he always had much to say. He saw the beginning of my Visions series in mid-February and was impressed.

"This bigger size is great," he said as he walked into the small studio. The paintings averaged about five by six feet.

"I like it," I said simply.

"If you keep painting like this, I'll support you all the way." He stepped up to study them more closely. "There are so many surprises now. You have the same viny things, but they're not so trite. You've created a more complex world, makes it exciting to look at. Remember how tight you used to be?"

"I am always fighting tight."

"What do you think happened? Why do you think they're different?"

"I know that I'm more satisfied with the outcome," I told him, "if I put Alzheimer's in the back of my head and put painting up front."

"I want to keep in touch," he said. "I want to see everything you've done, so that at the graduate review, there won't be any surprises."

"OK, thanks. I appreciate that."

When Bob and I met again for one last critique before the review, he said, "Such an improvement! Your work is harder now because we pushed you into this."

I placed my forefinger to his temple and said jokingly, "Just think thesis!"

He laughed. "Just remember, if you get passed on, it's because your work improved, not because of all those letters you wrote."

I did get passed on, finally, at the spring semester graduate review, but with one dissenting vote, one who said that the work was still "too illustrative" and added, "Do you even know what the form elements are?" The rest of the committee, however, were not persuaded by her comments, and gave constructive suggestions to consider when I pursue my thesis project. Luckily, I thought, I will be allowed to choose my own thesis committee for that project.

July 1991

The exhibit of my paintings at the Fine Arts Museum of the South in Mobile, Alabama, rounded out my spring semester and added just the right touch of sweetness to the news that I had been passed on at L.S.U. The Executive Director of the Southwest Alabama Alzheimer's Association, as well as her chapter treasurer, were just as efficient as Ruth Speirer had promised. They both arranged for tons of publicity, including a television interview and a lecture at one of their support group meetings. They gave me a reception at the close of the exhibit, so that I could dismantle the show on the same day, thus limiting the number of trips I would have to make to Mobile. Just like Ruth, they treated me as if I were doing them a favor.

My summer began on a positive note, yet Mom's disposition has moved in the opposite direction. She has reached the point in her disease where she needs help finding the bathroom and putting on her glasses. She wakes up every hour during the night now, and Pop is getting very little sleep. She won't go to bed unless Pop leaves on her shoes and socks because she is afraid of falling. I have bought her slippers with rubber soles, socks with scuff-proof bottoms, and soft boots that look like shoes, but she still insists on her regular shoes and socks. Mom could tie her shoes long after she forgot how to dress, but now she can't even do that. She has, however, finally allowed Pop to sell her 1983 Mercury that she has not driven for five years. He had kept it around solely as Mom's security blanket.

Mom's latest setback centers around our upcoming Hendry reunion in July. Whenever someone mentions it, she gets excited and is ready to go. Pop tells her, "Not this time, baby. It's too far away," and pats her on the knee.

She will say, "Oh, OK, I understand," but then turns away and pulls into herself. Even though Mom was able to go to the last one two years ago, she needs to get used to the idea that this one is out of the question. This summer's reunion will be at my oldest cousin Beth's in Virginia, and Pop knows better than to even attempt a plane trip, much less a trip by car. I set up my camcorder to make a tape of Mom to take with me to the reunion. I thought she might cheer up if she could at least send everyone a video hello. Instead, my good intentions backfired as her tears began to flow. Just bringing up the thought of talking to her nieces and nephews only reminded her of the fact that she was not going to be able to see them in July. We all made a pact not to mention the reunion in front of Mom again.

The reunion at Beth's was a warm get-together. Eleven of the thirteen first cousins arrived toting off-spring of all descriptions, cameras and camcorders, and ice chests full of beer. The weekend was calmer than expected, though; a sense of sadness seemed to keep the usually rowdy crowd to a mixture of soft laughter within small circles of chatter. Karen, Tricia's oldest, had been compiling facts about Bigmama's family tree on her computer back home in Chicago. As we watched her tape the finished printout to the outside wall of Beth's patio, our memories turned to old stories of Bigmama, of Dodo, or of Betty's husband, Irv. We finally collected our broods to return home, and passed hugs and kisses all around. It seemed, though, that Tricia squeezed me the tightest. When she let go, she looked at me with wet eyes. "Damn! I wish Lou and Bert could've been here."

"I know you do," I said and hugged her around the waist as we walked outside.

Some time after we returned from the reunion, Mom and I took a short walk and stopped to visit with one of her old friends, Mrs. Virgil McWilliams. Mom not only spoke reasonably well, but also walked up six steep steps easily to sit on Miss Virgil's front porch. I told her she was just showing off, but it made me realize that maybe a symptom of Alzheimer's is not as final as it first appears. What I mean is that about three years ago, Mom became afraid of stairs. Her depth perception had taken a tilt, compounded by the fact that her left eye has been blind since birth. It was becoming increasingly difficult for her to judge distances.

I remember Mom showing me what she had read was a typical symptom. She placed her right foot forward as if to take a step, but it seemed as if it were groping the ground ahead of it. When the foot was assured that it was on solid soil, it accepted the bulk of Mom's weight for the next step. She then turned to me.

"See? That's what people with Alzheimer's do. They walk like that because they're afraid of falling. They can't really tell what's in front of them." Since Mom fell on her walk two years ago, she has been afraid to step anywhere, much less up and down stairs. We have even had to add a stripe of yellow tape to each of the three steps by her own back door to assure Mom that she was home. After today, though, I'm sure Miss Virgil would find all of this hard to believe. Maybe Mom's lack of depth perception just comes and goes when it feels like it.

On Sunday morning, Mom arrived at my house with Pop at the usual 10:30 time. I could tell they had had a disagreement about something, but she and I went to church anyway. Our Mass routine has changed a bit in the last several months. Now, we always sit in the front pew, so Mom doesn't have to walk to Communion. I help her stand by pulling up her left hand to the railing in front of her; I help her sit by pulling down her right hand to the pew under her. I sit on the side of her good eye and hold her hand so that she will know I am there.

Today, however, within the first fifteen minutes after we arrived, Mom leaned over, told me that she was upset, but that she did not want to leave. Continuous heavy sighing on her part, however, told me that we were not going to get through Mass that day, so I stood her up to take her home. She agreed to go, but couldn't pry her foot from under the kneeler. I was behind her, coaxing her verbally; but Mom couldn't figure out how to dislodge her foot. Her breathing quickened as she became impatient with herself. Normally, when Mom needs help, the parishioners who sit around us are very attentive, always quick to help her with her jacket or help her to stand. Now, it seemed that the church was frozen in time. Everyone else was seated, but no one was offering to help this poor woman get out of her pew. Finally, an usher in his late seventies came up from the back of the church and gently took Mom's hand. He escorted her to the rear door, speaking softly as they walked.

Later that day, Ricky mentioned to me, "I saw you in Mass this morning. You sure were having trouble getting Mom out of that pew!" I cringed.

I guess I am being unfair to expect Fan and Ricky to participate as much as I do. Fan told me that I am different, that Mom and her Alzheimer's are a passion for me.

"You mean I'm obsessed with it."

"No," she said quietly, "obsessed means that you are consumed with one thing only and that you neglect other parts of your life. But that's not true with you, Kim. You are a passionate person about several things." She smiled. "You always have been. I'm just not as passionate as you are. I care, sure; I just care differently than you do."

August 1991

I sit in the studio alone for a long time before I am able to paint. The room is quiet; there is no din from a background television and never a sound from a radio. I have discovered that I cannot concentrate if there is any noise, including music, yet I enjoy the soft sounds of Kate playing in her room that drift every once in a while through my open door. As I tape down the four sides of the watercolor paper to a sheet of PVC plastic, my thoughts are relatively empty. I work on the floor, easily moving around the PVC, oblivious to the size or shape of the paper I am taping. I meander to the table that holds my collection of fluid acrylics, each bottle standing up taller as I approach. Choosing several at random, I place a few drops into a recycled margarine tub, then weaken them with water to make a light wash. The wash runs freely around the taped paper as I lift a corner, then a side of the PVC. I throw an old towel onto the runs, blotting the excess wash, and faces and textures begin to appear. The PVC then stands upright for the first time, and I sit down facing it about fifteen feet away. I am ready for our conversation to begin.

I wait; I listen; I study. The painting has to speak first; I know that. I can't force it to speak. But when my studio becomes too quiet, I walk over, turn the painting on another side, and sit back down in my studying chair. Then I wait again. Sometimes the conversation begins slowly, creeping out across the room. I have to listen intently, for if the conversation is not strong enough, I may have to add another wash and try again. On this day, however, the painting shouts at me. The images appear quickly and brazenly, impatiently begging to be developed. If I don't listen, if I ignore the images that are beginning to materialize, I know I'll lose my chance to make them come alive. It's as if the painting were punishing me for not listening, for taking a break during our conversation. Now, it is teasing me with its images, making them disappear as quickly as they appear. I realize I can't hold out any longer; so I start to paint while our conversation is still alive, even though it is difficult to work and talk at the same time.

It seems that I have allowed my emotions to take over my painting. I have no other choice, nor do I desire another choice. The rich times together that Mom and I share create in me a well of feelings that overflows into my work. Those experiences spark emotions that have settled deep within me like silt on the bottom of the river bed, disturbed each time a lazy catfish swims too close to the muddy floor. The emotions rise in brown clouds that lap the tips of my fingers like cypress knees catching the murky wake of a passing skiff. Oozing through palmetto hands, my feelings softly rest on the waiting surface of the bright white paper.

During this transfer of myself to the painting, my mind is in a dream-like state. Time means nothing to me as I watch the rounded surfaces form with each stroke of my brush. I look down, only to see drops of paint on the inner ankles of my socks as I sit cross-legged on the studio floor. It seems that someone else's hands are deepening the reds and yellows, while I watch helplessly in a vague, half-lit focus.

I have never dreamt of these images; yet, as Mom's emotions continue to dominate my spirit, more and more of these ambiguous shapes begin to emerge. I lose myself in the mystery of it all, oblivious to the fact that my work is no longer separate from my mother's feelings. As our experiences evolve, so do my paintings evolve. I have allowed myself to express freely, hoping that, in hindsight, my paintings will give me a clue as to what is propelling me to create these specific images.

Now, I am only clear on one fact, the source of my motivation: the emotional bond that exists between Mom and me, a psychological bridge that has been created by her venture into the surreal world of Alzheimer's disease. I can also imagine that my unconscious is in control of what occurs on the surface. It has created swollen as well as tentacular shapes interlocking within a hollow space. It has produced a mood within each painting, one of eerie calm, as the organic forms writhe slowly through the dark. I feel, too, that my unconscious has drawn me into the midst of these entangled tubes, crowding the picture plane, causing me to actually glide into Mom's diseased brain. I can see my mind floating among the tangled memories and dark voids of her confusing world.

Nevertheless, during the course of the painting process, I do remember several times at which my unconscious apparently released its hold on my senses. On those rare occasions, I was afforded short periods of time to make my own artistic decisions, to control a bit of the outcome of the painting. I was allowed time to emphasize a light, subordinate a shape, or create an illusion of texture. In these quiet awakenings, I enjoyed a feeling of power, of being in command of the mystery. I felt as if I could stand apart, as if I could become an objective observer, hovering overhead, critiquing the work's strengths and weaknesses. These moments of power, however, are brief. I find myself again lured in by the intense color and moving forms, only to be confronted once more by my mother's emotions of paranoia, delusion, and suicide. I can only assume at this point that these paintings must be necessary for this voyage on which Mom and I have embarked, possibly transitional elements needed to guide us back to the womb.

September 1991

The fall-semester meeting of my thesis committee took place in early September in my new, larger studio on campus. All five professors were seated except me. It was important for them to see my work, discuss its direction and approve my thesis proposal. After I explained my concept and my hopes for its future, I paused for what turned into an interesting half hour of debate.

Sidney Garrett was the first to speak. A shock of white hair crowned his bespeckled face made serious by years of stone carving. He leaned forward in his chair as if to get a better look at the large paintings tacked to the opposite wall.

"Wouldn't these paintings be more vague or foggy just as an Alzheimer's patient might see?"

"Not really. Images are crystal clear to Mom.

Especially at night, they're very real."

"Well, the most I know about Alzheimer's is that Joanne Woodward movie. Losing words and such?"

"Yes, as a matter of fact, it was that same movie that helped us realize what Mom had."

"I see a strong surrealist influence since you're working automotively. I like seeing the first strokes still show through in some places. Those images are coming from your subconscious?"

"Yes, thanks to your wife, Ann." I smiled at him. "She showed me how to release my feelings onto the paper."

"Really? I never knew that."

John Carambat spoke next. "Can your mother see these paintings?"

"I'm often asked that question. She can see the bright colors, but if you're asking if she looks at these and says 'Yes, you really got it; that's the way I feel,' no, she can't do that."

"I don't understand," a new voice chimed in. I guess Dr. Richard Cox was the only one in the room that actually looked like a typical university professor.

"It seems like you're trying to paint your mother's emotions. Are you getting too involved in her emotions and not your own?"

I smiled at him. "I have to be careful. Once I get started talking about Alzheimer's, it's hard to stop. But, no, I'm not just my mother's paintbrush. These works must come from me and my emotions. My emotions are formed, though, from my experiences with her. That's exactly why I work intuitively, so that I won't put too much Alzheimer's into the work on purpose. That would look contrived."

Then, I turned to John Malveto. "John, wouldn't you have to agree with me on this: that last semester my work improved once I put Alzheimer's on the back burner?" John Malveto seldom spoke in front of his fellow faculty members. I knew he had told me all I needed to know in our weekly critique sessions. I was hoping he would surprise me today and speak. He just nodded in agreement.

I directed my next sentence back to Richard. "When I give lectures about all of this, I like to steer the question-and-answer session toward the paintings,

even though people have so many questions about the disease."

"I think you've made a great breakthrough, Kim." Bob Warrens had been waiting so long to comment that I was beginning to get worried about what he was thinking. He continued, "I knew all along you had it in you, and I knew you would keep working until you pulled it out. What stage is your mother in now?"

"She's still at home, had it about eight years. I see her every day since she only lives about two blocks away with my dad."

"I like the second one from the right." He pointed to one that would later be titled *Nerves Kiss Before They Die II*. "It has a combination of flat and curved shapes. Some of the rest of the paintings seem all curves. See those nice shapes in the middle there?" I nodded.

"Do you think you'll get more figurative?" Richard asked me.

"I don't know. I pull out the shapes that appear. If the figure is there, I'll paint it, but I'm not going to force it to be there."

"Well, Kim," Bob was wrapping up the meeting, "these look great."

"Yes," John Carambat chimed in, "quite good. Do you mind if I take a few pictures of them? I'd like to see how they change over the course of the semester."

"Sure, go right ahead," I told him, "but let me get this straight before you all leave. The next time we meet will be for my orals?"

"Yes," Sid said, "we meet at the gallery the week of your show."

"The exhibit is set for March 7," I said. "I know it's early, but I don't like to wait until the last minute."

"Will your mother be able to come to the reception, or maybe you could have some pictures of her there?" John Carambat asked.

"I was going to see what you thought about having her journal on display. I'd also like to show a video during the reception of a short excerpt of Mom from a television special. She was part of a program on Alzheimer's for PBS. I just thought it would help the viewer to see her as human."

"I think it's a great idea," Richard said. "It would enrich the show."

Sid was not as confident. "I don't know. Are we taking too much away from the art?"

John Carambat added, "Yes, if the VCR were in the middle of the room."

"Oh, no," I broke in, "I always put it in a discreet spot, say, by the guest book. It's not viewed as an installation."

"Then, yes," John said, "it would be a good idea."

"I think it would add a personal touch to the show," Bob Warrens added, "a human interest we can all stand a little more of around here." They all nodded and laughed.

Sid laughed, too, and said, "Well, I lost that vote."

The five men left the studio amidst phrases such as "Thanks for inviting me to be on your committee" and "Keep up the good work." As I walked toward the door, I caught John Malveto's eye. He smiled at me from the edge of the group and gave me his nod of approval.

October 1991

One week after that meeting with my thesis committee, Betty came to Ponchatoula to spend a few weeks with Mom. Tricia and her husband, Hank, had already passed through earlier in the year. Both of their visits relieve Pop of some of the stress of caring for Mom. Tricia and Betty just take over, giving Pop an at-home vacation for several weeks, which includes a chance to catch up on his sleep.

On Saturday, Betty and Mom took their usual walk around the neighborhood, stopping to see me before their last few blocks back to the house. Since it was pleasant outside, we sat on my patio, Mom and I in the cypress glider, Betty in a black iron chair nearby. We chatted about nothing in particular. Mom seemed to have something she wanted to tell me, but it was difficult to piece together her broken sentences.

"I saw him walk to the edge, the corner by the grave," she began. Mom and Betty had just been to visit Bigmama's grave at the Arcola cemetery on Tuesday, and we thought she was telling us about that trip.

"You and Betty went to the cemetery, Mom?"

"No," she said indignantly, "Betty wasn't there."

I turned to Betty. "Maybe she's trying to tell us about one of her hallucinations."

"Then I saw, he went around the edge," Mom continued. "It was then I knew he was the man for me."

"Mom, are you talking about Pop?"

"Of course," she said, "a good lookin' man, still is."

"Did you dream this, Lou?" Betty asked.

"No, I'm trying to tell you, to explain. The Howes Cemetery, we were there," Mom said, and then leaned forward in the glider, so far that her outstretched forefinger almost touched the exposed rock on the surface of my patio. Betty looked at me and shrugged.

"I think this is something that really happened," I told her.

"He walked around the edges carefully, cleaning out corners right by the brick," Mom said, still leaning forward, her finger scraping the cement. "He told me, 'Let's get back in the car,' but I turned around and he was still picking up, straightening up."

"I think she's talking about Pop cleaning up the plots of his kin folk at the cemetery," I told Betty. Then to Mom, "So that's when you decided he was the one for you, huh, Mom?"

"Yep." She sat up straight. "A good-lookin' man, still is."

"What were you two doing in the cemetery, Mom, parking? No, what did y'all call it, sparking? Making out?" I asked her and winked at Betty.

Mom grinned at me, "That's nothing for you to know."

"Well, I'm glad you two finally figured out how to make out, or you wouldn't have three kids today. You're so lucky to have such wuniful chillen, huh, Mom?" I said facetiously, expecting some wisecrack in return. She and Betty just laughed as they got up to finish their walk back home.

Knowing I needed eighteen frames for my thesis exhibit in the spring, I decided to get an early start. On Monday, after Kate and Zab left for school and work, I brought the molding down to Pop's to run through his floor belt sander. I knew, too, that if he spotted me in the boathouse working on anything, he would come out to watch. He would bring Mom out to watch, too, sitting her close by in a folding aluminum chair. At

this stage, however, Mom preferred to match whistles with the birds overhead than to listen to the buzz of a belt sander. I also knew that Pop wouldn't watch for long because watching brings out those old creative urges to do. He eventually takes over, especially if the project involves wood. That's fine with me because I enjoy watching him do.

Pop still has sawdust in his cough from working in his boathouse void of ventilation. As an artist today, I am leery of hazards and toxins. Pop, on the other hand, has always believed that he is immortal and that nothing will kill him. "You gotta go sometime, baby, so why worry about it till you do?" is his common reply to my concern for his health. Now, as I watched the sander sawdust spray tan on his eyebrows and defenseless nostrils, I could see he had forgotten any close brush with his own mortality he had ever had. He may have been vulnerable years ago; but now, he was indestructible again. Nothing could hurt him. I stood nearby taking each newly sanded strip from him, making sure I had the next one ready to be placed in his other waiting hand. This time, though, when I turned around with a new board, I saw Pop leaning over with his hand pressed just below his belt buckle.

"Pop, are you OK?"

"It's just that hernia again. I'll be all right."

"Why don't you go on in and lie down," I told him, cautiously avoiding the word nap. "You'll feel better. Mom can stay out here with me. Go on."

"OK," he said and went inside.

As I finished the rest of the frames, my mind recuperated from the shock; not the shock of Pop being in pain, but the shock that he actually took one of my suggestions without arguing and that he went in to lie down during daylight hours.

November 1991

Without any nagging from me, Pop made his own appointment with Dr. Walker, who in turn scheduled X-rays of his hernia at the hospital the next Friday. I stayed with Mom while he was gone, and we found plenty to talk about sitting at our favorite spot, her kitchen table. On my side of the table, I was writing every word she said, while on her side, she was decid-

ing whether or not to honor my request of her to write her numbers.

"If I wanted to stop, right here, and say what, 18, 19, 20, 21, 22, I couldn't do it."

"Try it," I said.

She then counted perfectly from one to thirty and said, "Now, what were we doing?"

"I want you to write your numbers, not just say them."

"Those are the worst ones." She paused a moment. "We came over here to go with Pop. This is the kind of thing Alzheimer's likes to pick me up on. I get mad at myself and, dammit! Oh, dammits go round and round." After another pause, she said, "I forgot. What were we doing?"

"How about writing Lou Howes?" I wanted to offer her another option to see if she would write.

"I've gotta see about my glasses."

"How about this pad? It's larger than this white one." I pushed a clean, yellow legal tablet across the table.

"This upsets me. It hurts. These slips," she said

referring to the lines on the paper. Her fingers waved back and forth in the air above the tablet. "I try to get these that stay with me. This yellow, that really hurts me."

"Yellow now, too, huh?" I smiled at her as I took away the tablet. "No problem. We can do this some other time."

"I forgot you. Well, this is the kind of things Alzheimer's likes. That's why she gets me. I'm just bragging; I get tired of the story. I know it's down, going muchly. I'm surprised. I thought I died a long time. I thought I wouldn't last a long time with Alzheimer's and the rest. But I'm still here. It doesn't even bother me," she laughed. "Now I know I'm crazy. This is what I am; I'm sorry. I like to act silly."

Then, with her hands in the air, Mom added the drama of an actress on stage. "But you have to be something MORE!"

I finally laughed with her, shaking my head at this crazy lady. Now, even I was getting to the point where I couldn't quite tell if she were joking or not.

"What in the world are you talking about?" I said in an amused tone.

"*Je ne s'ai pas.* See? I remember *Je ne s'ai pas.* Isn't that right?" she asked smiling.

After I said yes, Mom paused for a long time, her thoughts too deep for me to read them. She began again, "Pop does everything. He sure can cook, can't he? You've seen his little . . . I've forgotten what he does. You've seen him, haven't you? You know what he does. He builds up. Let's see."

"You mean that conference table for Zab?" Pop had just put the finishing touches on a twelve-by-four-foot, solid-mahogany conference table for Zab's new office. He was so proud of it that he signed it underneath with a black marker.

"I don't know. I don't know. I don't know," she said looking down seemingly at the tablet, but her eyes penetrated beyond it. "I would like to have somebody get a, uh . . . a . . . what's wrong with me. I can't get on to what I can . . . what I can do and I can't do. It still makes me think, I'm not doing for me. Is that bad? Pop is getting his due. Well, that's just a thought that goes in the mind."

I thought to myself how much I loved Mom unconditionally, even when she's like this. Why should I dwell on the past or brood about the future of this goofy disease? People often want to help when they ask, "How do you keep so upbeat about all this?" I tell them that the disease is too slow to place too much emphasis on the sad parts. Sure, I cried the first year, but after that, I was so worn out that I knew I wouldn't be much good to anybody unless I took on Mom's optimistic attitude. That wasn't so difficult; optimism runs rampant in my family. I recently read another article on the latest Alzheimer's research. Apparently, scientists are beginning to think that early onset Alzheimer's, the kind that hits before the age of sixty-five, could possibly be hereditary. Fan, Ricky, and I, supposedly, would then have a chance of ending up in the same situation.

"But I can tell," Mom interrupted my thoughts as she popped out of her dream world, or as I've heard it affectionately called, Zombie Land. "Best thing I ever had in life were my girls. It keeps on getting worse, but you never stop. Thank you, darlin'."

"I don't stop because I kinda like you, not because you need me."

"You don't worry about yourself," she went on, wanting me to get serious. "You are the only person at this point in our Alzheimer's place. I think that you're the only one probably, maybe a couple every once in a while, yes, Fan, too. But particularly, but consistently. You are consistent with it. Hey! I got 'consistent' that time."

"See? You can still remember those big words." I smiled at her. "What about Pop? He does more than anybody."

"I hate to have, I hate to get my family . . . I know they all want you to, you know to . . . they want to help. But I hate to put them in situations like Pop, you know, can't leave from the house anymore. He's got to go get somebody to stay with me. It's hard for him."

"You didn't mention Ricky," I said softly.

"Men just don't have," she began. "Ricky's not a bad boy. He says 'I've got to do all this.' I don't know what he does. I don't bother about Ricky. I see him around."

I know in my heart that Alzheimer's is a family disease. It splashes into the victim with full force and drowns all family members in its wake, whether they like it or not. It drags the victim and her family slowly through a never-ending grieving process, sometimes lasting as long as fifteen years. Nevertheless, it's not the end of the world. It has been known to draw families closer together, making them aware of their own mortality. Pop said he can live with anything if he knows it is not going to last forever, and so can his kids.

Pop's return from the hospital lab was followed almost immediately by an appointment with a surgeon. It seemed that Pop's luck was still running high. If it hadn't been for the pain of a hernia causing Pop to get X-rays, we would never have known that he had an aneurysm in his aorta. We scheduled the surgery for the day before Thanksgiving, and I began the search for twenty-four-hour sitters for Mom.

Pop now had Emma sitting with Mom for three hours in the afternoon on Monday, Wednesday, and Friday. When Pop found out about his surgery, Emma quit her other job as a full-time cook at the truck stop to sit with Mom during the twelve-hour day shift. Even though she knew this job might be short-term, Emma thought Mom would adjust better to sitters if she had someone she already knew, and Emma certainly knew Mom. She had been considered a part of our family for so long that I thought she was really old, but she's only forty-nine.

We hired Emma's Aunt Mary to be the night sitter. Emma said that her aunt had been a nurse and was used to Alzheimer's patients. Besides, we thought that Mom might think she was Emma in the middle of the night and feel more secure. Mom wasn't fooled by our little scheme, but she didn't seem to mind. She liked Mary. I was hoping Emma had prepared Mary for Mom's nightly escapades. Mary assured me that she could handle that sort of thing. I don't think that she really understood how scary Mom's nights had become.

Before September, Mom's nightly hallucinations were accompanied by tears. Now, she screams. She screams for hours. Pop gets very little sleep and has tried everything he can think of to get her to stop.

"I wake up and she'll be sitting straight up in bed,"

he once told me. "If her eyes are wide, glassy, and wet, I know she's seeing something." His tired face creased into a small smile. "Last night, she woke me up to help her wrap all the Christmas presents. When I helped her to the bathroom, she wouldn't pull down her pants because she was afraid the kids would see her."

"And the screaming?" I asked.

"Loud. She won't stop," he said. "She walks around the house pulling the sheet from the bed behind her, just a-screamin'."

"What does she say? Any words or just sounds or what?"

"I knew you'd ask that." He reached to the edge of his papers on the kitchen table and pulled out a brown rectangle cut from a paper bag. "I didn't have any paper around, so I wrote on a bag." He slid it across the table to me.

In his typical choppy handwriting, Pop had written Mom's words from the night before: "He's killing me! Please God! Please God! Dr. Walker, please, please, please come help me! He lies; he lies! Where's Ricky? Aunt Dot, come help me! Please, God, where's

Kim? She can help me. You're going to kill me!"

I looked up at Pop, hoping that my tears were not showing. He just said, "Keep reading."

Pop had written his own words in parentheses: (You better take some water.) "No, you put something in it!" 12:35 AM Calming down, just talking. (Asked her if she wanted to lie down.) "No, I don't trust you."

"Pop, what did you do to get her to stop?"

"I had to hold down her arms and put my hand over her mouth. Then she just calmed down and went back to sleep. She woke up screaming again about 8:30 this morning. Ricky was here, had stopped by on his way to work, but she didn't know him either. She was crying. He was crying. Lasted about an hour." He paused a moment, then went on, "I want you to bring me a tape recorder."

"Why?"

"So you'll know she's really saying those things. I don't want y'all to think I'm hurting her or anything."

"Oh, Daddy, we'd never think that." My heart was filled with pain for him.

"No, I want to tape it."

"OK, but next time, call me, no matter how late it is. You don't have to go through that by yourself."

That night, Pop did call around eight o'clock. Mom had already been screaming for about ten minutes. When I answered the phone, I could hear Mom crying in the background. All Pop said was, "You said you wanted to hear it."

"I'll be right there."

As I got out of my car, I could hear her shrill yelling from outside. When I got into the bedroom, Mom was standing beside her bed with the sheet clinched tightly in both fists, pulling it back and forth. Pop was standing on the other side of the room. When he saw me, he shrugged his shoulders as if to say, "OK, your turn." I turned Mom around to face me, and her eyes widened, startled to see me.

I placed both of my hands on her upper arms and gently said, "Mom, it's Kim."

"You!" she yelled, "Kim! Kim! I've been calling you!"

"I'm here." I was trying to keep my voice from shaking. I knew she could not see my tears. Then I hugged her, even though her hands would not release their grip on the sheet. I kept saying things like, "It's OK. It's just Alzheimer's. It does crazy things. It's OK."

Pop and I finally got her to sit on the side of the bed, drink a sip of water and go back to sleep. He had taped her screaming that night, but I could only listen to it once. I then sent the tape to Fan.

Pop's operation lasted three and a half hours and, in Pop-like fashion, was a complete success. Fan, Ricky, and I sat it out in the waiting room and called Emma periodically so she could keep Mom posted at home. To Mom, this was a simple hernia operation; we had not told her about the more serious aneurism.

Emma had been doing fine with Mom during the day, taking their usual walks and talking about their children. Mary, on the other hand, was not prepared for Mom's wild nights, even though I had described both Pop's and my tactics that she was welcome to attempt on her own. She called me the first night at 1:00 AM telling me that Mom wanted her out of the house. Mary was afraid that Mom would hit her. I drove down, still in my nightshirt.

"Mom, it's Kim." I tried my method again.

"Are you sure?" she said in a screech.

"Yes, it's really Kim," I said softly and rubbed her arms. I wanted her to know I was the flesh-and-blood Kim, not some hallucination of me. "Pop's in the hospital, remember? You promised him you'd be good."

"That's the same thing *she* said!" Mom screamed, pointing at Mary. "She was doing just that."

"Here, why don't you sit on the bed. I know you're worried about Pop." I walked her to her side of the bed, the sheet trailing along behind her. She seemed to be slowly calming down because her voice changed from a high shrill to her normal deep pitch.

"I'm sorry," she started to whimper with big tears in her eyes. "Mary is so sweet, so wonderful. You, too. This Alzheimer's; it's this thing."

Mary sat beside Mom on the bed and put her arm around her. "I forgive you. I know it's just the disease."

"It was pretty bad, huh?"

"Yes, it was. You wanted me to see all these people on the walls." Mary pointed to Mom's picture wall behind me.

"Mom, do you have to go to the bathroom before you go back to sleep?"

She nodded, so I walked her to the bathroom and helped her sit down on the toilet. I sat on the floor in front of her so that she could focus on me through her bifocals.

"I can't stop crying," she told me.

"Just take long deep breaths." Her short breathing makes her sound even more upset than she is. "Now, close your mouth and breathe through your nose. When you talk, speak in your low voice, OK?"

"What are we doing here?" Her voice came out much deeper than usual, and we both laughed.

"Just a-chattin', Mom, havin' fun at two in the mornin' with you on the pot." Then she really laughed.

On weekends, Fan, Ricky, and I took shifts with Mom from 8:00 PM Saturday to 8:00 PM Sunday to give the sitters a day off. Since Fan took the night shift, I warned her of Mom's screaming, told her that Pop and I had tried half tablets of Haldol as prescribed by Dr. Walker, but we weren't having much success.

Fan called me the next morning to report that she

had to use her own method to calm Mom. She tried being gentle, tried playing a tape from *Fiddler on the Roof*, which Mom usually loves, and tried holding her, but nothing worked. Finally, Fan said that she stood directly eye-to-eye with Mom and began yelling back, "No, I'm not leaving here! This is my house, too!" and so on. She said that as long as she was yelling, Mom was not. Then Mom calmed down and went back to sleep. I'm going to have to try that next time.

Ricky took the Sunday morning shift and brought Mom to see Pop in the hospital after lunch. I met them there a little before two to see Pop and take Mom home with me. Mom was sitting on the side of Pop's hospital bed talking softly to Pop. Pop looked great even though he was lying down with a sheet over his mile-long bandage. Ricky was sitting in the visitor's chair, and I greeted all three of them when I came in.

"How do you feel, Pop?"

"Ready to go home."

I knew he would say that.

"Fan said Mom did fine last night," I told Pop as I patted Mom on the shoulder. "She has something new to calm her down."

"I know. She called me. Sounds good."

I walked over to the stool at the foot of the bed, and pulled out Pop's checkbook from my purse. "Pop, Emma and Mary asked if you could pay them every week instead of every two weeks. Is that OK? I brought your checkbook."

"Sure," he said and gently stroked Mom's knee.

"I told Pop," Ricky broke in, "that I would pay the sitters and he could just pay me back."

"That's OK," I said. "I brought his checkbook."

"No," he said, "I want to pay the sitters so I can claim it on my taxes."

"What?" I was stunned but not surprised. "But that's not ethical, Ricky." I avoided using the word illegal because there was probably some loophole that would enable him to get away with it.

"What boat did you just sail in on?" he asked sarcastically.

"Sorry, but I'm not going to let you screw Pop over." My voice quivered with anger.

"How am I screwing Pop over?" he asked. Pop and

Mom were listening, but not saying a word.

"You're taking advantage of Pop's situation."

"No, Kim, tell me. How am I screwing Pop over?"

"I just told you. You're taking advantage of Pop's situation."

That didn't seem to satisfy him, even though I thought I was making myself perfectly clear; so he asked me the same question a third time. I gave him the same answer and added, "Look, Ricky, I hired them. I'll write Pop's checks for them, and that's all there is to it. What do you mean what boat did I sail in on?" Even though I didn't want an answer.

Ricky didn't say anything else, just told us good-bye and left. Pop didn't mention it after Ricky was gone, so I took Mom home with me until Mary's shift that night. The next morning, I went to the hospital early to see Pop. He was already sitting up in a chair.

"I'm sorry you had to witness that fight with Ricky yesterday," I began.

"That's OK. You are just two different people. He thinks he's right, and you think you're right."

"I am right, Pop. What he wants to do is illegal."

"Everybody does little things they think are right, but just might not be by the law. I'm sure you've done things other people might think of as illegal."

"What things?" I asked almost naively.

He paused, thought for a long time, then laughed, "I can't think of any right now."

"Pop, why didn't you say anything yesterday?"

"I had already decided I wasn't going to let him do it," he said matter-of-factly.

"Then why didn't you tell him that?"

"Usually, I find if you don't say anything, things like that just have a habit of going away. And it did, didn't it?"

January 1992

Last semester ended in a mixture of chaos. We finally asked Dr. Walker if Mom could stop taking the Haldol. It had done nothing to prevent her nights of terror, yet it was making her into a zombie during the day. Even with her favorite holiday right around the corner, Mom had become withdrawn. Kate decorated Mom's tree while I wrote her Christmas cards for her. I usually write what she dictates, but this year, I had to keep getting her attention, bringing her back to the real world. For the last five Christmases, Mom would say certain key words that gave me ideas as to what she wanted me to write in the cards. This time, however, it was as if I were writing them without her. Every card carried the same paragraph, but as I read them back to her, each one sounded new to her. I expected that, but I didn't expect her to be so far away mentally. Bent over in the chair, she looked as if she were dozing, but her eyes were open. It seemed that Mom had closed out the world; she had retreated into herself.

Pop did get out of the hospital earlier than we had expected. He has always been a fast healer, so he told Mary he didn't need her anymore. He was going to change Emma's schedule to her former three days a week, but she instead had to go in the hospital herself. Two weeks before her fiftieth birthday, she found out that she had a tumor on one of her ovaries. Kate and I had been determined to make Emma a cake this year, and we had purchased all the ingredients. When Emma found out her operation was scheduled for the day of her birthday, we sent her a balloon bouquet instead. On December 30, a surgeon removed not one, but three cancerous tumors. Within three weeks, Emma was gone.

I knew Mom would not take the news of Emma's death lightly, but with an unpredictable disease such as Alzheimer's, I couldn't really tell. She was depressed for a while, crying about other things. She said Pop was ignoring her, and her friends didn't come to visit anymore. Mom even remembered one of her hallucinations.

"And there it was, staring me right in the face. It was holding me like this," Mom reached out and grabbed my wrist. "Then it started pouring in like water, and all I wanted was you. I wanted to call Kim. She knows I'm not crazy. Something, something. Did it do that or what? I didn't have anything in my hand. One thing I know. I cried you down. I said, 'I want Kim! I want Kim!'"

Two blocks down, at my house, December was not much better. We were looking forward to our first peaceful Christmas in about four years, since Grandpa,

Uncle Dodo, and Zab's father all died around the holidays. Apparently, God must think we can better handle the grief just because it's Christmas. This year, however, was just as depressing. Zab's best friend, Kate's godfather, died suddenly of heart failure one week before Christmas. He was just thirty-eight, and his only crime was making people laugh and loving his wife and daughter.

Needless to say, by this time, I was impatiently looking forward to the spring semester in the hope that life could only get better. Of course, for my optimistic family, life did begin to brighten up; it always does. Zab moved into his new office that we had been working on since October, Kate started playing basketball in the town league, and I was going back to my kids at Ponchatoula High School. The greatest news, however, had to be that the Federal Drug Administration was making plans to allow the experimental testing of the only Alzheimer's drug to date that has shown any hope—T.H.A., better known as Cognex or Tacrine. We kept our eyes peeled to the newspapers for any news of its distribution. Even Mom's mood was lifting,

not just because of the news about Cognex, but also because of the decrease of her screaming attacks at night. Pop said that she still cried, but he could handle that if he just took out his hearing aids. I'm not sure if Pop's sleeping through her whimpering was good for Mom, but I had to leave that up to Pop. He had to live with it.

Pop was still having to get up with Mom every hour or so because she said she had to go to the bathroom, but at least the screaming had subsided for a while. I don't know if I could last for very long on the little bit of deep sleep that Pop gets now. I did make an appointment for Mom as an outpatient at the hospital, so that she could be examined by a urologist. It turned out that her frequent urge to go every hour was physical and not related to Alzheimer's.

February 1992

The following Sunday, life seemed back to normal as Pop arrived to drop off Mom for Mass. Kate came with us this time, and as I watched her walk ahead of us down the aisle to the front pew, I thought to myself what remarkable poise she had for a ten year old. Her posture was perfect, and she seemed proud of the fact that her figure was in its early budding stages. I arched my back to stand up taller than my 5'8" and felt the stinging memory of Mom's palm hitting my shoulder blades each time I slumped to hide my own developing chest, slow as it was to develop.

Kate entered the pew first in order to sit on Mom's left, and together we edged Mom into her seat. Somewhere behind us, a baby cried out, and Mom spoke up loudly, "That's what I thought you said."

"Mom, look up," I whispered. "We're in church." In the midst of my wandering thoughts, I had forgotten to remind her that Mass was about to start.

"Oh, sorry," she whispered back. Kate and I smiled at each other.

I looked at Mom who then began to fool with the bottom button of her white blouse. She seemed to be picking at an imaginary piece of lint. Yesterday, as she sat in her favorite chair in the living room, she appeared to have the same thought on her mind.

"Clothes," she had said when I sat on the small hassock beside her.

"Clothes?" I asked.

"Some store in Ponchatoula. The only store," she stuttered.

"Alma's? Hotard and Goode?" I was trying to think of stores that were open when we were young.

"Hotard's. Kate could go there." Mom was trying to be helpful. Kate had just been talking aloud while skimming through a clothes catalogue.

"Hotard's is closed, Mom. It's an art gallery now. Remember at Hotard's, the clerks had to send the money in a can up a pulley to Mr. Hotard on his balcony just to get change?"

"I know what I wanted to ask you," Mom said, not acknowledging my nostalgia. "Why? People keep telling me to look up all the time. Why?"

"Because you're always bent over looking at the ground when you walk."

"Do I look stupid?" she looked up at me.

"Well," I said slowly, not knowing how to answer. "Even when you're sitting down, you're always looking at your stomach."

"My stomach? Why?"

"I don't know, just inspecting your clothes, I guess. Pop said that you're always griping about the clothes you have on."

"My stomach and I are friends," she laughed.

"I know, from all those busted gut operations." Mom has a veritable road map branded on her stomach from an appendectomy, a hysterectomy, a ruptured intestine, and the removal of a gall bladder and a hernia. I used to think she was hollow inside.

"OK, I'll have to work on it," Mom said. "Like this?" She bent her neck way back and looked up at the ceiling.

"Well, I guess so."

"But don't I look like an aaaaaasss," she sang the last letters so slowly that it wasn't until she laughed out loud that I realized what she had said.

"Yes," I was laughing, too. "But it does get rid of that double chin!"

"You better watch out. I'll show you where Hotard's really is."

I smiled as I remembered our laughter, thinking there was nothing wrong with this old lady. We stood up for the first hymn, and I curled my arm inside hers to sing the words into her ear. Mom still followed the tune with ease, but she was no longer singing the lyrics, any lyrics. Her words sounded like mumbling, but it was mumbling that resembled the vowel sounds that my lips formed.

We sat down for the readings, and Mom said, "Hot."

Kate and I helped her take off her green blazer, but that did not seem to be enough. She looked distressed about something.

"Are you OK?"

"No," she panted. "Pop."

"He's at home. He'll be waiting for you in the driveway right after Mass." St. Joseph's is only a block south of my house, and Pop always parks his gray truck in my driveway to wait for us to walk home.

"Pop. He's mad at me," Mom was getting more upset.

"Do you want to go home?"

"Yes." She seemed relieved.

"As soon as everyone stands up for the gospel, we'll go." I thought that would be the most inconspicuous time. I handed Kate my envelope for the collection and told her I'd see her at home. As the congregation stood, I gently led Mom out of the pew into the center aisle and began to walk to the big double doors in the rear of the packed church. Before we could take two steps, however, the Alleluia chorus began and Mom sang right along with it loudly all the way up the aisle. My eyes darted about catching the quick stares of the parishioners. I smiled meekly and cast my gaze to the carpet before us, thinking, "Mom, please don't sing now."

The usher, whose wife had coincidentally just been diagnosed with Alzheimer's, helped Mom down the front steps. When we reached the sunlight and the quiet of the walk back home, I let out a long sigh. We walked in silence for a little while, then Mom pulled back my hand.

"Did I do something wrong?" she asked.

"No, Mom, you just wanted to leave early. You missed Pop."

"I did?"

Just then, one of Mom's neighbors jogged by us and touched Mom on her arm.

"Hey, Mama Lou," he yelled.

"Hey, sweetheart," she yelled back. Then to me, she said, "It is so beautiful today, isn't it?"

"Yes, Mom, it is," I sighed again, but this time to myself.

March 1992

In the few weeks before my thesis exhibit, my nerves were at their most fragile, scraping at my sinuses with new sandpaper and tightening my neck muscles into burning rocks. Usually, when stress hits, I just moan around the house and have a good cry. Zab should be used to it by now, even though he never quite knows what to say. Just the other morning, I was rushing around the house getting together paintings and slides for a lecture I was giving to the Louisiana Mental Health Association. I was nervous because I knew I had to be away by 10:00. Zab was in a great mood, being the clown, the funny side of Zab that only

Kate and I see at home. I guess I was jealous; I wanted him to be as stressed-out as I was and help me load the car. My stress turned quickly to tears and I couldn't stop crying. Now, Zab does not console this kind of tears; he just gets quietly frustrated. After much yelling back and forth, I sat down across the table from him and asked him to do something to stop my tears. I couldn't go to my lecture in this condition, and time was running short.

Zab said simply, "Then, don't go. You can say 'no' once in a while. Call them up. Tell them you're not coming."

I felt my independence take over, and my tears began to pull back. I sat quietly listening to him for a while, then sat up straight and smiled.

"Thanks, Zab; I feel much better now."

"You're going, aren't you?"

"Of course," I said and laughed at the idiocy of the entire morning. Zab just smiled and shook his head.

Back on the L.S.U. front, my stress had already been compounded by the fact that my thesis chairperson, Robert Warrens, had decided to take a sabbatical this spring and travel to Germany. As soon as I found out he would be leaving, I went into double-time and finished both my paper and the paintings before Christmas. He called me at home after reading my paper and told me that he thought the writing was excellent and that he had only a couple of suggestions.

"There needs to be more about your painting process," he said. "Your ideas on color, space, maybe the transition from one piece to another."

"True," I told him. "I do think there's too much Alzheimer's in there and not enough art. I'll add more on that."

"May I suggest, too, that you refer to your relationship with your mother as a parallel journey, instead of a single journey?"

"I can't call it a parallel journey. This may sound spooky, Bob, but it's like Mom and I are one person. It's difficult to explain. It's just that we are so much together in this adventure, this voyage, that we seem to be almost one."

"That's great, then," he said sincerely. "You've

apparently landed onto something spiritual and unique. Keep at it."

By the middle of February, my body was rapidly beginning to show signs of exhaustion. My Art I students at the high school were being incredibly patient with the fact that their paintings were not getting graded with a reasonable amount of speed. My Art II's were understanding, yet restless. As for my upper-level class, whom I have taught for three and four years and who know me better than I know myself, they just said, "Get a grip, Miss Zab!"

The month was inconceivable. Mom was experiencing bouts of depression, thirty-five cousins were coming in for my show in only three weeks, and I had discovered a lump in my left breast the size of a quarter. Life was getting ridiculous! Even though my instincts told me that the lump was benign, I knew I still had to have it removed immediately just to be sure. I did, and sure enough, it was benign. Besides, it didn't make any sense for me to get cancer now. It would just distract from Mom's Alzheimer's, and I couldn't handle two diseases.

I knew it would happen eventually, and finally it did. It was late. I was already in bed with my calendar and its constant companion, my list of Things to Do, resting heavily on my lap. As Zab turned off the bathroom light and walked past my side of the bed, the tears came.

"What's the matter?"

"All of this is too much," I whined.

Zab sat down beside me on the edge of the bed. "What's all of this?"

"Everything! Why can't I just do art, just do it for the hell of it?" I sobbed. "People do it all the time. Just art for art's sake. Why does everything I do have to have a reason? Why do I have to have some big mission? I feel like I'm being pulled by everybody from all sides."

Zab didn't say anything, just handed me a Kleenex and waited for me to catch my breath. Then he reached over and hugged me in a tight squeeze. When I leaned back on my pillow, Zab stuck out his bottom lip in a big pout and said, "Life's a bitch, huh, baby?" I laughed and gave him a knuckle sandwich on his shoulder.

The day of my thesis exhibit finally arrived. We had a pre-reception party that afternoon so that everyone would get a chance to visit with Mom. Pop and I had decided that Mom shouldn't go to the opening reception because the noise would agitate her, but as it turned out, Kate couldn't go either. She broke out in chicken pox that morning and had to quarantine herself in my bedroom by the patio. Relatives waved to her splotchy face peering over a sign on the door that read, "If you've had chicken pox, come on in. If you haven't, just wave." She had used a marker to draw red dots all over the sign.

After the party, the entire crew caravaned to Baton Rouge to the gallery at L.S.U., only to find out that the air conditioner was broken. Most of the group politely stayed inside as long as they could before making their way to the keg of beer just beyond the front door. I remained inside to answer questions.

"Hey, these look great!" Fan and our cousins Tammie and David walked up from behind.

"Kim, some guy just came up to me and thought I was you," Fan smiled. "He said he loved my paintings."

"And what did you tell him?"

"I just said thank you," she grinned. "Did any of your professors come?"

"Only two. Look, Pop sure is hanging in there. He's been in here the whole time, even in a suit. Isn't he burning up?"

Tammie tilted her head. "Maybe he feels he has to substitute for your mom."

"Fan, be sure to show David Mom's journal," I said.

My cousin Steve barreled over to my side, followed closely by Ricky. These were the first paintings about Mom's Alzheimer's that Ricky had seen, in spite of the fact that I had painted fifty-two in the last two years.

Steve put his arm around my shoulder and shouted, "Kimmy, this is tremendous, just tremendous!"

"Congratulations," Ricky leaned over to kiss me on the cheek. "This is a lot of work here." The two of them paused, then looked at each other and let out a roaring laugh.

"Even if we can't tell what they're all about," Steve hugged my shoulder more tightly with each laugh. "Naw, Kim, naw, I just never have liked abstract art."

I smiled, shaking my head as they bounced off of each other with every guffaw. I caught a glimpse of Pop out of the corner of my eye.

"Well, Pop, what do you think?"

"Nice, but hot."

"I know. I'm really glad Mom didn't come now, but at least she's on TV." I pointed to the VCR setup in the far corner playing her six minute-interview over and over.

"Uh-huh."

"It's really hot in here. Why don't you go outside for a while?"

"Nah, I need to be here."

April 1992

After Emma's death in January, Pop hired another lady to sit with Mom three afternoons a week, but it's just not the same. Fan drives in on Tuesdays after school. Since she moved to Mandeville almost two years ago, she's been coming in every week to give Pop a couple of hours of freedom. She washes Mom's hair in the shower, and the two of them walk Mom's former route around the neighborhood and sing. On various Saturdays and holidays, Fan picks up Mom for the day, giving Pop enough time to run down the river or mend fences at his dad's old farm. Mom always enjoys these trips to Mandeville, not just for the change of scenery, but also for the pleasure she derives from watching Fan "run around the house," Mom's term for Fan catching up on errands and daily chores.

I know Tuesday is the one day I can skip my visit to Mom, but I go by there anyway, just to see Fan. As I walked into the back door last Tuesday, I could tell Fan already had Mom in the shower. My footsteps were drowned out by the high lyrics of "You'll Never Walk Alone" from *Carousel*, so I discreetly sat on the carpet of Mom's bedroom and watched the two songbirds through the open bathroom door.

Still dressed in her teacher clothes, Fan was standing on the same tiny chair Mom sat on to bathe a two, three, and four year old more than thirty-seven years ago. Today, Fan was on tiptoe, reaching over the glass door of the three-by-three-foot shower stall. The sound of water spraying against Mom's shampooed hair blended with the full scale the lyrics demanded. A long arm with a rolled-up sleeve disappeared into the steam as Fan turned off the water with a "Now, all finished." As she stepped off the chair to grab a towel, she noticed me sitting on the floor behind her.

"That's some mighty powerful singing going on in there," I said.

"That's our theme song. Mom may not remember all the words, but she never fails to hit those high notes. Hey, you, time to come out of there." Fan carefully pushed open the door, grasped a naked Mom's hand firmly, and helped her step out onto the bathroom rug. "What did you say last week, Mom, if you can't sing, you can't live?"

"That's right."

"I don't see how you do it, Fan."

"It's easier for Pop. He just gets in there with her." She began toweling the beads of water that were resting on Mom's chilly goose bumps. "I've been trying to get him to change the shower head to a hand-held model or at least to fix it so the door swings out instead of in."

"No, I mean I don't see how you can bathe her. I can take her to the bathroom fine. I got used to that part when I visited Grandpa in the nursing home, but I don't know about bathing my own mother."

"I don't even think about it." Fan powdered Mom's underarms. "We're lucky Mom never sweats. We can skip the deodorant."

"When I told Ricky he'd have to take turns sitting with Mom during Pop's operation, he said, 'Are you sure Mom would feel comfortable with me wiping her butt?' I told him it would be a breeze. Now, I can understand his reservations."

"OK, Mom, let's go sit on the bed and get you dressed."

"You sure are getting skinny, Mom," I said, then turned to Fan. "Can you believe she weighed over 170 pounds a year ago? She's down to 140."

"I know. She's just lost her appetite."

"Did you read about the man who was left at the race track with a box of diapers strapped to his wheelchair?"

"Yeah, where was that, Oregon?" Fan eased Mom down to the bed.

"I think so. Just left a note saying he had Alzheimer's, can you believe it?"

"Hey, pinkie," Mom noticed me on the floor at her feet. I was dressed in a hot pink knit shirt.

"I thought you had outgrown that red stage," I said. "You haven't mentioned it in months."

"It's pretty."

"You're somethin' else, Mom." I smiled up at her as Fan sailed a pair of white socks through the air to land in my lap. "OK, I get the hint. Here are your socks, Mom, can I have a foot?"

She raised up her right foot about three inches from the carpet.

"Fan, have you ever seen Pop do this? He used to go, 'Left! Left!' and get so outdone if Mom raised her right foot instead of her left. I convinced him that it was only natural for Mom not to know her left from her right, so now he just says, 'Foot! Foot!'"

She laughed. "Not only that. Have you noticed the pantry since Pop took over the kitchen? It is so dull. Mom used to have all kinds of neat snacks stashed everywhere, but Pop buys the same food every week. I don't see how he doesn't get bored with it."

"He just hates to go to the grocery store."

"Last Saturday, before he left," she went on, "he wrote detailed instructions as to how many seconds to warm her turkey and cheese sandwich in the microwave. It had to be thirty-two seconds because he chose two numbers close to each other on the dial. Then he wrote exactly how to brush her teeth and how to make her Instant Breakfast in a special glass he had marked with the milk line. He didn't even want me to clean the coffee pot too well because it would wash off his water mark on the inside."

"I know. He's really changed, hasn't he? Remember when Mom did everything? Whenever I speak to groups, someone in the audience will invariably say, 'Your mother is so lucky to have such a caring man. My husband would never do those things for me.' I just say, 'Let me tell you about the old Pop, the before-Alzheimer's Pop.'"

"Pop's such a butt," Mom whispered.

"Maybe so, Mom, but he sure loves you." Fan buttoned up her blue flannel shirt as I finished pulling on

Mom's sweatpants and shoes.

"Did you get a chance to talk to Betty or Tricia much while they were here?" I asked Fan.

"A little bit."

"Did Betty tell you that she's been checking into the Hendry side of the family to see if there was any Alzheimer's? We knew it wasn't on Bigmama's side."

"Yeah, everybody was just crazy," she laughed.

"I know, but not from Alzheimer's, so we started thinking about Bigdaddy. I hadn't even suspected his side until Betty said he died of arterial sclerosis. Sometimes, Alzheimer's was misdiagnosed as that."

"But is he the only one?"

"Betty said she thought his niece had something similar to it, but she wasn't sure. It would be worth looking into. If Mom's is hereditary, we've got a fifty-fifty chance of getting it, but I've already decided Ricky's going to get it and not us."

"That's good." Fan laughed with me. "Just our luck, we'd end up having to take care of him. No, seriously, stop and think of it. Why should I get my Ph.D., if I'm going to forget everything in twenty years?"

"But, by then, they're bound to have a cure, wouldn't you think? Did you know that I've been trying to get Mom hooked up with a neurologist to get her started on T.H.A.?"

"Really?" she said as we led Mom into the living room. "Don't you think it's too late for that now?"

"Maybe, but it's worth a try. Her back needs the attention now, though. It always hurts, and Dr. Walker won't give her anything strong. Apparently, it's her arthritis."

"Yeah, her spine is really twisted."

Mom finally spoke, "You two."

"What's the matter, Mom?" Fan smiled at her. "Are we talking about you?"

"It's all right," she said.

A couple of weeks later, Fan had to miss a Tuesday, so I decided to try giving Mom her shower. I was determined to do it just for the sole purpose of saying I could. I talked constantly the entire time, teasing Mom to keep her from noticing my inexperience.

"OK, Mom, this is Tuesday, and Fan always washes your hair on Tuesday. Who am I, Fan or Kim?"

"You're Fan or Kim." She smiled as the water ran over her shoulders.

"Not fair. Am I Fan or Kim?"

She laughed, "Is this fair?"

"Come on, Fan or Kim?"

"You're you."

"Cute, cute. OK, it's time to get out anyway. I didn't do so badly, did I?"

"You're a sweetie."

I wiped her glasses with a soft cloth and placed them on her newly dried face. "Now, am I Fan or Kim?"

"You're the beautiful one!"

I laughed, "No, that won't work either. How about this? Am I Fan, Kim, or Ricky?" I dried off her back and legs.

"That makes it harder." She smiled. "OK, not Ricky because he's a boy."

"Good, good, now, we're back to the original question: am I Fan or Kim?" I walked Mom to the edge of the bed to put on her pajamas, and I heard her murmur in a low groan.

"Kim."

I screamed in delight, "Mom, you really got it!"

She just nodded her head as I helped her get dressed, telling her which piece of clothing came next.

"OK, Mom, I'm putting on your undershirt over your head."

She looked at me out of the corner of her good eye and smiled. "Kim, you're always over my head."

May 1992

Mom and I took a longer walk than usual, but we were now within a block from her home.

"Hey, Lou." We heard a voice come from inside the dimly lit screen porch of a house to our left.

"Hey, Miss Ev," I called back, then said to Mom, "It's Mrs. Evelyn Disher, Mom. She comes to visit you all the time, remember? She's Fan's mother-in-law."

"No, I mean, yes," Mom said without looking up. She raised her hand to wave in no particular direction. I just shrugged a meek smile at Miss Evelyn who returned it and continued to sweep her porch. I knew Mom's lack of enthusiasm would not stop Miss Ev from visiting Mom every week. She had remained a faithful friend throughout.

We made it to the next sidewalk before Mom spoke again, "My nose . . . move my nose, up there."

"Your glasses falling down again?" I pushed her frames up the bridge of her nose.

"Yes, thanks."

"Ready to head home?"

"I think so. My back."

"Your back hurts again?" I rubbed it as we walked the half block to Mom's. In her living room, I placed a heating pad between her back and the chair and sat down beside her on the small yellow hassock that lifted me only a foot off the floor.

"Where's Pop?"

"He's at the farm with Kate and Zab. They should be back any minute."

"The farm . . ."

I sat listening long to Mom's rambling, piecing together phrases of broken thoughts, trying to read the incomplete sentences in the gestures of her hands, hands she always said were too stubby.

"You are so lucky, Sabe," Mom used to say. Her favorite nickname for me was Kemosabe, of "Lone Ranger" fame. "You have your daddy's hands—long, pretty fingers, an artist's hands. Here, let's do the commercial."

Then, she would place my teenaged hand next to her own distinctive hand, its bumpy veins mapping the years, recording the dry, ruddy mileage of her life's experiences.

"Which one is the mother and which one is the daughter?" Mom would laugh and say dramatically in an announcer's tone, "We can't tell! Isn't that amazing!"

I watched her hands now, still full of character, wandering through the air, walking from her knee until they found me sitting next to her. Her face brightened as her eyes raised to focus on me. "Oh, it's you! I'm so glad you came to see me," she said for the third or fourth time in the course of the visit. She began a new sentence searching with her hands to find an ending to her thought.

"Mom, do you remember about a year ago, a writer from New York wrote a story about your journal and my paintings for *Omni* magazine?"

"No."

"Well, it was finally published this month. Isn't that exciting?"

Mom's face grew serious, and she sat up in her chair away from the heating pad. "I know what I got. I know I can do it. Just remember, you can't do it all. This is a long time, but you're going to do it so well. They know you well, your family, all your people. You know you can."

"Thanks, Mom."

"It's not a little girl doing it," she continued. "You're a young lady. When you do it, don't try to keep: I can't do it. Think right up here," and she pointed to her temple. "You've been telling yourself you can't do it and you can. Don't let it do it halfway. You're a young lady, so don't get so upset about that. You've got it, you hear me?"

"Yes, ma'am."

"Don't push too much to people. Keep it down for the ladies. They'll be all dressed up, won't they? So," Mom stopped, her thoughts seemingly in another place. Then she looked straight into my eyes. "I didn't think I was a pusher."

"You're not, Mom, but thanks for the pep talk."

She chuckled. "I've talked so much, I've gotten my mouth all dry."

"I'll get you some water." I stood up from the hassock, but Mom stopped me.

"I know you can do it. I've watched you, and you do it, and you don't even think about it. Don't get to the point where, 'Oh, no, these women and people are going to look at us.' Go in there like this," and she sat up even straighter.

"I know I can do it, Mom, because you taught me how."

"I hope I did," she said slumping back in her chair. "I would love to be someone like you who could help."

"You are, Mom." I sat back down on the hassock and took her hand in mine. "You are."

Just then, the back door opened, and Kate bounced in, followed closely by Pop and Zab.

"Mama, I finished my Babysitters Club book."

"What? We just bought that one yesterday."

"I know, but it was good. In this one, they talk about Mallory's Uncle Joe who has Alzheimer's."

"Good grief! It's everywhere." I smiled at her, then as a quiet reminder, "Hello, Mom."

"Hello, Mom." Kate leaned down to kiss Mom on the cheek.

"Hi, honey."

"Well, guys, how were the cows?"

"Still out there." Zab crashed on the sofa next to Pop's chair. "All twenty-five of them."

"Isn't it about time to sell some?"

Pop sat down, too, propping his dusty shoes on his own hassock. "We've just been discussing that. You know, getting back to that dirt; I'd get a big bulldozer first before I bring the tractor in."

Mom leaned over to me and whispered, "Just act like you know what they're talking about. I do. They seem to have an answer to everything."

I laughed at her unexpected wit. "Come on, Mom, let's leave these two alone to their dirt and cows. How about that water I promised you?"

I helped her get up from the overstuffed chair and turned off the heating pad. By the time we made it to the kitchen table, Kate had papers spread out and a pen bobbing feverishly in her hand. I sat Mom in her place at the turquoise table facing Kate.

"What's going on here?" I asked, filling three glasses with ice.

"I'm making out new tests for Mom. The last time I asked her about spelling, like how to spell 'can,' Mom spelled it 'cn.' She would skip the vowels."

"I done, done," Mom began. "Ooh, my grammar is getting horrible."

"Mom, of all the things you remember." I sat in Fan's old chair between them. "So, Kate, what if she misses a word, does she get a grade or what?"

"Well, first I make her go over it to understand what she missed, but I always give her a B+ or an A-, so she won't give up."

"Why, thank you," Mom said clearly. Kate grinned.

"OK, Mom, I want you to say your ABC's."

"ABCGHIFKLMNOTUVXYZ and F. I think I forgot F."

"Very good, Mom." Kate scribbled some checks in

a row of boxes and went on. "Now, I'm going to say three numbers and you say them back to me." Then Kate whispered to me, "She used to do four."

"Ooh, my foot, my foot!" Mom frantically tried to find a pain.

"Got a pain, Mom? Where, here?" I pulled off her shoe and massaged the arch of her right foot. "Nerves acting up again?"

"Yes, it's so agalating."

"There's another one for your Alzheimer's dictionary: agalating." We all laughed. "Kate, write that one down: agalating for, I guess you meant, aggravating, huh, Mom?"

"Who knows?"

I left Kate testing Mom and went home to paint. It was too quiet in the studio, but I forced myself to get to work. As I painted, I heard the yodeling of a train whistle heading to New Orleans on tracks just two blocks from my studio window. I've always slept soundly through night trains, yet my friends complained of their unaccustomed restlessness when they spent the night with me.

Layer after layer of translucent color created a glow from within, an inner light that moved gradually from rich indigo shadows to acid yellow on the opposite edge. My eyes traveled around the forms, swallowing me in the deep chasms of their tangles. Dizzying shapes receded beyond the grasp of my brush and snuck into the dark recesses of lost color and blurred details.

A train whistle, no, a winged form emerged from the depths. I subordinated it quickly with a wash of Payne's gray, allowing it to fade quietly in its dignity only to float south with the rumbling caboose. An abandoned egg shape then requested a thin coat of Naphthol red to warm its shell, then yellow oxide, but never white, never white. The layering pulled the egg to the brink of cracking, the lips of its fracture tugging gently at my sponge. My brain awoke to a sobbing sound behind me. Kate had walked the two blocks home in tears.

"What's the matter?" I hugged her close and handed her a Kleenex.

"Mom really fussed at me, wouldn't let me do anything," Kate sobbed. "She didn't know who I was."

"Where were Pop and Daddy?"

"Out in the workshop."

"I'd better go down there."

When I entered the back door, Mom was in her living room chair whistling to herself.

"Hi, Mom." I sat on the yellow hassock again.

"Well, hey." She smiled at me, then looked into the air.

"Did Kate come to see you today?"

"No, not in a couple of days."

"Did anybody come to see you today?"

"A girl came," she frowned. "She kept wanting Pop."

"Have you seen this girl before?"

"Two, three times. Boy, she liked Pop. She almost told me something about her and Pop." Mom was getting angry. "The younger one was kinda ugly, kept saying 'I know Pop.' She wouldn't shut up. She was waiting for Pop to get back. I told her, 'I think it's time for you to go.'"

"Did this girl look like Kate?"

"No, this girl was a snotty little kid."

"Mom, do you want me to tell you what really happened?"

"No, it wasn't that young one. She liked Pop."

"Mom, it was Kate."

"No, this was somebody else."

June 1992

Kate put on one of Grandma's old straw hats and sat in a wooden camp chair on the black side of the checkerboard. Pop donned his own helmet, a bright yellow cap to cover his bald head, and positioned himself at the porch table ready to go to war for the red team. From where Mom and I sat on the swing, I could see only Kate's profile from her nose to her chin, the large brim of the hat shading the battlefield from the glare. As they set up the checkers, I gazed long at the narrow river that flowed only fifteen feet in front of the porch of the camp. It seemed different this time as I stared at it through forty-year-old eyes. I thought about the warning sign posted at the landing. The river had gradually become more polluted with the years. I guess Mom and the river had more in common than I realized.

She was singing now, softly to herself, making up the words as she went along, my toes and the breeze tipping the swing back and forth.

"Find there's a way
They don't really know,
Watch and wait
And see you again,
Hope there's a time
I'll need you,
Because I love you."

Her melody then turned to words, "Not too long ago, I started playing. Then I just make a little . . . keeping you from going. You just watch and go."

Mom began to sing again, stopping only at the end of a line to let out a dramatic "Ha, ha, ha," as if she were singing opera. She didn't notice me kill a mosquito that had landed on her left hand.

"One time, I didn't have a durn thing to do," she said, "and I just talked it. Gives me something to do. It's easy."

"Can't go wrong," I said.

"That's right."

In spite of the fact that it was eighty degrees in the shade, the humidity was low, and the breeze made shadows jump on the white ground. It was about to rain. The white undersides of the leaves had turned up to catch the moisture they thought would eventually flow from the southeast, but it seemed slow in coming. There was no current visible on the surface of the river either, a lone cypress branch floating patiently, waiting for its inevitable trip to the mouth downstream.

"Will you please move," Kate broke the silence with her impatience of Pop's concentration. He moved a red checker to a neighboring square, and Kate quickly attacked.

"Oh, you got me," Pop said after Kate had jumped his man on the board.

"We should go out to the lake soon," I told Pop, but he was more interested in the game.

Kate said, "That was pretty dumb. Now I can't move a thing."

"You give? You give?" Pop taunted.

"You outsmarted me."

"Oh, me," Pop sighed, very pleased with his victory.

"Whatcha say we go get some fish?"

As I watched them untie the boat, I thought how much they looked like Pop and me taking off fishing when I was little. We would take turns paddling while the other one fly-fished toward the bank, and we'd never catch a thing but a lily pad. When we'd return to the camp, he would show me how to tie the line into a half hitch to hold the boat firmly against the wharf.

"Promise me something," Mom spoke up as they left.

"Sure, what?"

"The first time Pop, Bert—whatever you want to call him—he was one to himself, like he didn't know what to do. A couple of things as it might be. We talked a little bit. Then he found out he still was the same way. He thought, 'What if I do?' I think he's much better at relaxing. And I was just . . ." she trailed off.

"Go on," I said, even though I had no idea what she was talking about.

"It's nothing. It's fine," she said. "He hadn't been much. Then he kind of moved on like he put something over here." She reached her left hand toward the floor below our swing. "He got better, much better. Probably the reason is he's . . . It's raining?"

"No, Mom."

"He's just kind of, what's the word when somebody's scared? No, that's not the word." She was giving up on the thought. "He really . . . doesn't say much at all. When kids come, he goes. He loves them."

"Yes, Mom, he does."

Kate and Pop returned within what seemed like minutes. It had been minutes.

"Already?" I looked surprised.

"I traded a dozen tomatoes for a dozen catfish," Pop smiled.

I should have known. Pop liked to fish only when he was positive that they were biting; he's too impatient a man to wait on a fish. I watched as he showed Kate how to tie a half hitch.

"Is Kate going to get to skin 'em?"

"If she wants to," Pop said as he and Kate got out the ice chest full of tomorrow night's supper, still wiggling around in the bottom. With a distorted face and partially closed eyes, Kate pulled off the skin of the first fish Pop hung on a hook on the oak tree. I took appropriate pictures as she slung the skin into the river behind her.

"The crabs will like that," Pop said, trying not to sound too proud of Kate's handiwork. "Not bad, not bad."

Finally, the rain did come, and Kate and Pop had to delay their fish cleaning for a while. The wind was blowing much harder now, and it eventually knocked out the electrical power. Boats began to race back to their dry, though darkened, camps. I brought Mom a sweater and again sat next to her on the swing. We had decided to stay on the front porch to enjoy the chaos of the afternoon summer storm. Normally lazy moss flew wildly in the trees above our heads. Lightning cracked through the clouds as the rain pelted the carcasses of the abandoned camps on either side of us. One had been deserted so long that the swamp had swallowed all but the peak of its collapsed gable roof.

"Pop, where are snakes now?" Kate asked, knowing that I was not wild about them since a moccasin had crawled over my foot in that same side yard when I was a kid.

"People have been shooting them."

"That's good," I said.

"No, it's not. There's a king snake that lives under that wharf sometimes. He kills rats."

"OK, king snakes are good," I said, not really believing it.

"Pop," Kate had more questions, "how did this river happen? Steep hills?"

"No, all this land was flat, except the river. It was probably just the lowest part of the land."

"Why are those places in the river darker?"

"Not raining as hard; wind blowing it." Then Pop turned to Mom and patted her on the knee. "You OK, baby?"

"Yeah, fine,"

"Like it down the river?"

"Oh, yeah, beautiful down here."

Pop looked at me and smiled. "She always says

everything is beautiful. I guess that's better than her griping all the time."

The electricity came back on about 8:00, after I had fixed supper using a kerosene lantern and a battery-powered bulb that Pop had rigged up over the kitchen table. Mom and Pop went to bed at 9:00, but Kate was not at all sleepy, so she and I read till ten. I had suggested to her that she take a nap earlier that day because we might not get much sleep if Mom woke up; but Kate didn't want to miss any exciting moments being down the river. Kate slept with me in the bed closest to the noisy air conditioner, hoping that if Mom did cry out that night, we wouldn't hear her. There's not much Pop can do to stop her tears at night. He sometimes just goes into the next room and lets her carry on. We dozed easily until midnight, when we were awakened by the quiet of a dead air conditioner. Kate saw that I was awake and said, "Mama, you're hogging the bed."

"Then why don't you sleep in the other bed?"

She crawled into the empty double bed next to mine and turned off the light. I lay awake thinking about my nights down the river as a kid when I slept in the bed with Fan while Ricky took the other bed or the front porch sofa if the night was cool enough. I would lay in the dark listening to the firecracker pops of the rain hitting the tin roof overhead and the creak of the rain frogs as they suctioned their little spider feet to the window pane. A stray mosquito or two would eventually buzz around my ear, and I would slowly plot its demise. I had it all figured out. If the sheet covered up every inch of biteable skin except my head, I could kill each mosquito that dared float too close to my ear with one smooth sweep of my open palm onto the pillow below. The next morning, I would see several dead black specks on the pillow case, victims of my ingenious trap. As I watched Fan already in the bathroom rubbing pink Calamine lotion on her red welts, I thought she should try my trap. No, I decided to keep it to myself.

I guess I was about ten, Kate's age now. I devised these inventive schemes to obliterate those obnoxious little featherweights simply because I was too scared to go to sleep. My vicious imagination made the floor squirm with dozens of water moccasins. I couldn't hang my hand beside my bed because there was an alligator under there waiting to gnaw it off. Every swamp noise I heard was the boogie-man, whose dusky shadow moved past the back screen door every time a breeze disturbed the sleeping moss in the cypress tree by my window.

Kate startled me when she appeared at the edge of my bed with tears in her eyes.

"Are you scared, sweetie?" I asked.

With a nod, she climbed under the musty sheet beside me. I gave her a Kleenex and watched her get settled. I could feel my eyes smile as I wondered if she were experiencing any of those same fears I had had as a child. Wouldn't it be ironic, I thought, if Kate were having the same fears? I had to know.

"What were you afraid of, hon?"

"Mom screaming."

My smile disappeared as I hugged her sniffling body close to mine.

Mom did wake up that night about two hours later. She cried and talked incessantly, but Pop seemed to be handling it. I heard him get up to take her to the bathroom at least a half dozen times and order her to go back to sleep. He would then have about twenty minutes of rest before she would start crying again. I wondered at the time how could he sleep like that every night? When I asked him the next day, he said, "Oh, last night wasn't bad."

July 1992

In spite of an unusually busy summer, I was still more preoccupied with getting Mom started on T.H.A. It took me five months of preliminary running around before Mom was able to participate in the testing of the drug. In March, the first two appointments were canceled by the neurologists themselves for various reasons, then rescheduled. In May, we finally met with a neurologist, who one month later received a Fellow and left his practice to go back to school. We were again at square one. I then decided to go straight to the source and contacted the rep from the drug company who immediately connected us with Dr. Richard Gold in Baton Rouge. Even after we scheduled an appointment with Dr. Gold,

Pop had reservations about the treatment.

"What if it screws up her liver?" he asked me as I was helping him pick up the kitchen dishes. We had already walked Mom to her chair in the living room.

"Do you remember when Mom was going to Bethesda to test drugs, and she was just getting ready to test T.H.A.? They canceled the test because it was found to have too many side effects, one of which was liver damage in one out of every two patients. Well, since then, they've improved it enough to where it only damages one liver in every four. If the drug begins to hurt Mom's liver, we'll just stop it."

"What if it doesn't help her, just makes her stay the same? I don't want that." His eyes never left mine.

"We won't know if we don't try. From what I've read so far, it's supposed to help her, but only a little bit. But wouldn't a little bit be better than nothing? Maybe she'll just be able to feed herself again, who knows?"

"That would be a help. I can't even get her to open her mouth wide enough."

"Well, Pop, you do give her gigantic bites." I smiled at him.

"Gets supper over with faster."

"Seeing this doctor couldn't hurt." I plugged his percolator into the timer and walked ahead of him toward the living room. "If nothing else, maybe he could give Mom something to help her sleep at night."

"Honey?" Mom called.

"Yeah, baby," Pop answered nonchalantly.

"Honey?"

"Yeah, baby." His answer was as routine as his settling in his favorite chair. I found my own perch on the yellow hassock by Mom's feet.

"Mom, tomorrow, we're going to take you to the doctor for a checkup."

"What?" she stiffened. "There's nothing wrong with me."

"No, Mom, this is an Alzheimer's doctor, a neurologist."

"He's that goofy one. He doesn't know anything about Alzheimer's."

"You're thinking about that first one we saw over seven years ago. Who said you lost your memory?" I smiled at Pop who just shook his head.

"I'm scared," she whimpered. "What does Pop think?"

"Go for it, baby!"

Mom half-turned in her chair toward Pop's voice but couldn't focus on him. "Will you be there?"

"If I have to." Pop was expecting me to take Mom to Baton Rouge giving him a free afternoon.

"What about Dr. Walker?"

"He's sent you to a specialist before, Mom," I said firmly. "This isn't like you. You're usually so positive. Why don't you just give it a try? If you don't like him, we'll leave."

In a low voice, she whispered a reluctant OK.

The next morning, I arrived to pick up a very drowsy Pop and an alert, cheerful Mom.

"Hey, you look terrible, Pop."

"The screaming started again last night," he yawned. "Call the police. Get these people out of here." He mimicked Mom's hallucination.

Mom grinned, "I missed it all. Slept like a baby." Pop and I just laughed.

As soon as we got into the car, I approached a subject that I had been meaning to discuss with Pop for several months. Fan and I had already talked about it, and she suggested I pass it through Pop.

"Pop," I had to talk loudly since he was in the back seat. "Last semester, I had a student in one of my classes that could never sit still. His body was in constant motion, blinking, clearing his throat, coughing, twitching. After a few weeks of watching this boy, I thought that he really looked familiar."

"Sounds like Ricky," he said.

"Exactly, I felt like I was watching Ricky every day. He was a sweet kid, just couldn't stop twitching. Anyway, one day, this boy shows up with a letter from his mother apologizing that she hadn't realized that her son had a new art teacher at midterm. She wanted me to be aware of the fact that her son had a mild case of Tourette's syndrome and told me what to expect. The information she sent me described all of Ricky's habits."

"Hmph," was all Pop said.

"Anyway, I just thought that Ricky might want to look into it."

"But you shouldn't be the one to tell him."

"I know that. That's why I'm telling you. You could tell him."

"Is there a cure?"

"I don't know. I don't even know if there are any drugs he could take."

"Then why tell him?"

"I think he'd be relieved to know he might have something specific, just like Mom was relieved to find out she had Alzheimer's—you know, something with a name. Besides, he might find out he's not alone or that there is some drug out there. I'm sure it's very frustrating for him, like a terrible itch he can't scratch."

"OK, bring me the stuff and I'll talk to him about it." He leaned his head on the seat cushion and fell asleep.

Mom and I drove along in silence for a while. My thoughts moved toward the subject at hand, Mom's appointment with Dr. Gold, and I remembered something Alan Stevens told me about two weeks ago. He described our first visit to the neurologist by saying that the doctor would probably ask Mom about fifteen questions, everyday things she should know. This way, he could judge her condition based on the number of correct responses.

"Mom," I broke the quiet. "Today, the doctor is going to ask you a bunch of questions to see how much you remember. For example, what's your address?"

"480 North Seventh Street," she said without hesitation.

"Great! Who's the president of the United States?"

"Don't know that one."

"George Bush, Mom, George Bush."

"That pill! I don't like him."

"Well, the doctor will probably accept that one if he's a Democrat. OK, let's try a different one. How old are you?"

"I've never known that."

"You're sixty-seven."

"I'm that old?" Her eyes squinted at a quick ray of sunlight shooting through the windshield. I pulled down the visor above her head.

"How many children do you have?"

"Fan, Kim, and Ricky."

From the back seat, I heard a low voice mumble, "Y'all are cheating."

"Aw, Pop, she'll probably forget them anyway."

Once inside his office, Mom sat quietly in a small cushioned chair while Pop paced to the window and back, jingling the change in his pockets. Suddenly, the door burst open as if a hard wind had pounced on it from the outside, and a big burly man with wild black hair stepped inside the tiny room.

"So, this is Mrs. Howes. I'm Dr. Gold, and what makes you think she has Alzheimer's disease?" He talked rapidly, breathing very little from beginning to end. Pop nodded to me to answer.

"She was diagnosed over seven years ago and has been through three years of drug testing at the National Institutes of Health."

"That's easy enough. I can just get their records."

"Good luck. They usually don't part with them."

"Well, we can try. Mrs. Howes," he said loudly, standing directly in front of Mom who was not looking at him. "May I ask you some questions? I'd like to give you a test."

"OK."

"Can you tell me where you are right now?"

"480 North Seventh Street." She seemed pleased with herself.

"No, what city are you in right now?"

"Ponchatoula!"

"Let's go on to something else." He leaned over as if to shake Mom's hand. "Mrs. Howes, can you give me your right hand?"

Mom raised her right hand.

Pop said, "That's the only hand she'll use. She never has used her left one."

"Mrs. Howes, can you give me your left thumb?"

Again, Mom raised her right hand.

"That's great! That's great!" Dr. Gold wrote some notes quickly on his folder.

"Does that mean she fails?" I asked.

"No, the more she gets wrong today, the more we can see how she improves next time."

"So, she can start taking T.H.A.?"

"Sure, sure. We'll schedule some blood work and fill out all the necessary papers."

Pop finally spoke, "What's it supposed to do?"

"Oh, I've had patients who used to wander off who can now take walks by themselves or, say, a patient who wouldn't eat, now sits at the dinner table with the rest of the family. Then, I've had some patients that have shown no improvements whatsoever, but my patients have yet to show any liver damage. She'll start off on forty milligrams a day for six weeks, getting a blood test every week. Then, if her liver remains unharmed, she'll increase the dosage to eighty milligrams a day for six weeks. Then, she'll move to the highest dosage, 120 milligrams. You may not see any improvement until she reaches that level. After that, blood tests move from once a week to once a month."

Pop looked at me still sitting beside Mom. "What about sleeping at night?"

"What Pop means is that Mom seldom sleeps, has nightly hallucinations, some screaming. It's difficult for them to get any rest."

"Has she ever tried Mellaril?" When I shook my head, he went on. "Then we'll try that. If it doesn't work, we'll try something else. There's a long line of medicines that can help that."

As we rode the elevator back to the first floor, Pop said, "That wasn't so bad."

"Yes," I told him. "But I was just disappointed that he didn't ask Mom the name of the president of the United States."

Mom's face lit up, and her eyes widened. She squeezed my hand and grinned, "480 North Seventh Street!"

"That's it, Mom. There's nothing wrong with you."

September 1992

From their carport, I could see Mom sitting alone in the living room, leaning to the right side of her chair. Her hands were jerking a bit, and when I opened the back door, I realized she was crying and talking in that high pitch she uses only when she's upset.

"Mom, what's the matter?" As I walked a few steps toward her, I looked to my left through the dining room and into the kitchen. I could see Pop and Ricky visiting at the table. "Hey, guys, Mom's all alone in here."

"She's all right," Pop told me.

"But she's crying." I didn't expect them to hurry in there, but I did want them to know she was upset. Ricky waved a hello, then turned around to continue his conversation with Pop. I sat down by Mom's side and patted her leg.

"You don't look very happy, Mom."

"My back, my back," she sobbed.

"I can fix that. Let me get the heating pad again." I maneuvered the gray pad to the base of Mom's back, and clicked on the M switch. I then bent over her, rubbing the tight muscles that were impatiently waiting for the heat. She became quiet enough for her right hand to settle onto her lap like the head of a loyal puppy. When I returned to my hassock, I made the tone of my voice sound as if all was normal again.

"Pop's in the kitchen."

"Who?"

"Remember Pop, your husband? That cute skinny sailor you married?"

"I'm not married," Mom said matter-of-factly. "I've never been married."

"Only for forty-seven years. What about your three kids?"

"I don't have any kids." Her eyes gazed so deeply into the open air that I felt for a minute that she could see clearly into another time, another dimension.

"Have you graduated from Southeastern yet, Mom?"

"No, no," she smiled as if I were kidding.

"Have you graduated from high school yet?"

"Oh, yeah, long time ago."

As Ricky and Pop continued to talk, their voices carried into the living room, Ricky's much louder so that Pop's weak ears could hear him. I could hear Pop's low voice in bits of mumbles. I recognized the word Tourette's, then heard Ricky say he hadn't heard anything about it. Another few sentences of Pop's blurbs were followed by responses like "Really?" and "I'll check into it." I then heard them push back their chairs across the linoleum floor and walk into the room by Mom and me.

"Mom tells me she's not married," I said as Pop sat in his chair while Ricky stood, seemingly ready to leave.

"Yeah?" Pop smiled. "Last night, I said, 'C'mon, baby, we're going to have fish for supper' and she said, 'We don't have any money.' I just told her, 'We can write a check.' She just said, 'OK.'"

Ricky coughed a laugh, then began in the middle of a discussion he and Pop must have started in the kitchen, something about finishing the white, picket fence in his back yard. He hadn't said but a few sentences before Mom started whining again.

"Ooh, the noise."

"Mom, it's just those old boys talking."

"Too loud," she said, then her whines turned into tears. The louder Mom cried, the louder Ricky talked to Pop, so much so that I was beginning to wish they had stayed in the kitchen. I placed a Kleenex to Mom's nose and told her to blow. She sniffed instead, then continued to half cry, half whine. Ricky finally walked toward the back door to leave, saying good-bye to Pop as his long fingers reached for the knob. Then, as a second thought, he backtracked his steps to Mom's chair.

"Bye, Lucy," he leaned down and gave her a kiss on the cheek and hugged her shoulders.

Mom stopped crying almost immediately, then said clearly, "Bye, honey."

After he left, I shook my head at Pop and turned back to Mom. "Now, tell me again about not having any children?"

October 1992

For the last four Sundays, Kate and I have been preoccupied with getting Mom to endure an entire Mass without having to take her home before the end of the hour. Each Sunday brings a different excuse to leave: either Mom's back hurts or the music is too loud or she's too hot or too cold. Kate has hung in there with me each time.

"You know, you don't have to sit with us, sweetie," I told her as she washed out her cereal bowl in the sink. "You can sit wherever you like and just walk home with us."

"No, that's OK. I don't mind." At that, we heard the back French doors open, and looked up to see Pop helping Mom cross the threshold.

"Step up," Pop said as he lifted her elbow with his

hand. "That's right. We're at Kim's." Mom didn't say anything. Kate left me quickly to walk to the door. She caught Mom's right hand and pulled her gently toward one of our bent-wood dining chairs. When Kate spoke, her voice was not depressed but pleasant, as if she were afraid her tired voice would affect Mom's mood.

"Good morning, Mom, did you sleep OK last night?" Kate held the back of the chair while Pop eased Mom down.

"About three, four hours," Pop sighed. "Then sat up about three hours talking and whistling. I finally had to go sleep on the sofa."

"So you did get a little sleep?" I asked, handing him a mug of coffee before walking to Mom's chair. "Hey, Mom." I kissed her on the cheek and stood behind her with my hands on her shoulders waiting for Pop to answer.

"Hey," was all that Mom said.

"Nah." Pop flipped up his yellow cap as if it were the visor in his gray truck. "Then I couldn't go back to sleep."

"Well, you can take a nap while we're at Mass." I slipped a few extra Kleenex in my sweater pocket.

"Can't nap. Never could."

"I thought that medicine Dr. Gold gave her, Mellaril is it, was making her sleep too much."

"Sure, she sleeps off and on all day long. Dr. Gold told me to give it to her four times a day. She just doesn't sleep that great at night."

"Come on, Mom," I said, "let's get to Mass before somebody takes our front row seat." I walked around to face her, then pulled up both of her hands to help her float to a standing position.

In church, Mom sat in between us, and Kate held her hand to the railing in front of our pew. When Mom groaned slightly, Kate leaned toward her and rubbed the base of her back, hoping it was just her arthritis flaring up again. Mom's eyes were half shut as if she were hypnotized, and her lips didn't even try to sing. I could feel my composure weakening, but took a deep breath instead. Just before Communion, I dropped my hymnal to the floor, but let it stay there, more concerned with Mom's growing zombie-like state.

When Father walked up to our pew to hand Mom

Communion, he smiled at me and offered me the hymnal from the floor. His kind eyes didn't flinch when Mom dropped the Communion wafer, nor when he saw my eyes begin to water. He just calmly took it back and handed Mom another. A lump grew in my throat as I tried to whisper to Mom to at least open her mouth. I finally squeezed her elbow enough for her eyes to widen and her lips parted to take the host.

I remember thinking I had dried up by the end of Mass, but I felt people pat me on the back as they left the church and not say anything—a sign, I guess, that they understood what Mom was going through. Kate and I walked Mom back to our house, and this time, happened to get there before Pop. I brought Mom into my living room and lay her on the sofa on her back. I closed the curtains to help shield the sunshine and covered her legs with a lap blanket. I sat on the arm of the sofa by her head, stroking her cheek to calm the muscles of her frustrated face.

At that moment, as Mom lay just that way with her hands folded across her waist, I thought how much she resembled Bigmama lying still in her casket. Mom's face was cold and dry, just like Bigmama's hand had been when I touched it that day five years ago. This time, however, I didn't feel the same relief I felt when I realized Bigmama's spirit wasn't trapped inside. This time, I knew Mom's was.

When Pop drove up, I met him at the back door in tears. "Pop, you've got to get her off of that Mellaril. She dropped Communion, didn't even try to sing. It was so pitiful. Pop, I don't like her like this."

"OK, OK, call Dr. Gold tomorrow and ask him what to do."

After Pop and Mom left, I felt a soft hand on my elbow. Kate was pulling me to follow her down the hall to my bedroom. She walked me into my bathroom and wiped a Kleenex over my eyes. I smiled through my sniffles at the thought of her taking care of me for a change.

"Now, Mommy, this is what you're going to do," she said with authority. "You're going to paint." She stepped into my closet and pulled out my favorite painting clothes, an old pair of loose gray pants and a big white tuxedo shirt, both of which were decorated in absent-minded smears of whatever was on my brush at the time.

"Oh, yeah?"

"Yes, go in there and let it out." She held up the clothes and deliberately shut her eyes, an indication that I was supposed to change. I obliged.

"Thank you, Miss Kate. Anything else?"

"Your shoes?" She offered me my stained high-tops and a pair of white socks garnished with colorful drops on the inside of each ankle. "And the earrings have to go. They aren't arty."

Kate then escorted me to my studio and sat me in the black studying chair opposite a large sheet of white paper I had prepared earlier with preliminary drips of watery paint. I smiled as I watched her fill two bowls with clean water and place them on the floor in their usual positions. I nodded to her as she arranged my paints about four feet away, and I looked up to her determined face as she handed me my two favorite brushes.

"Now, paint."

"Yes, ma'am."

Kate kissed me on the cheek and closed the studio door behind her.

I thought I'd at least make the effort, so I studied the drips in front of me looking for anything that might voluntarily appear. I saw a flexed arm bent at the elbow, a long ribbon draping over the bicep and behind a shoulder. Then I stopped. This wasn't going to work today. As much as I wanted to please Kate with a surge of creativity, I couldn't bring myself to paint.

The next day, a call to Dr. Gold's nurse cleared up the Mellaril problem. He had told Pop to adjust the dosage from one to four tablets at a time, just at bedtime. Pop thought he meant four a day. Pop immediately cut Mom back to only two at bedtime.

As for Mom's continuous backaches, the urologist scheduled X-rays of her kidneys in the hopes of finding an infection that may have been causing the pain. She was confused throughout the procedure, constantly lifting her head from the pillow, not understanding where she was. It turned out her kidneys were fine, but the doctor noticed marked scoliosis and severe rheumatoid arthritis in her spine. Mom began taking Lodine the next day, and her back pains subsided.

February 1993

In my Christmas cards to Betty and Tricia, I told them that I expected Mom to be in a nursing home within a year. She showed little, if any, signs of life at her birthday party in late October. Her face remained expressionless as we sang "Happy Birthday," and Kate could barely get her to open her mouth for a bite of her own cake.

Mom was no better at Christmas. Pop insisted that we celebrate as a family on Christmas day and no other, yet Mom didn't even notice when a present was placed in her lap. She dozed through much of Pop's birthday party in January, waking only to complain that she wanted to go home. She was home.

Mom's rapid decline hit Pop and me so quickly that we weren't sure what to do next. We checked into a day-care center for the elderly and met with the head nurse who was excited about the prospect of Mom joining their group. The next morning when the nurse saw Mom for the first time, she turned her down. She said Mom was too far gone, meaning she was now in need of more individual care.

The adjustment of Mom's medication several months ago did take away her arthritis pains which helped her sleep through the night. She has continued to take T.H.A., showing no ill side effects that we can tell. We're just struggling at this point to keep her happy so that the tears and the whining won't start.

Last Saturday, I stayed with Mom so that Pop could take a break. In that excruciating two-hour period, I tried more than ten different activities to try to calm her, to distract her, to satisfy whatever itch was inside.

"What about a little music, Mom? Here are your big band tapes, or what about these Broadway musicals? Fan made you one from the *Sound of Music* and here's one from *Carousel*." I pressed "play" on the cassette recorder, thinking that the stream of nostalgia those songs always created would this time prove true.

"No, no, no." Mom waved her hand in the air in front of her face.

"How about a snack? Come on, hop up, Mom. Let's go see what Pop's got in the pantry."

She walked slowly beside me, my left arm around her waist, my right hand in hers. When I stopped halfway, she stopped, too. She wouldn't take a step unless I did. The snack was not the answer. She wouldn't drink the Coca-cola I fixed and wouldn't let me place a cookie in her mouth.

"I know. We can sing. How about our old Girl Scout song, huh, Mom?" and then I broke into "Girl Scouts together / That is our song / Winding the old trails / Rocky and long." Mom stopped crying for just a moment and smiled.

"Girl Scouts," she sighed.

"Yeah, Girl Scouts, that's right, Mom!" then in song, "Learning our motto / Living our—"

"Oh, no," and she began crying again, not tears actually, just a kind of whining, whimpering sound mixed with muffled words.

"It's such a great song. Come on, Mom, let's dance." By this time, I must have been brainstorming for anything that would help her calm down. We swirled slowly around the kitchen, but Mom's moves were stiff. "You need exercise, Mom, let's lift these arms and take a deep breath."

She did as I stretched her hands high above her head and swung them down in a crisscross. She didn't like that and wouldn't do it a second time. I remembered when Kate had nonstop colic in her first five weeks, we used to try taking her outside for a walk.

"A walk, Mom, sure, I should have thought of this before. Let's go outside."

We did make it the few blocks to my house. After that, I tried a pause at the swing, a chat in my studio, and a ten-minute car ride in the country. Out of desperation, I took her home, hoping selfishly that Pop had possibly decided to come back early. No luck.

"Mom, we're home."

"This isn't my home," she whined as I took off her jacket.

"Of course, it is. I'll show you. See, this is the kitchen where you used to cook. This is the living room. See? All of your Oriental stuff is still on the mantel. Next stop, the hall, then my room. Remember, this is the room where you wrote most of your journals. And this is Ricky's old room, and let's go back to the hall and go to your room. Look. There are all of your family pictures on the wall. They're still in those same old eight-by-ten plexiglass boxes. Nothing's changed. This is your house."

"You think so, huh?" She seemed to be talking in a deeper voice now.

"Here's your bed, Mom. Why don't you lie down and take a little nap?" I sat her on her side of the bed and took off her tennis shoes. Then I lifted her legs and thought how light they were. She's already down to 124 pounds.

By the time Pop came home, Mom had finally fallen asleep. My first question was, "How can you take this?"

"Sometimes, I think it's a problem, like getting her to the bathroom and stuff," he said quietly. "But then I think I should be grateful that she can still walk. It would be tough if she were in a wheelchair."

"You know, Pop, it might be time to take Dr. Gold's suggestion. Putting her in the Geriatric Behavioral Center for a few weeks would give you a chance to rest and maybe make Mom a little happier."

"Uh-huh."

"It would give you an idea of what it would be like to . . ." I paused a moment, "to put Mom in a nursing home."

"I've been thinking about it."

"I've received some booklets from the Alzheimer's Association about choosing a nursing home. This center is designed to get Mom as healthy as she can be before moving to one, so I guess it's not too early to check around. What do you think, Pop? Just tell me what you want to do, and I'll do it."

He smiled at me then nodded, "Go ahead. Call them. Then call Dr. Gold."

The next day, after a phone call from me, Dr. Gold scheduled Mom to enter the Geriatric Behavioral Center almost immediately. I had two days to get Mom ready to go and to convince Pop that he had made the right decision. The night before we were to leave, I stopped by to help Pop pack Mom's suitcase. I tried to remain as cheerful as I could knowing that any hesitation in my voice might change the plans. I wasn't even sure if we were doing the right thing.

I sat at the kitchen table next to Mom, waiting for Pop to count out the pills she would take with her last swallow of milk. My fingers fondled the five tips of the white Formica star still embedded in the turquoise and thought about that family of five that used to sit in these same five chairs by this same window that looked out on that same back yard. The back yard was dark now. The neighborhood kids had all gone inside. The edge of the window glowed from the streetlight that crept through a crack in the kitchen curtain and joined the bright florescent bulbs over my head. I reached down to my waist and felt the drawer that still held the phone book when it wasn't being used to remind me to straighten up. Mom sat quietly now in her usual chair at that same Formica table, the chair in which, after today, she would no longer sit.

"OK, let's see, I knew there was something I wanted to tell you two," I said with forced good spirits. "I'm having my first solo exhibit at a New Orleans gallery next month."

Pop said, "Really?" Mom just sat there quietly with her hands in her lap.

"Sure am. I'll put in about twenty-four paintings and set up Mom's journal on the side." Mom remained expressionless even when I said the word "journal."

"OK, baby, time for your pills. Open up." Pop placed them inside her lips, then wrapped her fingers around the glass and raised it to her mouth. "That's a good girl." Then to me, he said, "How'd you get there?"

"Well, remember Charlotte's little brother, Alan Stevens? He's graduating with his Ph.D. this semester. Anyway, he met a man at a fund-raiser. One thing led to another. The man said he owned a gallery, and Alan told him about my work. It seems Alan has been a great spokesman for me. I'm so bad at selling myself."

"Honey?" Mom said.

"Yeah, baby." Pop got up to place the milk glass in the sink knowing Mom wouldn't answer.

"Pop," I said, "Kate said you should send a tape recorder with Mom, that every time she would say 'Honey?' it would say 'Yeah, baby.'"

He smiled. "I should have thought of that a long

time ago." Pop sat down next to Mom and patted her on the knee. "Baby? Tomorrow, Kim and I are going to take you to the hospital."

"Why? There's nothing wrong with me."

Pop looked at me to explain it to her.

"Mom," I said, turning her knees so that she would face me. "Mom, your Alzheimer's doctor wants to check out your brain, see how you're coming along with that new drug."

"Yeah?"

Pop broke in, "He's going to get your medicine straight."

"Yes, Mom, remember when you went to Bethesda to help Dr. Morale? Well, this is similar to that. You'll be helping Dr. Gold see how his drug works."

Then, as clearly as her old self, Mom said, "He must be a poor man if he has to depend on me."

"He just knows how smart you are, Mom. Come on, let's go pack your clothes. We have to mark your name on everything and get your shower. We have a lot to do."

"OK, OK." She walked slowly beside me to her room. Pop followed close behind.

I whispered to him, "When she's like this, I wonder if we're doing the right thing."

He nodded. "I know, but this won't last long."

"Mom, aren't you excited?"

She just gave me a sarcastic smirk.

The next morning, Mom's zombie state quickly reminded me of the reasons we were taking her to the center in the first place. It was a quiet ride to Baton Rouge, for Mom slept most of the way. Pop didn't say much, but I knew he wasn't sleeping. Through my rearview mirror, I could see him staring blankly out of the car window.

Once there, we spent an hour with the nurse, answering endless questions while Mom slept in a nearby chair. I stayed dry-eyed until the nurse looked soulfully into my eyes and said, "I know this is hard for you." I guess it wasn't until I heard those words that I realized how difficult this was going to be for me. I had thought often about Pop and how he would handle being alone, but I hadn't thought of how I would feel without being with Mom every day. For the last four years, I had visited with her almost daily, and now? Well, now, it was hitting me, especially since Dr. Gold had said specifically not to visit for a couple of weeks, to give her time to get used to her surroundings. I realized then that the time would be my adjustment period, too.

As we prepared to leave, the nurse put her arm around Mom, who was awake, and said, "Your daughter has to get back to teaching now."

Mom looked puzzled. "She's not a teacher."

I tried to make my voice sound normal. "Yes, she is, Mom. Both of your daughters are teachers."

The nurse turned to me and said softly, "Don't worry. We'll take care of her. I know. I've been through this myself."

I leaned over to kiss Mom good-bye. "We have to go, Mom."

"I don't understand," she whimpered.

I couldn't answer because my throat was full. I had hoped Pop would say something, but he couldn't speak either. He just bent over and kissed Mom on the forehead. I watched my tears drip onto her pants leg, then we turned and pushed past the swinging doors to the outside hall.

When we reached the car, I looked at Pop and smiled. "That wasn't fun at all." He just smiled, and we rode home talking very little. When I pulled into his familiar driveway, Pop reached for the car door handle, but just sat there for a moment.

"Well?" I asked, trying to sound cheerful. "Are you going down the river now?"

"No, not just yet. I want to get all this straight, make sure she's OK." Then he looked at me and said, "Thank you, baby," before getting out of the car and walking slowly inside.

Even though I had completely dried up on the hour-long drive from Baton Rouge, I knew I couldn't go home just yet. I had to see Zab. When I stepped inside his office, it seemed he knew I was coming. He was talking to his partner, but stopped with "Well, how did it go?"

When I couldn't answer, he said, "Let's go in here." We walked into a vacant room next to the kitchenette, and Zab closed both doors. I began to cry again as I related the details of Mom's good-bye, and

Zab's eyes filled with tears, too.

"Zab, I didn't think it would be this hard," I sobbed and he pulled me close. It felt good to have arms around me; I knew Pop didn't have that waiting for him anymore. I pulled back to wipe my eyes on the pieces of tissue I had left, but Zab fished in his pocket to offer me his handkerchief instead.

"Uh-oh," he smiled, "it's not here. Wait just a minute." He disappeared into the kitchenette and returned with a rough, blue paper napkin.

"We're down to this, huh?" We both laughed through our tears.

Back at home, I sat alone in my studio. It would be several hours before Kate arrived from school, and I needed this release before she got here. I knew I had to work. I thought about Mom as I rolled around the dripping paint on the stretched sheet of watercolor paper. The paint took on a life of its own as my mind blanked to another place, to a hospital room, to a whimpering woman sitting alone in an overstuffed chair. The paint made no sound as it formed long tendrils and twisted around itself, yet I heard a voice saying, "I don't under-stand." The paint began to grow into large fetus shapes connected by cords of red and yellow. They crept deeply into the flat surface to transform into vague images of eggs and tangles. With each layer of translucent acrylic, I felt my pain turn to calm, my anguish turn to acceptance. Mom was finally reaching the womb, and I was still with her, brush in hand, visualizing our emotional struggle, painting a diary for the rest of the world to read.

Journal Entry
March 1993
(Posted above Lou Howes's bed)
To all my visitors,
nurses, and nursing assistants
at Audubon Living Center

Hi, my name is Lou Howes, but I answer to Miss Lou. Even though I am only 68 years old, I have early onset Alzheimer's Disease and can no longer do anything for myself. Just like an infant, I cannot tell you what I need or where it hurts, so if I am crying, something is wrong.

Check for the following:

1. Dry Mouth: *The medicine I am taking makes me very thirsty for water or apple juice. I hate those glycerine sticks and drink better with a straw.*

2. Pain in my Back and Hands: *I have bad arthritis. Sometimes a heating pad works.*

3. Pain in Lower Abdomen: *Try lying me flat on my back to allow gas to escape and do not feed me any food rich in fiber. I have an old case of Crohn's Disease.*

4. Dirty Diaper: *When I have to potty, I may get agitated because I still know I'm not supposed to wet my pants. Just tell me I am wearing a diaper, and that it's OK "to go."*

5. Fear and Depression: *I get scared if I'm left alone too long. Sometimes all I need is a hug and a few comforting words. Loud noises upset me, but my door has to stay open so you can hear me if I cry out. (Sorry for the disturbance.) Try just telling me to stop talking. Do not say stop crying, or why am I crying, because I'll say I'm not crying. (Stubborn Southern pride, I guess.)*

6. Loneliness: *Even if I don't always respond with a clear answer, I love to hear about old times and familiar people. Some names ring a bell, like Bert or Pop (my husband), Fan, Kim, & Ricky (my children), Betty and Tricia (my sisters), Dodo (my brother), or Bigmama (my mother).*

Please don't ask me, "Do you remember . . ." Now, isn't that cruel?

Thanks for taking such good care of me in this last stage of my Alzheimer's disease. Believe me, I'd much rather be down the Tangipahoa River at our camp enjoying the fresh air and sunshine, but Al has decided he wants me here. You remember Al? He's Mrs. Zheimer's son.

Lou Howes

```
=================================================

              PATHOLOGY GROUP OF LOUISIANA
                    AUTOPSY REPORT

NAME:  Margaret Lou Howes
AUTOPSY NO.:  PLA-9401
AGE:  69      SEX:  F      RACE:  Caucasian
EXPIRED:  August 27, 1994, 2215 Hours
PATHOLOGIST:  David A. Boudreaux, M.D.
COMMENTS:  The morphologic changes identified
on macroscopic and microscopic examination of
this brain are fully consistent with the clinical
diagnosis of classical Alzheimer's disease.


=================================================
```